AF552552

PRIMARY SCHOOL TEACHER EDUCATION PROGRAMME
(An Evaluative Study of DIETs)

PRIMARY SCHOOL TEACHER EDUCATION PROGRAMME

(An Evaluative Study of DIETs)

Dr. K. CHANDRASEKHAR
Department of Education
Regional Institute of Education
Mysore – 570 006

Discovery Publishing House
New Delhi–110002

First Published-2001
Reprinted-2010

ISBN 81-7141-588-1

Published by :
DISCOVERY PUBLISHING HOUSE
4831/24, Ansari Road, Prahlad Street,
Darya Ganj, New Delhi-110002 (India)
☎ : 3279245 • Fax: 91-11-3253475
E-mail : dphtemp@indiatimes.com

Printed at :
Mehra Offset Press
Delhi

FOREWORD

It gives me great pleasure, indeed, in writing foreword to the book entitled "Primary School Teacher Education Programme—An Evaluative Study of DIETs", which is in the printed form of the Ph. D. Thesis of the author.

Education is a perennial concern for all the time all over the world. Evaluation is an essential barometer to find out the conditioning of existing education, its process and product, its outcome for human development. The present study is a formidable venture to probe into the inside territory of primary school teacher education programme in Andhra Pradesh.

The author focussed his attention on various crucial aspects of teacher education, such as status of elementary school teachers, practice teaching, use of audio-visual aids, library facilities, physical education and many other variables. But the major emphasis is on the perception and attitude of student teachers, teacher educators and principals of teacher training institutions. It is true that teachers are human tools and the attitude they harbour in the inner region of their mind regarding all facets of education is the key stone of all teaching enterprise including daily ritual of classroom teaching and so on.

The investigator tried his best to reach the hinterland spread over 23 districts of Andhra Pradesh. The wealth of information regarding the existing paraphernalia connected with the DIETs is immense.

The salient features of the study are : The research problem studied is topical in nature. It has sound methodology. The conclusions are precise. The educational implications are feasible. The study could also enable to identify the weaknesses of the DIETs.

I sincerely believe that readers will enjoy reading this book and that it will provide with a lot of important points to ponder over and discuss with their colleagues and that all this will ultimately contribute significantly for the primary school teacher education.

No education is worth its name unless it helps the students feel at home in the world of books. With the explosion in knowledge no educationist can acquire or impart all the information pertaining to a subject. The best that one can do is to make the students cultivate a taste for reading. For cultivating the habit of reading, good books within the reach of students are essential. I am of the opinion that this book disseminates useful information to the students about the DIETs.

I hope the Universities, the State Departments of Education and Teacher Education Institutions will make the best use of this book. Further I hope that advanced students, teachers and learned scholars interested in teacher education at primary level will find this publication of great value and interest.

Prof. N. Venkataiah
Faculty of Education
University of Mysore
Manasagangotri
Mysore—570 006

PREFACE

The teacher training institutes of primary level now called as district Institutes of Education and Training (DIETs) play an important role in producing quality teachers for primary and upper primary schools. Great is the task and dynamic is the role of the DIETs to produce quality teachers. Are these institutions producing quality teachers? Is the pre-service training programme provided by the DIETs effective in all respects? What are the deficiencies in DIETs? A variety of such questions are to be answered with empirical evidences.

The research study was conducted in 1997-98 to collected data about the perceptions and attitudes of student teachers, teacher educators and principals about their training so as to get a better picture of the situation and to identify means to improve the teacher education further. The present study is, therefore, an ardent effort in this direction

Some of the major findings of the study are as follows: 1. The present day teacher education curriculum is outdated and it should be restructured and reorganised keeping in view the present day needs and aspirations of the young trainees. 2. Teaching profession is not well recognised for which student teachers are unhappy. 3. The DIETs are ill-equipped with regard to the physical and academic facilities. 4. There is deterioration of standard in teacher education. 5. Diets have not conducted workshops to improve primary school curriculum. 6. Majority of the trainees have not been able to acquire any teaching skills during the brief span of one month's teaching practice period. It is hoped that the findings of the study provide an insight into the problems of Primary School Teacher Education Programme to the planners, administrators as well as academicians.

I am grateful to Dr. N. Venkataiah, Learned Professor of Education, Department of Studies in Education, University of Mysore, Mysore for writing a valuable foreword to the publication.

I express my sense of gratitude to Dr. S. Padmanabhaiah, Principal, I.A.S.E., Dean, Faculty of Education, S. V. University, Tirupati for having given me an opportunity to work for my Ph. D. Degree under his guidance and also for his continued interest and encouragement for the publication of this book.

My grateful thanks are due to all those who have helped me for completing the study and publication of this book.

K. Chandra Sekhar

CONTENTS

1 INTRODUCTION

1.1 WHAT IS EDUCATION?

Education, according to Indian tradition, is not merely a means to earn a living; nor is it only a nursery of thought or a school for citizenship. It is an initiation into the life of spirit, a training of human soul in pursuit of truth and the practice of virtue. Aristotle, however, held that education exists exclusively to develop man's intellect in a world of reality which men can know and understand.

The word 'education' has a very wide connotation. It is hard to define. There is no single objective which can cover the whole of life with its various manifestations. The two poles of our concern : the temporal and the world of spirit are widely apart. Philosophers and thinkers from Socrates to Dewey in the West and from Yajnavalkya to Gandhi in the East have defined education in accordance with their philosophy of life with the result that there emerged divergent concepts and definitions of education. The concept of education is like a diamond which appears to be of a different colour when seen from a different angle.

Like the proverbial elephant and the blind men everybody i.e., a biologist, a priest, a philosopher, a psychologist, a statesman, a teacher, a shopkeeper, a merchant, an artisan seems to have his own concept of education which is influenced by his own outlook on life and his past experiences in a limited field.

"Education to be complete, must be humane; it must include not only the training of the intellect but the refinement of the heart and the discipline of the spirit. No education can be regarded as complete if it neglects the heart and the spirit".

1.2 PLACE OF TEACHER IN ANY EDUCATIONAL SYSTEM

"No system of education, no syllabus, no methodology, no text book can rise above the level of its teachers. If a country wants to have quality education it must have quality teachers".

—*V.S.Mathews*

According to the Department of Teacher Education, the educationists, teachers, administrators thought that a teacher should know the objectives before the nation in terms of the economic, social, political and cultural growth, which should engender in him the ability to train present generation of students into enlightened citizens of India.

A teacher should have good information about Indian thought and culture from ancient times to the present, which will help him to have an adequate and healthy personal philosophy of life. He should have a clear perception of the importance of his job for the nation and should take consequent pride in the teaching profession. A teacher should have healthy emotional development and cheerful disposition. If a teacher is joyful he will rejoice in life with all its variety. A teacher should be well informed, curious and alert. He should not only have a thorough knowledge of the subject taught or skills imparted by him but also habits of wide reading including current journals and magazines.

"Of all the different factors which influence the quality of education and its contribution to national development, the quality, competence and character of teachers are undoubtedly the most significant...".

—Indian Education Commission, 1966, (p.46)

The importance of the teachers in the educational programme of a country is too great. The greatness of a country does not depend on lofty buildings, gigantic projects and large armies but on the quality of its citizens. If a nation has youngmen of sterling character and unimpeachable patriotism, she is found to make rapid progress in all fields. Youngmen are entrusted to the care of the teacher and it is therefore the sacred duty of the teacher to impart the right type of knowledge and make them good citizens. It is the teacher who impresses his children with his personality.

The framers of Second Five Year Plan observed "At all times the teacher is pivot in the system of education". This is especially true in the case of a nation in its transition. The Secondary Education Commission of 1952-53 also points out that every teacher and educationist of experience knows that even the best curriculum and the perfect syllabus remain dead unless quickened into life by the right methods of teaching and the right kind of teachers. For imparting good education a good teacher is needed. All other things related to infrastructure are secondary.

The teacher, a national integrator as he is, is the backbone of society, particularly so in the remote villages. He stands as an outstanding figure among the illiterate and semi-illiterate families. He is their friend, philosopher and guide. The teacher actively shares the responsibility of reconstructing a social order, with all the cherished values and traditional beliefs, which are being eroded by the surge of new ideals and practices. He acts as a social reformer and counsellor to the community.

The role of the modern teacher is not confined to teaching alone. He/she is expected to participate in the development programmes of the community life. The question arises as to how this could be integrated with the teacher education programmes. Mudaliar Report (1952) stated rightly "We are convinced that the most important factor in the contemplated education reconstruction is the teacher—his personal qualities, his educational qualifications, his professional training and the place that he occupies in the school as well as in the community". On similar lines Kothari Commission stated that "nothing is more important than securing a sufficient supply of high quality recruits to the teaching profession, providing them with the best possible professional preparation and creating satisfactory conditions of work in which they can be fully effective".

1.3 THE CONCEPT OF TEACHER EDUCATION

Teacher Education has been defined as "all formal and informal activities and experiences that help to qualify a person to assume the responsibilities as a member of the educational profession and to discharge his responsibilities more effectively". The concept of "Teacher Education" is not new. However, scholarliness was considered the sole criterian for becoming a teacher. The concept that teachers are born and not made was also prevalent in those days.

But the teachers were not given any sort of formal training. Only scholarliness was expected from a prospective teacher. In the Gurukula system which prevailed in India during the vedic and upanishad times and even later children from the upper strata of society would go and spend their formative years of life in the hermitage of a teacher located on the outskirts of a village or on the bank of a river or in a forest. The teachers of such Gurukulas were men of high integrity and sterling character. Having renounced the worldly life they pursued the spiritual path and dedicated their life to acquisition of Jnana or learning. Education was thus a highly personalised arrangement.

It may be worthwhile to recall that till a century ago teaching was mastered mainly by gaining experience. No formal, theoretical or professional training was considered necessary. Even a new teacher learnt under the guidance of an elderly and experienced person. Usually, this was taken up after the completion of academic study of a subject. Gradually, physiological and pedagogical knowledge relevant to the work of teachers developed. It came to be felt that acquisition of this knowledge could lead to professionalisation of teacher education.

The desire of increasing number of people to come to the fold of education resulted in the need for training of teachers. For long, it was generally accepted that acquisition of relevant knowledge base was sufficient for good teaching and the rest could be learnt during the job practice. However, there was sufficient proof of the poor application of this knowledge base. Teacher education was viewed as a translation of theory of good teaching into practice. The questions that usually arise in this context are : how to implement academic knowledge in the practical setting? how to make teachers aware of their practical knowledge —conceptions, beliefs, and personal theory embedded in their every day teaching and how to develop in teaching both a feeling of responsibility for the goals and effects of their teaching and the skills required to work towards those goals?

Teacher Education now includes every aspect of the student-teacher's personality. We may define teacher education as such institutionalised educational procedures that are aimed at the purposeful organised preparation or further education of teachers who are engaged directly or indirectly in educational activity as their life work. This concept of teacher education does not exclude members of other professions who prepare for teaching as secondary or supplementary activity.

The aim of teacher education is the formation of educated and cultured persons concerned with education. The aims and objectives of teacher education are intimately related to the ideals of education. In the past it was believed that those who had acquired knowledge needed no particular skill to transmit it. It follows, therefore, that any one who knows a subject well can teach others. Without any training a teacher may teach well, but with training he may do still better, since he learns the scientific aspect of teaching which includes the skill of handling various teaching aids, art of questioning and treatment of answers, class management, etc.

Teachers in India have come to assume new roles for which the traditionally designed age-old teacher training programmes would not be adequate. For instance, the expanded function of education in India when it is directly linked to national development requires a broadening and deepening of the teacher's own knowledge and understanding. It also requires that the teacher sees himself not as a prime source of knowledge but as an organiser of learning and learning experiences. This calls for a change in the concept of teacher education and a consequent reorientation of the teacher education curriculum, both for enhancing the teacher's educability as well as his contribution to development. While there is a growing awareness that education can make important contributions in respect of the national development programme, the curricula of teacher training institutions have yet to be revised and reoriented with respect to the requirement that teachers are to be involved in programmes of education for national development. Teacher education, thus, will have to find an entirely different focal point in planning and implementing the various aspects of its programmes. Again, the organisation, content and methods of teacher education may have to be updated in the context of the developmental programmes. The teacher education curricula would necessitate courses on national development, information about agencies undertaking programmes of this kind, and activities which will assist teachers in developing a clear understanding of the national educational goals of development. Likewise the methods of teacher education will have to undergo a new orientation as they come under the influence of the new objectives of education for development. In-service programmes for teachers and teacher educators would have to be planned in the context of the knowledge and skills required for the new challenge of development.

1.4 ORIGIN OF TEACHER EDUCATION

It was only during the British period that the teacher education had its birth. As early as 1802, William Carey set up a Normal School for primary teachers at Serampore. The Calcutta school society established in 1819 took early steps to train teachers on the Lanchesterian system. In 1825, the Court of Directors awarded the society a monthly grant of Rs.500/- and expressed their approbation for the education of persons working as teachers in native schools. The need for training secondary teachers draw the attention of Sir Thomas Munro, Governor of Madras. In his Minute of 10th March, 1826 he observed, 'No progress in education can be made without a body of better instructed teachers'. He further recommended the establishment of central school for educating teachers. The Calcutta Ladies Society also organised a training class in 1828 for women teachers in the Calcutta Central School for girls. In 1829 the Native Education Society of Bombay started a training class for primary teachers. Training classes were also started at the Elphinstone Institution as the society's primary schools increased and more and more trained teachers were needed to run them. These institutions and organisations were primarily meant for primary teachers. Later the need for training secondary teachers attracted the attention of the new Department of Education, established in 1855. As early as in 1856, Mr. Howard, the Director of Public Instruction, Bombay, proposed the establishment of regular training college in Bombay for the professional preparation of assistant masters of English Schools. The Government Normal School, Madras, out of which the present teachers college at Saidapet developed, was established in 1856. To it was attached a 'model and practical school'. The institution distinguished itself by having on its staff eminent personalities like Dr.S. Radhakrishnan, Sir Samuel Ranganathan and the late Right Hon'ble V.S.Srinivasa

Sastri. Similarly, the first Normal School in the present Andhra Pradesh (erstwhile Madras Province) was established at Rajahmundry in 1894. The Stanley Despatch of 1859 declared that salary grant would be given only to those schools which had trained staff. Consequently the training of teachers was given more attention. During this period, a controversy arose regarding the place of subject matter and methodology in the curriculum. There were two schools of thought—one school believed that the knowledge of the subject matter was enough to make the teacher effective, while the other school advocated the study of principles and practices of teaching in a training school. The second teacher's institute was the Lahore Training college established in 1881, and later it formed the nucleus of the Central Training College, Labore. Both these institutions, however, admitted graduates and under-graduates in the same class. The courses included what the teachers had to teach in schools and very little of professional subjects. This was the state of affairs when the Indian Education Commission of 1882 was appointed by Hunter. In 1882 the British announced a policy of universalisation of education in India which required an increased number of schools and qualified or trained teachers in equal proportion. So the history of teacher education in India can be traced back to 1882.

1.5 TEACHER EDUCATION AT VARIOUS LEVELS

Teacher Education in our country exists at various levels.

(i) Teacher Education at Pre-Primary Level

Although pre-primary education is not a state responsibility, it has been accepted that the education at this level is more important than at the other stages of education. Unfortunately facilities for pre-primary teacher education are meagre in our country. Though the successive governments and different private agencies set up a number of pre-primary schools they neglected the area of training the pre-primary school teachers. Except few private organisations, Indian Government made a little effort in preparing teachers for pre-primary schools.

(ii) Teacher Education at Primary Level (T.T.C.)

The teacher training programme for the primary stage is different from that of the pre-primary stage, since the objectives of teaching in a primary school are different from those of pre-primary education. Here the emphasis is on literacy, numeracy and other social and emotional objectives.

This training course is open to matriculates and is of two years duration in most of the states of the country. Normally, the first year is devoted to the subject-matter and the second year to the methodology of teaching. This training leads to a certificate or diploma under the name of J.B.T. (Junior Basic Teacher's Training) or D.Ed. (Diploma in Education) or T.D. (Teaching Diploma).

At the Primary Teacher Education level, the Government introduced a number of courses such as non-basic secondary grade training, non-basic elementary grade training, basic senior grade training, basic junior grade training, secondary grade basic training, elementary grade basic training, pre-basic training, emergency training, etc. Later all these courses were clubbed together and a two year teacher training certificate course was set up in the Teacher Training Institutions (TTIs). Further they were improved resulting in the present form of District Institute of Education and Training (DIETs) for in-service and pre-service teacher education of primary teachers. The detailed description of DIETs is dealt within a succeeding section as the area of research of the present investigation is primary teacher education institutions.

(iii) Teacher Education at Secondary Level (B.Ed.)

This training course is open to graduates and is of one year's duration with an emphasis on the principles and methodology of teaching, leading to the B.T. (Bachelor of Teaching), subsequently renamed as B.Ed. (Bachelor of

Education) degree. In some states, particularly in Uttar Pradesh, the Education Department issues a diploma known as Licentiate Course (L.T.) which is considered equivalent to the B.Ed. degree. Teachers having this diploma are competent to teach middle, high or higher secondary classes. There has been a large expansion in the number of institutions teaching this course, ranging from 42 in 1947 to more than 400 in 1985.

Apart from this one-year course after graduation, the four year integrated course leading to the B.A.Ed. and B.Sc.Ed., has been continued in the four Regional Institutes of Education, located at Ajmer, Mysore, Bhopal and Bhubaneswar. It is open to those who have passed the pre-university or the higher secondary examination. Kurukshetra University, too, tried this experiment but could not continue it due to various reasons. However, it has been found that the product of four year integrated course is definitely superior to that of the one year B.Ed. course after graduation. For preparing teachers for secondary schools, university departments of education, government colleges of education (B.Ed. colleges), private colleges of education are there.

(iv) Teacher Education at Higher Secondary Level (B.Ed.)

Since it has been recommended by the Education Commission as well as the NCERT that the +2 stage of education is to fall within the purview of school education and is to be given a vocational bias, it has been suggested that a separate structure of teacher education for the higher secondary stage should be evolved.

The NCTE Framework has proposed a new structure for this stage of education. It has offered four models covering the academic and the vocational streams. One model has been suggested for collegiate education with a weightage of 30 per cent for pedagogical theory, 20 per cent for working with the community and the remaining 50 per cent for content-cum-methodology and practice teaching, including related practical work.

(v) Master's Degree in Teacher Education (M.Ed.)

At higher education level there are the University Departments of Education to provide M.Ed. degree course for preparing teacher educators and administrators of both primary and secondary levels. Through M.Phil. and Ph.D. courses they take up research work and inculcate research attitude among prospective teacher educators and administrators. In addition to these, almost all the universities offer graduate and post-graduate courses in Teacher Education through Distance Education.

(vi) Teacher Education for Special Subjects [B.Ed.(Spl.), M.Ed.(Spl.), B.P.Ed. etc.]

Special training institutions are there for preparing teachers for educating the physically handicapped and the mentally retarded children. There are also special institutions like J.J. School of Arts, Bombay and Kalakshetra, Adayar for preparing physical education teachers, music teachers, craft teachers, dance teachers, fine arts teachers. In some states there are special courses for preparing specialists in English, Science, Mathematics; Geography, Agriculture; Languages, etc.

1.6 ESTABLISHMENT OF DIET, OBJECTIVES AND THEIR FUNCTIONS

The 1986 National Policy on Education (NPE) gives paramount importance to teacher's status and training. In fact, the NPE has stressed that attention will be given to overhauling the system of teacher education, bearing in mind the pivotal importance of teacher education. Keeping in mind the highest priority given to teacher education programmes in NPE and Programme Of Action (POA), the Department of Education, Ministry of Human Resource Development, Government of India has prepared a centrally sponsored scheme of teacher education which has five parts:

— large scale orientation of teachers;

— establishment of District Institutes of Education and Training;

— strengthening Colleges of Teacher Education and upgrading of the Institute for Advanced Study in Education;

— strengthening SCERTs; and

— strengthening University Departments of educational studies.

Central assistance, for these schemes, will be provided on the basis of: systematic identification of institutions; determination of requirements of each institution; and preparation of a proper programme of teacher education, including the phasing out and closing down of sub-standard and redundant institutions.

A new type of educational institution called the District Institute of Education and Training (DIET) has been conceived within the NPE and POA as one of the major steps towards effective teacher education at the primary level. The DIET is designed to improve and enrich the academic background of elementary school teachers, non-formal and adult education functionaries and other personnel at the lowest level of the educational system.

Thus, facilities for qualitative improvement are to be made available at the very doorstep of the teachers and others involved. DIETs aim is to extend to the remotest parts of the country, with relative ease, the advantages of the educational knowledge available about management and planning, research and experimentation and the existing variety of rich resources and learning materials. It will provide academic support to the proposed District Boards of Education.

The DIET is a step towards the decentralisation of opportunities of professional preparation and extension of excellence from 'urban' to 'rural' areas, from the 'elite' to the 'general' population of teachers, from 'higher' to 'lower' levels of education, and from the 'academic' to the 'teacher'. It will provide guidance and leadership to ensure that effective measures are adopted in the four aspects of the Universalization of Elementary Education (UEE) through access, enrolment, retention and standards. The DIET should be in a position to devise, for local situations, specific ways to increase enrolment and more importantly, drastically reduce the alarming drop-out rate at the primary school level. It should also facilitate the education and literacy of adults and others who, unfortunately, drop out of the formal system due to economic and social handicaps.

While existing teacher education institutions are largely concerned with only pre-service preparation, the DIET concept is based on the premise that teacher education is a continuous process and its pre-service and in-service components are inseparable. It will have the capability of organising pre-service and in-service courses not only for elementary school teachers but also for personnel working in non-formal and adult education sectors. It would therefore break the isolation of the non-formal system from the formal system and integrate them to mutual advantage to improve efficiency.

The DIET has been conceived as a vibrant instrument for bringing about qualitative change in the quality of life of the community through education. It aims at energizing the educational climate of the district by providing rich training and resources and improving the professional competence of teachers and other educational functionaries. It has the following major objectives:

a. To provide pre-service and in-service education of elementary school teachers;

b. To provide teacher induction and the continuing education of instructors and supervisors for non-formal education, and the provision of resources to support them;

c. To provide planning and management support for District Boards of Education (DBE), school complexes and educational institutions;

d. To serve as an evaluation centre for primary and upper primary schools, as well as for non-formal and adult education centres;

e. To act as a resource and learning centre for teachers and instructors;

f. To act as a centre of experimentation and research; and

g. To support educational technology and computer educational programmes in the district.

To effectively perform their major functions, the DIETs have the following seven academic branches :

1. Pre-service Teacher Education Branch (PSTE);
2. In-service programmes, Field Interaction and Innovation Coordination Branch (IFIC);
3. District Resource Unit (DRU) for Adult and Non-Formal Education;
4. Work Experience (WE) Branch;
5. Curriculum, Material Development and Evaluation (CMDE) Branch;
6. Educational Technology (ET) Branch;
7. Planning and Management (P&M) Branch.

The National Policy on Education (1986) has reset the target which is reflected in its assertion that all children who attain the age of about 11 years by 1990 will have five years of schooling or its equivalent through the non-formal stream; like-wise by 1995 all children will be provided free and compulsory education up to 14 years of age. The NPE, therefore called for i) universal enrolment and universal retention of children up to 14 years of age ii) a substantial improvement in the quality of elementary education and provision of support services. The measures proposed to improve the quality of elementary education include reform of the content and process of education, improvement of school buildings and other facilities, provision of additional teachers and the comprehensive programme of teacher education.

The success of an education programme in schools

depends on the quality of teachers, which in turn, largely depends on the quality of their professional preparation. If prospective teachers acquire a real understanding of children and of the subjects they teach and if they have rich preparatory experiences in the class room, they will progress well towards professionalizing the teaching. One, therefore, expects the institutions of teacher education to turn out competent teachers with sound knowledge of school subjects, awareness of the nature and significance of the subjects, insight into the learning processes and ability to design and implement appropriate instructional strategies for the harmonious development of the children.

1.7 CURRICULUM FOR PRE-SERVICE TRAINING PROGRAMME

As explained earlier, DIETs are responsible for both pre-service and in-service primary teacher education programmes. This investigation is concerned with pre-service training programme. The curriculum for pre-service training programme includes both curricular and co-curricular activities.

Curricular activities cover the content and pedagogy where as the co-curricular activities are concerned with the other roles to be played by the prospective teachers when they are appointed in primary schools.

Under content and pedagogy the student teachers are exposed to four theory papers out of which two are common to all and are related to foundations of education. The other two are related to teaching subjects—one of the four school subjects namely, mathematics, physical sciences, biological sciences and social sciences and the second is a language namely, English or Telugu.

All these four theory papers are included for the purpose of evaluation of the ability gained by the student teachers during the training programme through assignments, unit tests and final state-wide Teacher Training Certificate (T.T.C.) examinations. The total marks allocated to theory are 400.

Under practical component the student teachers are exposed to demonstration lessons by subject methodology experts, usually by the teacher educators and observation lessons given by school masters and co-trainees. After these two events the student teachers are to go to different primary schools for block teaching or practice teaching. They have to teach ten periods in each one of the electives and five periods each in the remaining four school subjects. The evaluation of the practical work done by the student teachers is done for a total of 600 marks on the basis of their practice teaching, lesson plan writing, observation records, preparation of aids, etc. Thus, the total marks for the purpose of deciding the grade obtained by the student teacher are 1000.

Apart from the above curricular activities the student teachers are giving training in the activities related to physical education, health education, or special education, community participation, work experience, etc., through the conduct of both theory and practical classes. The student teachers are supposed to prepare records on each one of the co-curricular activities wherein they have to project their gain in the theoretical aspects as well as in their field experiences in the respective activities. These records are also included for evaluation under 600 marks mentioned earlier. Thus, the curriculum for pre-service training programme consists of the entire package of activities which are supposed to develop both general and specific skills required to be an effective teacher. But to what extent the curriculum is transacted during the period of training ? and what are the lapses in the existing training programme are to be evaluated objectively so as to improve the quality of teacher preparation in the state of Andhra Pradesh.

1.8 THE PRESENT STUDY

Any research in the field of education should bring an increased understanding of the existing phenomenon and lead to further refinement or improvement in the educational practices if it is an applied research and it should add to the existing stock of knowledge if it is a fundamental research. The present study virtually analyses the existing pattern of teacher preparation at primary level and so it falls under the category of applied research.

The present study is an evaluation of the existing pre-service training programme for primary teacher preparation with the broader objective of bringing qualitative improvement in it and hence, the study may be a survey type in its nature. As it aims at identifying the lapses or weaknesses in the existing programme and suggesting remedies, it may also be called an explorative and remedial research.

Any evaluative study aims at collecting information (data) from different sources—both primary and secondary. To evaluate a programme under implementation one may wish to follow different approaches, such as systems analysis approach, individualistic approach, comprehensive approach, etc. Whatever may be the approach that can be adapted the basic data are to be collected from all possible sources—functionaries and beneficiaries, organisations, records and registers. What type of data are to be collected ? From what sources the data are to be collected ? What approach is to be followed to evaluate ? and what techniques are to be employed in the analysis of data?—all these queries are quite common to any researcher which probably can be answered only after a thorough review of related literature in the specific area of research.

2

REVIEW OF RELATED LITERATURE

2.1 HISTORICAL DEVELOPMENT OF TEACHER EDUCATION IN INDIA

Teaching has been one of the oldest and most respected professions in the world. When a systematically organised human society came into existence the need to mould its children on proper lines arose requiring persons who could perform this role, that is teachers. The task of shaping the future citizens is a noble one and so the teacher has always occupied a place of honour and reverence in the Indian society over the ages.

The preparation of teachers has changed with the passage of time and with the changes in expectations of the society whereas in ancient India the teacher was a Guru who was well versed in temporal knowledge and deeply steeped in spiritual knowledge and he commanded great respect for his high personal qualities of head and heart; in the medieval times the expectations of society changed his role, making him a master of his subject area;

in the modern times he has come to perform yet different roles to meet the challenges of the present day demands. What interests us is to find out how he has been prepared for the different roles at different times and how he has failed to come upto expectations.

1) Preparation of teachers in the Upanishadic period

In ancient India the teacher was held in high esteem by the society by virtue of his being an embodiment of good qualities, a fountain of knowledge, and an abode of spirituality. Max Muller, quoting the Rig Veda, states that the teacher was a brahmachari who passed through the recognised curriculum and who was also deeply spiritual. The teacher was not only to impart knowledge but also to live in it; thus knowledge for knowledge sake was not sought, but knowledge for spiritual realisation was aimed at. Thus, the teacher in the ancient days did not simply teach precepts but practised them in real life inspite of the difficulties involved in the process.

The scholarly class of teachers, who invariably belonged to the Brahmin caste got stratified with the passage of time and lost its original grandeur. Later, it became a hereditary profession. Manu refers to this system when he remarks that the son of the teacher sometimes helped his father, by acting as a teacher in his absence. At times some of the older and abler pupils acted as monitors and assisted the teacher in his work. This monitorial system of inducting senior pupils to the position of teachers, was a contribution of the ancient Indian education system.

In the ancient period when knowledge was transmitted orally (since writing developed later) the students memorized the spoken lessons and repeated them orally. Teachers gave explanations whenever required by the pupils, and this method of teaching increased with the induction of other subjects and sciences. For instance, the Sutras were written in a language so condensed that without explanation they could not be comprehended. The teacher used parables from nature, and stories such as Panchatantra and Hitopadesa to explain the deep philosophical concepts of the Upanishads. Thus, various methods were used by teachers in ancient India to explain and expound difficult philosophical concepts. These methods were picked up by the disciples and handed down from one generation of teachers to another. Though a formal programme of training did not exist, the transmission of methods through imitation and repetition continued, and the teachers were well aware of what they had to do.

2) The Buddhist period

In the Buddhist period there was a major change in the educational system. The disciple would choose his teacher with much care, and show him utmost respect and the teacher was responsible for his alround development. With the development of knowledge in various fields the teacher's role also changed; he was expected to be a master of his special branch of knowledge. He employed other methods besides oral recitation—such as exposition, debate, discussion, question-answer, use of stories and parables, etc. Thus teaching became more systematised. In viharas and monastic schools, the inductive method was adopted and the intellect of the disciple was sharpened through it.

3) The Medieval period

According to the Koran, education is a duty. Though education was not widespread among Muslims, education was given a place of importance. The Mohammedan rulers in India founded schools (Maktabs), Colleges (Madrassahs) and libraries in their dominions.

The teachers teaching in the Maktabs were mostly Moulvis; in the Madrassahs scholarly persons were employed. The method of teacher preparation was mostly imitation of what the old teachers practised. Good and experienced teachers appointed talented students as tutors to look after and teach the junior students in their absence. Thus the monitorial system a preparation for the would be teachers was in vogue during the medieval times too.

4) The Modern period

With the advent of the Western powers in India a new type of educational system, quite different from the existing indigenous system came to be established. European missionaries took lead by starting schools first and teacher training institutions later. The Danish Mission under the inspiring leadership of Zienbalg and his colleagues opened an institution for the training of teachers at Tranquebar in 1716, and opened two charity schools in 1717, one for the Portuguese and the other for Tamil children.

Prior to the advent of the European powers the 'Monitorial System' remained an important method of training teachers for quite a number of years. But very soon the system was found to be inadequate and so steps were taken in India as well as abroad for systematizing the training of teachers.

5) Developments from 1800 to 1947

As early as 1802, William Carey set up a normal school for primary teachers in Serampore. School societies and school book societies made attempts for the training of teachers. The Calcutta School Society, established in 1819 took early steps to train teachers on Lanchesterian system.

Mr. Campbell, Collector of Bellary, in his minute dated 17th August, 1823, commended this system. He says : "The system by which the more advanced scholars are caused to teach the less advanced and at the same time to confirm their knowledge, is certainly admirable, and has well deserved the imitation it has received in England". Such schools for training teachers were established earlier in Calcutta and Bombay.

Later the need for training secondary teachers appears to have drawn the attention of Sir Thomas Munro, the Governor of Madras. In his Minute of 10th March, 1826 he observed, 'No progress in education can be made without a body of better instructed teachers'. He further recommended the establishment of central school for educating teachers.

In June 1826, the first normal school was started under the management and with the finances of the government in Madras. Initially, it prepared teachers for the District Schools (secondary schools). Later, this normal school developed into the Presidency College. The Calcutta Ladies Society also organised a training class in 1828 for women teachers in the Calcutta Central School for girls.

In August 1828, the Committee of Public Instruction in Madras suggested an increase in the salary of teachers and an improvement in their training. It was suggested that two superior schools (called Collectorate schools) and fifteen subordinate schools (called Tehsildarry schools) be established.

In 1829 the Native Education Society of Bombay started a training class for primary teachers. In 1847, Bombay started a normal school in the Elphinstone Institution, and in 1849, Calcutta too had a normal school. Normal schools were also started in Poona, Agra, Meerut and Benaras between 1850-1857. Mass education gained momentum with the recommendations of Wood's Despatch, 1854.

Wood's Despatch, an important educational document, was released on 19th July, 1854. It urged the establishment of training schools in each presidency in India. The despatch suggested the introduction of the pupil-teacher system (as prevailed in England) in India and an award/stipend to the pupil teachers and a small payment to the masters of the school to which they were attached. On successful completion of the training programme they were to be given certificates and employment. So the despatch introduced sufficient incentive for the would be teachers.

The need for training secondary teachers attracted the attention of the new Department of Education, established in 1855. As early as in 1856, Mr.Howard, the Director of Public Instruction, Bombay, proposed the establishment of regular training college in Bombay for the professional preparation of assistant masters of English schools.

The Government Normal School, Madras out of which the present teachers college at Saidapet developed was established in 1856 with a model and practical school were attached to it.

On 7th April, 1859, Lord Stanley, Secretary of State for India, in his Despatch set forth an examination of the operation of the 1854 Despatch and very emphatically stated that the administration should resist from procuring teachers from England and that teachers for vernacular schools should be made available locally.

During this period, a controversy arose regarding the place of subject matter and methodology in the curriculum. There were two schools of thought—one school believed that the knowledge of the subject matter was enough to make the teacher effective, while the other school advocated the study of principles and practices of teaching in a training school. This was the state of affairs when the Indian Education Commission of 1882 was appointed by Hunter.

The Hunter Commission, known as the Indian Education Commission, was appointed to study the working of the existing system of public instruction and it submitted a voluminous report, comprising 13 chapters of 639 pages. It laid at rest some of the controversies on the teacher training programme, and recommended the establishment of normal schools, whether government or aided, to provide for the local requirements of all primary schools.

In very specific terms it recommended a pass in the examination in the principles and practice of teaching for permanent employment as a teacher in any secondary school, government aided. For graduates it suggested a shorter course of training than for others. So the anomaly that had persisted in teacher training was done away with.

The Commission's insistence on a certificate in teacher training led to tightening of the rules. Pedagogical courses became more prominent. This also led to the opening of new teacher training institutions, and by 1892 there were 116 training institutions for men and 15 for women.

In 1886, the Madras Normal School was raised to the status of a college and was affiliated to the Madras University. It was removed to Saidapet in 1887. A training college was established at Rajahmundry in 1894. It then consisted of the Licentiate course (L.T.).

A secondary training college was found in Bombay in 1906 and prepared secondary teachers for its own diploma known as the Secondary Teachers Certificate Diploma (S.T.C.D.) until it was affiliated to the University of Bombay in 1922, for teaching courses leading to the B.T. Degree.

In 1917 the Government of India appointed a commission known as the Saddler Commission. The Commission, studied all aspects of University education and presented its voluminous report in 1919. It pointed out the painful inadequacy of training institutions and the poor quality of the training provided in them. It also pointed out that the B.T. and the L.T. courses were similar but the calibre of the pupils was not upto the mark. It also suggested that the training programme should not only make the trainee a competent classroom teacher but also a good administrator. Some of the important recommendations of the commission are :

1. To open a Department of Education in Universities to develop systematic and practical study of the science and art of education.
2. To equip each Department of Education with a Professor, a Reader and a number of Assistants. The Department should consult and collaborate with Departments of Experimental Psychology, History and Economics.
3. There should be a demonstration school under the direction of the University for practical trial of

new methods of teaching, new combinations of school subjects and new plans of school organisations. Such a school would serve as a laboratory for educational experiments.

4. The Department should have a good Library with good books, reports and journals.
5. The Department should bring out publications and promote research on training. It should also work as a link between Boards of Education and Intermediate Colleges and Committees of High Schools.
6. The Department should facilitate the professional growth of the teachers in services and also encourage the progress of the new educational movement whenever possible.
7. There should be a post-graduate degree in education.

The commission woefully observed that "the three essential components of teacher education were knowledge of the subject-matter, practical training and theoretical training but under the existing conditions, the first is often unfulfilled, second rarely possible and third too little regarded by the university in framing the regulation".

It recommended the introduction of Education as an optional subject at the B.A. level. The Commission also recommended that a post-graduate degree in education should be introduced.

The recommendations of the Saddler Commission had a salutary effect on the teacher training programme in India.

The work initiated by the Saddler Commission was further carried on by the Hartog Committee. The Committee was primarily concerned with primary education. The committee learnt that only 44 per cent of primary teachers were trained, and that only 28 per cent had passed the middle examination. It rightly observed that the success of education depended on the quality of the training, the status and pay of the teachers. It suggested that teachers for rural areas should be inducted from persons close to rural society. It identified a very dismal picture of the teachers and their training. It said "The period of training is too short, the curriculum is too narrow and the teaching staff is inadequately qualified".

Working on the recommendations of the Saddler Commission, 13 out of 18 Universities set up faculties of education. The Lady Irwin College was established in New Delhi. Andhra University started a new Degree the B.Ed. in 1932. Bombay launched a post-graduate degree the M.Ed. in 1936.

Some other important changes in the field of education also took place in the thirties. The act of 1935 introduced provincial autonomy under which the Indian Minister of Education had considerable powers.

In 1935, the Central Advisory Board of Education (CABE) was revised. Basic Education was started by Mahatma Gandhi in 1937, leading to the training of teachers for basic schools. In 1938, a Basic Training College was set up at Allahabad, and the Vidya Mandir Training School was started at Wardha in 1938.

In 1941, there were 612 normal schools out of which 376 were for men and 236 for women. These schools provided one or two year's training. There were 25 training colleges for graduates, which were inadequate to meet the needs of the time.

In 1941, the Vidya Bhawan Teachers College was started in Rajasthan, and the Tilak College of Education in Poona. Bombay which took the lead in starting a Doctorate Degree in Education the same year.

In 1944, the Central Advisory Board of Education presented a scheme of education "Post-war Educational Development in India", popularly known as the "Sargent Plan"

A broad based educational plan, it made some practical suggestions for teacher's training programme as follows :

1. Suitable boys and girls should be inducted into the teaching profession during the last two years of their high school course and they should be given stipends for receiving teacher training.
2. Provision should be made for training different categories of teachers—2 years course for pre-primary, 2 years course for Junior Basic School teachers (after High School), 3 years course for Senior Basic School Teachers, 2 year course for under graduate teachers in High School and 1 year course for graduate teachers.
3. Refresher courses should be organised for giving in-service education to teachers.
4. Research facilities should be provided.
5. Practical training should be provided.
6. The first year of the two years training should be devoted to the study of the general and professional subjects. It should be supported by school visits, discussions and other experiences to kindle the trainee's interest in education.
7. It proposed revised pay scales for all categories of teachers, to attract better teachers.

In 1948, the Central Institute of Education was established in Delhi, and the Government Training College at Allahabad was developed into the Central Pedagogical Institute.

6) Teacher Education in Free India

The changed social, economic and political conditions after our independence necessitated the revamping of the traditional system of education as well as the teacher education programmes. It will be interesting to observe the recommendations of various committees and commissions appointed by the Government of India for the improvement of teacher education in free India.

(a) The University Education Commission (1948-49)

Just after independence the University Education Commission was constituted under the Chairmanship of Dr. S. Radhakrishnan. The Commission submitted its report in 1949.

The Commission observed that there was no difference in the theory courses offered in the various teacher training colleges, but much difference was observed in the practices followed. The number of supervised lessons varied from ten to sixty. It observed that the training colleges had no basic orientation in the essentials. For improvement of teacher training, the Commission suggested that the teacher educators must look at the whole course from a different angle; that the theory and practice should support each other; that courses in the theory of education must be flexible and adaptable to local circumstances; that original work by professors and lecturers in education should not suffer from isolation and lack of inter-university planning. The Commission also recommended the following with teacher preparation:

— Starting the training institutes of teachers and diverting a large number of students into them;

— Organising refresher courses of school and college teachers;

— Improving lecture method of teaching;

— Transforming the teacher training colleges into constituent colleges of universities.

(b) The Secondary Education Commission (1952-53)

One of the important events of the decade was the Report of the Secondary Education Commission. It analysed the problems of teachers and the training programme in great depth. It observed : "We are, however, convinced that the most important factor in the contemplated educational reconstruction is the teacher, his personal qualities, his educational qualifications, his professional training, and the place that he occupies in the school as well in the community". So the commission made recommendations on all these aspects. It found that two types of teacher training institutions existed : (a) Primary (Basic) Teacher Training (b) Secondary Teacher Training Institutions.

It recommended that :

1. There should be only two types of institutions for teacher training—
   - (i) for those who have taken the School Leaving Certificate or Higher Secondary School Leaving Certificate, for whom the period of training should be two years, the secondary grade training institutions should be under the control of a separate board.
   - (ii) for graduates, for whom the training may, for the present, be one academic year but extended as a long term programme to two academic years. The graduate teacher training institutions should be recognised by the affiliated universities which should award the degree.
2. The teacher trainees should receive training in co-curricular activities.
3. The training colleges as a normal part of their work should conduct refresher courses, short time intensive courses in special subjects, practical training, etc.
4. Special part-time training for women teachers should be conducted.
5. The Master's Degree in education, should be availed of by trained graduates with three years teaching experience.

(c) The Kothari Commission (1964-66)

In 1964 an Education Commission was set up by the Government of India under the Chairmanship of Dr. D.S. Kothari to advise on the educational development. The commission observed that a sound programme of professional education for teachers was essential for the qualitative improvement of education. The commission pointed out the weaknesses of the existing system and suggested ways to improve it.

The general recommendations of the Kothari Commission are as follows:

— It recommended that isolation of teachers colleges from the universities, schools and the teacher's colleges themselves should be removed;

— It suggested ways to improve the quality of teacher educators;

— It advised the State Governments to prepare a plan for the expansion of training facilities.

However, the commission made specific recommendations relating to primary teacher preparation and they are presented below :

Recommendations on the Primary Teachers Training

1. The staff in institutions for training primary teachers should hold a Master's Degree either in education or in an academic subject as well as B.Ed. and should have undergone special induction courses in teacher education at the primary level.

2. New appointments of primary teachers should be restricted to those who have completed at least 10 years of general education, exceptions may be made for women teachers in tribal areas.

3. Correspondence courses and liberal concessions for study leave should be made available to

unqualified teachers for improving their qualifications.

4. Special courses should be organised for graduates entering primary teaching.

5. The duration of the training course for primary teachers should be uniformly two years for those who have completed the secondary school course.

Consequently, some welcome changes have been introduced in teacher education. An M.A. degree in education has been introduced in some universities such as Aligarh, Kurukshetra, Kanpur and some others. Some universities have introduced summer schools and correspondence courses to meet the backlog of untrained teachers and some states have set up State Boards of Teacher Education.

(d) National Policy on Education (1968)

Incorporating the recommendations of Kothari Commission, the Indian Parliament adapted the National Policy on Education in 1967. The NPE, 1968 included the following suggestions as far as education of teachers is concerned.

1. The emoluments and other service conditions should be adequate and satisfactory having regard to their qualifications and responsibilities.
2. The academic freedom of teachers and researchers should be protected.
3. Teacher Education, particularly in-service education, should receive due emphasis.

(e) National Policy on Education (1986)

The Government of India announced a New Educational Policy in 1985. Accordingly National Policy on Education was produced in the year 1986. It made the following recommendations on Teacher Education.

1. The New Knowledge, skills and favourable attitudes

should be developed among teachers to meet the present needs.

2. Orientation of teachers should be a continuous process of teacher education.

3. Like SCERT at State level, the district level body may be established and it may be called as the District Institute of Education and Training (DIET).

Thus, through successive committees and commissions teacher education has undergone a number of changes.

Commission & Committees and their recommendations

On the basis of the recommendations of various committees and commissions, many changes were effected in the system of education in general and teacher education in particular. Moreover, the Indian Government started the five year plans to achieve sustained economic development by developing different sectors of the economy in balanced manner. Education was regarded as one of the basic sectors of the economy and thereby in all plans education was given due importance. With all these, the following important events took place.

The Planning Fifties

The first conference of training colleges in India was held at Baroda in 1950 and it discussed programmes and functions of the training colleges. In the following year, 1951, the second All India Conference was held at Mysore. It discussed the teacher training programme in a broader perspective and suggested substituting the term "Education" for "Training", and widened its scope. In the same year, a six week summer course in education was organised for college teachers at Mysore.

The syllabi in teacher education were revised, new areas of specialisation added, and practical work enhanced.

The enthusiasm for seminars, workshops, etc., led to the establishment of extension centres. In 1955, the All

India Council for Secondary Education was established. The Council through its Extension Centres (within a year 24 centres started functioning) imparted in-service education. In 1957, the All India Council for Elementary Education was formed.

The second five year plan launched in 1955-56, contemplated training of 68 per cent of the teachers by 1960 and an amount of Rs. 17 crores was apportioned for increasing the training facilities.

The All India Council for Secondary Education established an Examination Reform Unit in 1957. The Directorate of Extension programme for Secondary Education was set up in 1959 to coordinate the extension programmes. In the same year the Central Institute of English was established at Hyderabad to train teachers in English and to provide research facilities in that field.

The sixties started on a note of new ventures and ideas. The first National Seminar on the Education of Primary Teachers was held in October, 1960. The findings of the seminar reflected a sad state of affairs, for example, the supply of trained teachers was not correlated to the requirements; the training institutions were not well planned; the small institutions were poorly staffed and ill-equipped, etc. The seminar suggested that every teacher should be trained, and that the State Government should plan a phased programme to attain the targets. It recommended selection of some training institutions as models for developing primary teacher education on the right lines. The seminar suggested that the optimum size of a training institution should be 200 trainees. It recommended that primary school teachers should also be included in the extension programmes. It advocated the setting up of State Institutes of Education. During 1962-63, Extension Training Centres in Primary Teacher Education Institutions started functioning. The State Institutes of Education were established by 1965, and a Department of Teacher Education was established at the National Institute of Education.

One important achievement of this period was the establishment of the National Council of Educational Research and Training (NCERT) devoted to training, research and coordination. In 1964, at the Seventh Conference of All India Association of Teachers Colleges, it was proposed that comprehensive colleges be set up to bridge the gulf between primary and secondary teacher training institutions. The conference recommended the setting up of State Councils of Teacher Education.

In 1961, four Regional Colleges of Education specifically meant to integrate professional and general programmes by running content-cum-pedagogy courses of four year duration were started.

These colleges are experimenting with new programmes of teachers education, new instructional materials and new ways of teaching with special emphasis on skill development.

A panel on teacher education has been set up by the UGC to advise it on measures to be taken up for the improvement of standards of teaching and research in education in Universities, departments of education and colleges of education. The panel recommends proposals for promotion and supports of studies/research which may draw special attention in relation to the educational and developmental needs of the country and the community.

The panel has suggested that the resources available to the department of education should be extended to the community with special reference to surveys which may serve as a basis for determining the learning needs of the community; preparation of curriculum and teaching materials in functional literacy, organisation of training for various categories of functionaries and mid-term appraisal. The department of education could also work with the secondary and elementary schools in the neighbourhood and help them to improve their standards.

The setting up of the N.C.E.R.T. on 1st September, 1961 is an outstanding land-mark in the history of education in the post-independence period. Several institutes and bureaus working under the Ministry of Education were merged in to it. These were the Central Institute of Education, Central Bureau of Text-Book Research, Central Bureau of Educational and Vocational Guidance and National Institute of Basic Education.

Presently it comprises the National Institute of Education, New Delhi, four Regional Colleges of Education, one each at Ajmer, Bhopal, Bhubaneshwar and Mysore, and Field Advisors units in state capitals or main educational centres of various states.

Further, it works in close co-operation with the education departments in the states, State Council for Educational Research and Training (SCERT) and the universities and with all the institutions and agencies set up in the country for furthering the objectives of school education. It also maintains close contacts with similar international agencies.

The Ministry of Education, Government of India, established in May, 1973, the National Council for Teacher Education, usually termed as the NCTE, for maintaining the standards in teacher education in the country. The NCTE was established with the assumption that it would advice the central as well as state governments on all matters pertaining to teacher eduction and would review the progress of plan schemes to maintain the sanctity of the high standards in teacher education. However, only in 1993 the NCTE was given the statutory status as an apex body at national level.

The main functions of the NCTE are :

— To survey the whole field of teacher education at all levels in consultation with state councils from time to time and suggest ways and means of qualitative improvement as well as quantitative expansion of teacher education;

— To coordinate the activities of State Councils and to recommend to the Union Ministry of Education to provide maintenance and development grants to them;

— To suggest proposals to central ministry for planned development of teacher education in the country;

— To set national standards in terms of curricular requirements, equipment, facilities, staff requirements, etc., for teacher education;

— To establish inter-state parity in standards and survey the position from time to time to assess the nature and extent of new developments in the field;

— To promote measures for improvement of standards of teacher education in the country by setting up study teams, arranging for development grants, promoting research, etc;

— To coordinate, at the national levels, education research conducted by teacher training colleges, departments of education and other agencies;

— To plan and sponsor in-service training programmes for teacher educators at the inter state level in certain subject areas as may be decided from time to time in consultation with the state councils;

— To maintain international contacts in the field of teacher education.

Besides many other activities, the NCTE has been taking interest in initiating novel academic activities. Some of these are: Proposal of closing down of B.Ed. correspondence courses; code of professional ethics, etc.,

Education has now been accepted as a discipline. That is why the UGC now takes more interest in professional education and teacher education. The future expansion of professional education depends upon the adequate training of top level educational administrators, teacher educators, experts in curriculum construction, evaluation methods of teaching, etc. M.Ed. and Ph.D. programmes conducted by universities would need the growing demand for experts in all branches of education. On realising this growing demand, the idea of establishing a department of education was first mooted by the Culcutta University Commission in 1919. The idea took root slowly. But by 1966, the number of universities having departments of education reached the figure of 31. These departments had much better resources and better qualified staff than the Colleges of Education in their state. All of them conducted the B.Ed., M.Ed. and Ph.D. courses in the education programmes.

2.2 THE PRESENT STATUS OF PRIMARY SCHOOL TEACHER EDUCATION IN ANDHRA PRADESH

The teacher training institutes of primary level now modified into District Institutes of Education and Training (DIETs) play an important role in producing required teachers for primary and upper primary schools. Great is the task and dynamic is the role of the DIET's to produce quality teachers for primary and upper primary schools. Do these institutes produce quality teachers ? Is the pre-service training programme provided by DIETs effective in all respects ? What are the deficiencies in DIETs ? A variety of such questions are to be answered with empirical evidences for further improvement of quality of teacher education at the primary level.

In the past Basic Training Schools, later Teacher Training Institutions (T.T.Is) used to play an important role in producing required teachers for elementary schools. Now, in the place of T.T.Is, District Institutes of Education and Training (DIETs) have come into existence to produce effective teachers for primary and upper primary schools. At present there are 23 DIETs in 23 districts of Andhra Pradesh. Apart from these 23 DIETs, there are two T.T.Is located one at Araku Valley (Visakhapatnam district) and another one is at Utnur (Adilabad district). These two T.T.Is are established to provide training for tribal students under Integrated Tribal Development Agency (ITDA) areas for their requirements. Hence, there are 25 teacher education institutions for primary school teachers in Andhra Pradesh. The state government is providing finances to the DIETs. The present study is limited to primary school teacher education in Andhra Pradesh.

The historical review reveals that the teacher preparation in ancient period was not systematic but concentrated on practical aspects of teacher preparation. However, with the advent of British, the teacher training became more systematic step by step, and the emphasis was shifted from practical aspects to mere theory. At present 'Education' has gained the status of an independent discipline with the contributions from various branches like Philosophy, Sociology, Public Administration, Psychology, Economics, Statistics, etc. These changes appear to be a strong reason for the shift from practical aspects to mere theory. To overcome this, the National Council of Teacher Education (NCTE) prepared a draft curriculum for teacher preparation at different stages where equal importance is given to both theoretical orientation and training in practical aspects and skills which are essential for an effective teacher.

2.3 RESEARCH STUDIES ON TEACHER EDUCATION

The most neglected area in the field of education is teacher education. It has been recognised and stressed by almost all committees and commissions on education. Still the status of teacher education has not changed much due to non allocation of funds and non availability of quality teacher educators. Research on teacher education is also sparse. This part of the review tries to give a brief summary of the research work done on teacher education in India by which one can understand easily the status of teacher education in our country and what best can be done to better it. The present study is aims at identifying the shortcomings in the pre-service training programme of primary teachers conducted by the DIETs. The research studies related to pre-service training of primary teachers alone are given priority in the presentation of this part.

Tripathi (1964) made an evaluative study of the then existing basic training institutes in the states of Bihar, Gujarath, Madhya Pradesh and Maharastra and found number of deficiencies in them. Of course, the programme of basic training does not exist anywhere in the country at present. But, creating 'work experience' among the student teachers has become a real problem without the basic training approach for teacher preparation.

State Institute of Education (Gujarat) (1965) conducted an investigation into the problems of the Trainees of the Primary Teachers. The main objective of the study was to know the then position of primary education in Gujarat with special reference to the primary teacher trainees. The main findings of the study were : (i) the syllabus needed some modification; (ii) the trainees had some financial problems; (iii) the attitude of the trainees to the basic education was positive; (iv) the trainees liked the community life activities very much; and (v) the quota of the craft was too much for the trainees.

State Institute of Education (Gujarat) (1966) made case studies of Primary Teacher Training Institutions of Gujarat. The objective of the study was to get a representative picture of the position of primary teacher training institutions of Gujarat. A representative sample including ten per cent of the total number of primary teachers training institutions was selected for the study. A case study proforma was prepared and used to collect the data.

The study revealed that (i) more physical facilities were needed for the trainees, as these institutions were residential units; (ii) all the institutions had adequate number of basic trained staff members; (iii) no institution had a science laboratory; (iv) there was no reading facility in these institutions; (v) there was a great need for adequate reading room for students and staff members; (vi) fifty per cent of the staff members needed refresher courses; and (vii) there was no proper planning in the provision of facilities for the teacher training.

SIERT, Rajasthan (1966) conducted an investigation into Teacher Education at the Primary Level in Rajasthan. In the state of Rajasthan, where out of 63 BSTC training institutions, 47 were under the government and 16 under the private management. Thirteen training institutes did not respond to the questionnaire. Forty-two government and eight private institutions responded. Fourteen of them were situated in rural, 23 in sub-urban and 13 in urban areas and they were evenly distributed all over the whole state.

The study revealed : 1. The average intake was about 130. The qualification prescribed for admission to the STC course was the High/Higher Secondary Examination. 2. About two-thirds of the trainees belonged to the rural area. 3. The minimum age prescribed for freshers was 18 years whereas the ages of the trainees ranged from 18 to 45 years. 4. There were headmasters, subject teachers, and craft, agriculture, physical education and drawing instructors on the teaching staff. 5. The syllabus was prescribed by the Department of Primary and Secondary Education of the state government and was followed in all the institutions. 6. Some of the institutions felt that the syllabus was somewhat ambitious. The syllabus for craft was heavy, its teaching required a lot of funds, and the teaching staff had inadequate training. 7. Many difficulties in making arrangements for practice teaching were faced because they did not have demonstration schools. 8. Out of 50 training institutions, 37 had their own buildings. Eleven were housed in rented buildings. Out of the remaining, one was functioning in a Dharmasala and the other one was located in a high school building. 9. The expenses of the government training institutions were met by the government. Aided institutions got grants-in-aid from the government. Stipends to pupil teachers were paid by the state government. The State Institute of Education provided guidance to the training schools.

Upasani (1966) evaluated the Existing Teacher Training Programme for Primary Teachers in the State of Maharashtra with special reference to Rural Areas. The study is an attempt to evaluate the existing primary teacher training programme in the state of Maharashtra with special reference to rural areas. The purposes of the study were : (a) to identify the major strengths and weaknesses of the training programmes from an analysis of the self-evaluation reports; (b) to compare these reports of the principals with the annual inspection reports of the parishad education officers to find out the extent of usefulness of such an external inspection; (c) to examine and analyse the opinions of the parishad education officers and the principals concerned; (i) the adequacy of the preparation of the newly trained primary teachers, (ii) the understanding, skills and abilities expected of the rural primary teachers, and (d) to examine and analyse the existing teacher training programmes and to propose suggestions for their improvement. The major aim of the present study was to examine the hypothesis : 'The existing primary teacher training programme in Maharashtra did not achieve fully the objectives of the training and that the present inspections of the training colleges fail to evaluate the effectiveness or otherwise of the training programmes in all aspects'. The aspects taken into consideration were : (i) instructional objectives; (ii) curricular programme; (iii) organisation of the programme; (iv) staff; (v) student personnel services; and (vi) inspection.

One hundred and eight principals participated in this study. Opinionnaire and questionnaires were prepared by the investigator and used for the collection of data. Interviews and inspection reports were the other sources of data. Percentages, correlation coefficients, and chi-square test were used for the analysis of the data.

The author has recommended the following : (i) The minimum qualifications prescribed for recruitment as primary teachers or for admission to training institutions should be the completion of a secondary school course. (ii) The present position of the professional training of primary teachers is far from satisfactory especially if it is evaluated in the light of the new challenges in elementary education. (iii) A very serious defect in the practical training is the tendency to confine the practical training to the prescribed number of practical lessons; what is actually needed is a wider conception of teacher education and provision of opportunities to student teachers to acquire various skills. The Indian child needs down to earth grassroots knowledge of the country's condition. So the teacher has to be a well informed, well grounded, effectively participating citizen and he has to bring into action special resources of scholarship and practical competence. (iv) There should be a special agency for the supervision of training colleges (other than the education officers who are otherwise busy) with a special officer at the directorate level. (v) The duration of the primary teacher training should be extended to two years.

Banerjee (1967) studied the training of primary teacher in India. An interview schedule was prepared covering the different aspects of training of primary teachers, viz., aims and objectives of training, organisation, curriculum and syllabus, practice teaching, community living, examination, teaching staff, wastage, supervision, community development, in-service training and pay allowances. Different authorities in the sixteen states of India were interviewed with the help of this schedule.

The following observations were made on the basis of the data collected: (a) There were weaknesses and shortcomings in the professional education of primary teachers and vigorous attempts were needed to put the programme on the right track. (b) Basic education attached great value to the child and real development would take place only under conditions of freedom. (c) In the new age, the school, the teacher, the training institutions had to pay a great role in changing the old patterns of education. (d) The number of student teachers, explosion of knowledge and democratic living all these placed upon the training institutions a responsibility of unprecedented magnitude. (e) A training college had to address itself to the task with a spirit of high adventure and faith.

Mallaya (1968) studied the modern trends in the

teacher training programmes and the problems of teacher training in Madhya Pradesh with a view to suggesting ways and means to make it more effective. Several official reports, documents and magazines provided the main sources of information. Visits to various teacher training institutions were made in order to collect the views of heads and other staff members.

The study revealed that : (i) the pre-primary teacher training facilities were insufficient in Madhya Pradesh and Montessori training was very costly and it needed reorganisation; (ii) the existing teacher training facilities at the primary and secondary levels which were considered sufficient, could be made more effective by strengthening the science teacher's training at all the three levels, rationalising the selection of candidates for training and introducing practical aspects of teacher's training such as practice teaching, community life, preparation of teaching aids, games and sports, and cultural activities; (iii) it was observed that there was no proper dissemination of research findings in the field and traditional teaching methods were followed; (iv) evaluation techniques were mostly of routine type and showed large variations in internal and external assessment; (v) since Madhya Pradesh is mainly an agricultural state, agriculture, cooperation and rural upliftment activities could be included in the teacher training programme and more of outdoor activities be organised; (vi) better coordination in the programme of teacher training at various levels could make them more effective; (vii) the teacher training institutions in the state did not have adequate library facilities and the periodicals and magazines to which they subscribed were less in number; (viii) coordination at different levels of teacher training was lacking; and (ix) there was no provision for training the inspectors of schools and social education organisers.

Srivastava (1970) conducted an investigation into the Evaluation of Practice Teaching in Teacher Training Institutions to find out the place of practice teaching in the total programme of teacher preparation and the manner in which the evaluation methods and practices influenced the student-teachers' performance in teaching, to study their attitude towards practice teaching and to study teacher pupil relationship.

The information gathered in this study revealed that practice teaching formed an essential and compulsory item in all the teacher preparation programmes irrespective of the fact that the requirement of study and activities for obtaining degree in education were not the same in all the institutions. The place of practice teaching was determined either by relative weightage in terms of examination marks allotted for practice teaching in the total programme or the amount of time or hours of work a student had to put in to complete the requirements of practice teaching in relation to the time used for completing all the requirements of the programme. However, majority of the teacher educators were not satisfied with the system of practice teaching evaluation in their own institutions. Majority of the institutions had some system of internal assessment and most of the institutions did not give more than fifty per cent of the total marks for practice teaching in internal assessment. Except two universities, the other examining agencies did not define and outline the scheme of marks distribution over the contents of class teaching. The satisfaction of student-teachers about the evaluation practices correlated highly with their perception of the presence or absence of the element of subjectivity in the evaluation system.

Gupta (1971) examined the admission procedures in elementary and secondary teacher training institutions. The purpose of study was to examine the admission procedure in teacher training institutes and suggest a suitable admission procedure. The major findings of the study were : (1) minimum qualification required for admission was matriculation or S.S.L.C. (2) age limit was 15 to 30 years for freshers and upto 35 years for untrained teachers, and (3) admissions were given on the basis of written test, interview, academic record and teaching experience.

Arora et.al., (1974) undertook a study of the National Survey of teacher education at elementary level with the objective of collecting data concerning major areas of elementary teacher education such as students and staff, facilities and services, programmes, administration and supervision, etc., with a view to (i) compiling a national report which could be used as a reference document, and (ii) locating weak areas which needed strengthening and thus required special attention of the NCERT. A comprehensive questionnaire was used for the purpose of the survey. Data was collected from all the elementary teacher training institutions of India. The draft report which emerged out of the data was sent to the SIEs, Directors of Public Instructions, and the field advisors for comments and suggestions. The final report was prepared after their incorporation.

The following were the major findings of the survey: (i) about 59.9 per cent institutions were located in the urban areas while 48.3 per cent in the rural areas; 54.71 per cent institutions were residential in nature, 22.84 per cent were partially residential and the rest were not residential; 46.30 per cent of the institutions were co-educational, 35.89 per cent were for men only and 17.01 per cent were for women only; 63.18 per cent institutions were run by the state government, 27.34 per cent were run as private aided and 9.47 per cent were as private unaided; (ii) quite a fair justice was done in the selection of candidates for admission to training institutions, the main criterion being the marks obtained at the matriculation examination; some seats were kept reserved for scheduled castes, scheduled tribes and deputed teachers too; there was a good provision for stipend in almost all the government training institutes; in majority of the states, no tuition fee was charged; (iii) in majority of the states, the minimum qualification required for the recruitment to the post of principal as well as to the teacher educator was trained graduate; (iv) in most of the states the syllabus was prescribed by the state department of education; most of the theory papers in different states were almost the same; the common papers were Principles of Education, Educational Psychology, Teaching of Mathematics, Teaching of Science, Teaching of Social Studies and Teaching of Languages; in many states, there were optional theory papers; practice teaching prgramme had a vital place in all the states; a little more than fifty per cent training institutions had demonstration schools inside their campuses but most of them had inadequate accommodation and ill-equipped staff; (v) in many of the states, the trainees had to practice one major and one subsidiary craft;(vi) in most of the states, the final examination was conducted by the state departments of education; usually, there were internal and external assessment for theory papers, practice teaching and crafts; (vii) poor physical facilities were observed in many respects, viz., lack of science laboratories, inadequate buildings, inadequate accommodation in the hostels, no good libraries, no trained librarians and no adequate number of books and magazines; (viii) in case of government institutions, the grant from the government formed the only source of income; in the case of the private aided institutions also, considerable responsibility was born by the government and in the case of the private unaided institutions the main source of income was contribution from the management, donations, income from fees, etc.; and (ix) some senior officers from the Directorates of Education inspected the institutions and provided academic as well as administrative guidance.

Department of Post-graduate Studies in Education (1974) conducted a study of the Role Expectations of Teachers Under Training in the City of Bangalore. The main objectives of the study were : (i) to find out the attitude of pupil teachers towards different functions of teaching profession; (ii) to find out the interest pattern of pupil teachers in respect of teaching as a profession; and (iii) to assess the role expectation of pupil teachers regarding the functions of a teacher. The sample consisted of all the pupil teachers enrolled in the four teacher training colleges of Bangalore city during the session 1972-73. The total sample included 350 pupil teachers of which 124 were experienced male and female pupil teachers, 226 were fresh male and female pupil teachers, (157 male and 193 female).

The major findings of the study were as follows : (i) both the groups expressed high degree of favourable attitude; (ii) the female pupil teachers were more favourable towards the academic aspect of teaching than the male pupil teachers; (iii) the fresh pupil teachers were found to indicate higher degree of positive attitude than the deputed pupil teachers towards teaching as a whole; (iv) the deputed pupil teachers were inclined towards administrative aspects more than the freshers; (v) even among the female pupil teachers the freshers had registered a higher degree of positive attitude than the deputed pupil teachers; (vi) the experienced female pupil teachers were more favourable towards the academic aspect than the deputed female pupil teachers; (vii) the female pupil teachers were found to be more interested in cocurricular and community activities than the male pupil teachers; (viii) the experienced pupil teachers were more interested in teaching than their counterpart; (ix) experience had no effect on the role expectations of male pupil teachers; and (x) the fresh female pupil teachers exhibited a higher degree of role expectation than the experienced.

Joshi (1974) conducted a study of Innovations in Teacher Training Institutions. The objectives of the study were to find out (i) innovations in teacher education programme pertaining to curriculum, methods of teaching and in-service education; (ii) the types of courses followed in different states; and (iii) the resisting factors of innovations. The method followed was the descriptive survey method. A preliminary survey of fifty teacher training institutions was made and eleven institutions were selected by stratified random sample basis for intensive study. Questionnaires were mailed and a sample of principals and teachers was also interviewed.

The findings of the investigation were : (i) In the area of methodology of teaching, popularly used methods were question-answer and objective based teaching. (ii) The use of micro-teaching, programmed learning, interaction analysis and self-learning projects were negligible. (iii) Nearly eightyone per cent of the instructors frequently used lecture method in their theory classes. (iv) Not many institutions and instructors were involved in the in-service programme of elementary teachers. (v) In Rajasthan some innovations were reported. For example there were three institutions to organise regular programmes of in-service education, the teacher training institutes provided training on ungraded unit and a new experiment on first introduction to teaching was undertaken. (vi) In Gujarat and Jamia Millia Islamia, block teaching was one of the components of the teacher education programme. (vii) In Gujarat and Rajasthan separate institutions for linguistic minorities existed. (viii) The most significant factors of resistance to innovations as reported were : lack of facilities, lack of funds, lack of time to pursue the new ideas, lack of professional guidance and lack of support from education department.

Prakash and Mehrotra (1974) made an exploratory study of the use of audio-cassette recordings in the supervision of student-teachers. The major objectives of the study were : (i) to find out the feasibility of the use of a cassette recorder in practice teaching lessons of student teachers, and (ii) to evaluate the effectiveness of its use in improving the skill in the teaching of student teachers.

The findings were : (i) The use of cassette recorder caused a little commotion in a class when used for the first time; but after the novelty wore off, it disturbed neither the student teacher nor the pupils (ii) It provided an accurate record of the verbal interactions in the lesson (iii) It resulted in (a) Confirmation of good practices and consequently student teachers gaining more confidence; and (b) readiness to accept shortcomings (iv) The student teachers could locate different types of shortcomings in their lessons after listening to the audio-cassette recorder. Some of these shortcomings were related to (a) unnecessary reframing of questions asked by the teacher, (b) question elaboration, (c) lapses regarding content, facts, figures and concepts, (d) mistakes in the use language, (e) unnecessary pauses in the development of the lesson, (f) teachers voice, (g) his delivery, (h) mannerism, (i) not allowing pupils sufficient time to respond, (j) finding out that pupil participation was not sought where it could have been, (k) realization of not having adequately removed wrong concepts held by pupils, (l) not giving sufficient attention to desirable details, (m) lack of variety in approach, and (n) teacher domination.

Safia Sultana (1976) conducted a study of the Academic Difficulties of Student Teachers. The results revealed the following as the major difficulties of student teachers : (i) Course content of the theory papers especially philosophy and psychology, is difficult. (ii) The students had no chance to express their difficulties in understanding the lesson during the class. (iii) Majority of the students, who did not study in English medium found it difficult to understand what was being taught in English. (This difficulty was especially mentioned by the students in the Department of Education). (iv) On the basis of their experience of practice teaching, their main difficulty was that what was being taught in methodology classes was not acceptable to school teachers and they hardly agreed to try new methods in actual classroom teaching. (v) The whole programme was so over crowded that they did not get enough time for other activities. (vi) Most of their difficulties persist because the teacher educators never tried to have interaction with them outside the class.

Krupa Latha (1979) conducted a study of the relative effectiveness of micro teaching technique in developing teacher competence among trainees at the teachers training institute level. The sample of the study consisted of 200 student teachers from a teacher training institution.

The major findings of this study are : (1) The training of skills through micro teaching resulted in better teaching competency. (2) The training given to the student teachers through micro teaching before the post test and the macro lesson given after the post test resulted in better teaching ability. (3) The treatment through micro teaching had no direct effect on the attitude of student teachers of the experimental group. (4) The treatment through micro teaching had no direct effect on the attitude of student teachers of the controlled group. (5) The latency period did not effect the skill already acquired. (6) The training in interaction of skills improved general teaching competence.

Sujatha (1979) conducted An Enquiry into the undergraduate Teacher Training Programme in the State of Karnataka. Data were collected through questionnaires and a teacher efficiency inventory. The sample for the questionnaire included 200 experts in the field of education.

The facilities provided in the teacher training institutes in respect of teaching personnel, admission procedure, institutional plant, time allotment to the teaching of different subjects and practice teaching were not adequate to carry out the curricular programme effectively. The performance of the trainees in the teacher's efficiency inventory showed that the training programme had failed to develop a teacher of desired quality.

Verma (1979) conducted A Study of Teacher Training as a Catalyst of Change in Professional Attitudes of Student-Teachers. The sample consisted of 500 student-teachers undergoing training in seven teacher training institutions of Uttar Pradesh. The tools used were Teacher Attitude Inventory prepared and standardized by the investigator, follow-up questionnaire, personal data sheet and Instructor Rating Questionnaire.

The main findings of the study were: (i) The teacher training programme was a catalyst of change in the professional attitudes of the teacher-trainees. (ii) Sex, age, marital status, caste, rural-urban residence, income and source of income of the family, size of the family, parental education, presence of a teacher-member in the family, political affiliation, party affiliation, academic qualification, courses of study of the teacher-trainees were not correlated with their attitudinal change. (iii) Pre-training teaching experience, place of graduation and post-graduation and the teacher training institutions attended by the teacher-trainees were significantly correlated with their attitudinal change. (iv) The teacher-training programme was very effective for attitudinal change of those teacher-trainees who had pre-training teaching experience of one year or less. It was less fruitful to freshers and almost useless to teacher-trainees with pre-training teaching experience of more than five years. (v) The teacher training programme was more effective for attitudinal change among the trainees who had completed their education privately and also those trainees who had come from families where the source of income was business.

Jangira (1982) conducted a study of social cohesion in Elementary Teacher Training Institutions and its Relationship with their Efficiency.The study involved thirty-three elementary teacher training institutions drawn at random from 185 institutions in the State of Uttar Pradesh. The main findings of the investigation were : (i) Social cohesion had significant correlation with the student-teacher's achievement in theory as well as in practice. (ii) It's correlations with the student-teachers' adjustment and attitudes were not significant. (iii) Social cohesion in the teacher training institutions turned out to be a predictor of student-teachers' achievement in practice teaching explaining 48.23 per cent of the variance. (iv) It was a comparatively weak predictor of student-teachers' achievement in theory explaining merely 11.69 per cent of the variance in achievement. (v) Student teachers' achievement in theory in institutions with high and low social cohesion differed significantly. (vi) Student-teachers' attitude to teachers (teacher-educators in this case) differed significantly in institutions with high and low social cohesion.

Rai (1982) conducted a survey of the problems of Teacher's Training Colleges situated in Uttar Pradesh and Gujarat with regard to practising schools. The sampling technique used was a combination of random and cluster sampling. It included 730 respondents consisting of 20 principals, 100 teacher-educators, 500 student-teachers,

30 school headmasters, 70 teachers and 10 educationists. The tools used included questionnaires, a checklist and an opinionnaire. Chi-square test, critical ratio and percentages were the statistical techniques used.

The findings of the investigation were : (i) Fifty three per cent of the student-teachers of Uttar Pradesh and 31 per cent of Gujarat admitted that they failed to discharge their responsibilities satisfactorily due to lack of time. (ii) Sixty-four per cent student-teachers of Uttar Pradesh and 82 per cent of Gujarat opined that demonstration lessons were useful for them. Introducing and dividing the unit in a proper way were the problems of student-teachers of Uttar Pradesh and Gujarat, respectively. The student-teachers stated that the teacher educators generally lacked competence in respect of giving guidance. (iii) Seventy-four per cent of the teacher educators of Uttar Pradesh and 36 per cent of Gujarat reported that they failed to perform their responsibilities during student teaching satisfactorily.

Of the teacher educators of Gujarat 76 per cent against 28 per cent of Uttar Pradesh expressed their satisfaction with their supervisory functions. The most difficult problems were in regard to establishing good relationship with practising schools and framing suitable time-tables. The teacher educators of Uttar Pradesh and Gujarat admitted that they lacked professional efficiency to guide the student-teachers properly. They felt that the student-teachers wanted spoon-feeding. They faced the problem of limited periods of practice teaching allowed by schools. Internal assessment was another problem.

Principals of the training colleges admitted that they were unsuccessful in realizing the objectives of student teaching because of lack of cooperation from the schools and inadequate time. The headmasters of practising schools of Uttar Pradesh and Gujarat were not happy with the teaching by student-teachers. The school teachers felt that the programme of student teaching upset their plan of work.

Educationists felt that the objectives of student teaching were not realized, the quantum of student teaching was inadequate, supervision was defective, the relationship between colleges and schools was not harmonious and the evaluation process was defective.

Sharma (1982) investigated into the progress and problems of Teacher Education in India. The progress and development of teacher education was examined on the basis of the data collected from reports and journals on teacher education. The information was collected in the light of the modern concept of teacher education, the qualities of a teacher, the teacher's role in modern society and pre-service and in-service teacher education programems. Progress and programmes of teacher education during the Five Year Plans in India were also examined.

The main findings of the study were : (i) Even after a lapse of sixteen years, from the publication of the Education Commission Report (1966), teacher education programmes had not undergone any marked improvement. (ii) Methods of teaching and evaluation being used in training institutions were traditional. (iii) There was evidence to show that there was lack of research data in the field of teacher education. (iv) There was dire need for organising refresher coursers, short-term intensive courses in special subjects, practical training, workshops and professional conferences at both the levels (primary and secondary) of teacher education programmes. (v) If education was to meet the demands of our time and of coming decades, the organisation, content and methods of teacher education must be constantly improved. (vi) Search for new education strategies and concepts should be undertaken, taking into account the special social and cultural conditions under which the school and the teacher must perform their basic functions. (vii) Since it was not possible to equip the student-teacher with knowledge and skills which would be sufficient for his whole professional life, the initial preparation for the profession in the form of pre-service education and training, should be considered only as the first fundamental stage in the process of continuous education of teachers.

Sinha (1982) conducted An Evaluative Study of Teacher Education in Bihar. The study was based on a randomly selected sample of forty-four primary teacher education colleges out of a total of eighty-four colleges and all the ten secondary teacher education colleges in Bihar. Data were collected from the principals and the teacher educators of the college.

The main findings of the study were : (i) At the primary level, about 60 per cent of the teacher-educators were trained graduates and their performance was not satisfactory. (ii) Over 77 per cent colleges had no buildings of their own while 65 per cent colleges had their own buildings in poor condition. (iii) A majority of the colleges had inadequate staff, library, equipments and laboratory. (iv) Recent innovations in teacher education were not incorporated into the system. (v) In-service programmes were not carried on effectively and there was little attention paid to follow up programmes. (vi) The evaluation process had remained traditional. (vii) Practice teaching in colleges of education was being neglected by the methodology masters.

Gopalacharyulu (1984) studied the Relationship between certain psycho-sociological factors and achievements of student-teachers in the Teacher Training Institutes of Andhra Pradesh. The major findings of the study were: (1) Socio-economic status and caste influenced all the three achievement variables, namely, theory, practical and total achievement. (2) Attitude towards teaching profession and attitude towards training influenced the theory and total achievement significantly. (3) Age and locality of student-teachers were found to have significant influence on the theory and total achievement.

Sharma (1984) conducted a study of Teaching Aptitude, Intellectual Level and Morality of Prospective Teachers. The sample of the study included 412 student-teachers who were studying in ten teachers' colleges of three universities of Rajasthan. The findings were : 1. About 75 per cent of student-teachers were below average in aptitude and intellectual ability. 2. An insignificant difference was found in teaching aptitude ability in sex-wise and discipline-wise comparison. 3. A positive correlation was found between teaching aptitude, intellectual level and morality of prospective teachers.

Mohammed Pasha (1988) studied the problems faced by the primary teacher training institutes in practice-teaching in practising schools. A sample consisting 28 heads of practising schools, 56 cooperating teachers, 30 teacher educators and 120 student teachers was taken on the basis of purposive random sampling. A self prepared questionnaire and interview were used as tools. Data was analysed and presented in percentages and tables.

The major findings of the survey are : (1) About 50% of headmasters of practising schools considered practice teaching an obstacle in their school programme. (2) A majority of student teachers found it is difficult to manage the classes, since they were novices. (3) 72% of schools did not allow the student teachers to use their equipment for teaching. (4) 72% of schools alloted only the periods of non-academic subjects for practice teaching. (5) 92% of headmasters did not supervise the practice teaching lessons. (6) A majority of co-operating teachers did not evince interest in teaching practice as it was not remunerative. (7) A majority of teacher educators observed more than 20 lessons per week. (8) A majority of student teachers got experience of single teacher schools.

Kollur, Sheela Bai (1990) made a study of the opinion of the teacher educators regarding the new Teacher Certificate Higher (TCH) syllabus of 1989. An opinionnaire prepared by the researcher was used as tool. Data was analysed and presented using frequencies, percentages and tables.

The major findings of this study are : (1) 87% teacher educators desired TCH to be called as D.Ed. (2) 93% agreed for making PUC as minimum qualification for TCH. (3) 87% of teacher educators welcomed the idea of having a co-ordination board. (4) 56% of them welcomed innovative ideas like micro-teaching and un-supervised lesson for the

TCH course. (5) 60% teacher educators supported practical exam in teaching for the I year TCH. (6) 52% teacher educators opposed the idea of cancellation of specialisation subjects in the II year TCH. (7) 66% welcomed the introduction of the new subject, Educational Evaluation and Measurement.

Reddy (1991) examined the quality improvement in the pre-service education of the primary school teachers in Andhra Pradesh. The study revealed that : (1) Out of 11 Teacher Training Institutes (TTIs), only one TTI had enough classrooms, others had 2 to 3 classrooms, and 2 TTIs had no classroom at all. (2) Out of 11 TTIs, only 9 TTIs had library facilities and 2 TTIs did not have library facility at all. (3) All TTIs had office rooms, 9 TTIs had staff rooms, 5 TTIs had laboratory facilities, 7 TTIs had toilet facilities, 4 TTIs had better play-ground facilities, 3 TTIs had no play-ground facilities. (4) Only 4 TTIs had workshops and 3 TTIs had tools for work experience activities, only 4 TTIs had A.V.rooms and 5 TTIs had some electronic equipment like T.V., V.C.R., V.C.P., Two in-one, etc. Only 2 TTIs had common meeting halls. (5) The teacher educators strongly felt that the TTIs were under-staffed. The teacher educators recommended for one lecturer for one subject and teacher pupil ratio should not exceed 1:30 to maintain the quality in PSTE. (6) The teacher educators were not in favour of the present teaching practice. They were in favour of introducing internship in teaching and they suggested 3-4 weeks of period on internship. (7) The teacher educators felt that the duration of pre-service teacher education programme had to be 2 years after intermediate course (ie., + 2 level).(8) The present evaluation system of PSTE had to be modified to include the evaluation of acquired skills. (9) Internal and external, continuous and comprehensive evaluation had to be adopted. (10) Regular and immediate feed back had to be given to trainees. The syllabus of PSTE had to be designed for 50 per cent content and 50 per cent for methodology. The investigator suggested that the existing curriculum should be revised and the primary school should be attached to the TTI.

Viswanathappa (1992) made 'An evaluation of pre-service teacher education programme of the DIETs in Andhra Pradesh'. Major findings of the study were : 1. Out of 148 objectives from various sources, 144 were identified as important. 2. Out of these 144 the existing curriculum programme were found to be adequate for the realisation of 64 objectives only. 3.(a) Though the DIET Guidelines (1989) suggested that PSTE branch should possess one senior lecturer and 8 lecturers, it was observed that there were only 4-5 lecturers in each branch. It means that every PSTE Branch was run with inadequate teaching staff. (b) DIET Guidelines (1989) indicate that the teaching staff should have special training in elementary education. It was found that majority of the teaching staff in the DIETs had no specialised training in the elementary education. (c) Most of the faculty members were having high school teaching experience but not elementary school teaching experience. (d) The time allotted for theory and practice teaching was in the ratio of 3:1. Teachers suggested that the allotment should be in the ratio of 3:2. (e) Majority of the teacher educators suggested 45 days of practice teaching in each of the two years for PSTE programme. (f) The state level common entrance test for admission into the DIETs consisting of the components: test of general knowledge, test of language ability and test of non-language subjects. The supplementary assessment relating to verbal and non-verbal intelligence tests, attitude towards teaching and aptitude for teaching was ignored. (g) Among 27 physical facilities to be available only classrooms, seminar rooms, physical science and biological science method laboratories, play-ground, library, hostel facilities were available in majority of DIETs. The remaining physical facilities were poorly available in the DIETs. (h) Among the student personnel services, individual guidance for subject knowledge improvement and guidance in personal problems were provided with the organisation of co-curricular activities. Among the 15 desirable co-curricular activities organised in the DIETs, nearly three fourth of teachers were dissatisfied with the co-curricular activities like N.C.C. Karate, Judo training. (i) Only 4 DIETs had demonstration school of their own. (j) Majority of demonstration schools concentrated on practice teaching and paid little efforts for carrying out research programme.4.(a) The male and female student teachers differed significantly in their average teaching competence and the female teachers had an edge over the male student-teachers. (b) The difference between the teaching competence of student teachers in the subjects was not significant though the teaching competence of student teachers in social studies was higher than in the remaining subjects, viz., mathematics, science. (c) Teaching competence of the students was high in lesson planning and low in recapitulation and evaluation. (d) The teaching competence of student teachers belonging to the DIETs with the partially adequate staff was higher than that of those belonging to the DIETs with adequate staff. 5. There was no significant impact of the number of (a) Co-curricular activities organised by the DIETs. (b) Co-operating schools used for practice teaching.(c) Difficulties experienced by the DIETs in making arrangements for practice teaching on the teaching competence of student teachers.

Gopalan, Beena (1993) carried out a case study of a few District Institutes of Education and Training in Kerala. Major findings of the study were: (1) The literacy percentage ranged from 58.32 to 78.82 among districts which were against the belief that Kerala had achieved 100% literacy. The female literacy percentage was less than that of the men. (2) Audio-visual aids such as slides, slide projector, maps, charts, cassettes, radio were available in all the DIETs. But some of the DIETs did not have films, video cassettes, VCR, TV etc. (3) Reference material, books, newspaper were available in all the DIETs. (4) In all the five DIETs the pre-service offered was the Teacher Training Course (TTC). (5) Training programme for head teachers was also undertaken by DIETs. (6) District Resource Units of all the DIETs had organised programmes for adult education.

Manoj (1993) studied the "Competencies and training needs of DIET faculty members in DPEP districts of Kerala". The major findings of the study were : 1. Most of the faculty members working in DPEP-DIETs were men. 2. Majority of the DPEP-DIET faculty members were from teaching background. 3. Almost all the faculty members of Kerala had a double post-graduation. 4. One third of the total DPEP-DIET faculty members were not willing to continue in the DIET. 5. DIET faculty members did not consider themselves least competent or not competent with regard to any of the competencies. 6. DIET faculty members did not perceive the need for a long term training with respect to any of the competencies. 7. The DPEP-DIET faculty members in Kerala preferred to have : (a) Training programme outside the DIET.(b) Seven to ten days for short term training. (c) Less than one month or one to three months duration for long term training. (d) Institutionalised type of programme.

Ramamurthy (1994) made a study of the problems faced by the trainees in schools during the practice teaching programme. 50 Teacher Certificate Higher (TCH) trainees of one teacher training institute were chosen as the sample on the principle of purposive sampling. A self-made questionnaire was used as tool for collection of data, which was analysed in terms of percentages.

The major findings of the study are : (1) 92% of trainees got the experience of teaching in a single teacher school. (2) A majority of trainees did not get sufficient co-operation in schools. (3) A majority of schools split the classes for practice teaching. (4) 92% trainees got opportunity to act as class teachers for large classes. (5) Very few trainees organised co-curricular activities in schools. (6) A majority of trainees got guidance from their teacher supervisors.

Betageri (1996) studied the competencies and training needs of DIET faculty members in DPEP districts of Karnataka. The major findings were :1. Most of the DIET faculty members did not have post-graduation in education and their professional qualification was B.Ed. 2. All the faculty members had undergone one or the other training in elementary education. 3. DIET faculty members did not consider themselves least competent, not competent or highly competent. All of them considered themselves fairly competent. 4. Most of the faculty members required a short term training programme with theoretical orientation. For a few competencies they did not require training at all. 5. The faculty members working in a particular wing of the DPEP perceived training as required to certain identified competencies. 6. Even though a DIET faculty member was likely to have more than 10 years of previous experience, his experience in DIET was below 2 years.

The review relating to research studies conducted in the area of teacher education discloses that the efforts of Central and State Governments in making teacher education more effective resulted in marginal modifications only. The status of teacher education is still in bad shape. The present study is also an attempt to highlight the deficiencies in the pre-service programme conducted by the DIETs in Andhra Pradesh so as to suggest suitable remedial measures and make the process of preparing teachers more effective as quality teacher input is most important to bring qualitative improvement in primary education.

3

Statement of the Problem, Hypotheses and Variables

With the knowledge and experience gained through the analytical observations reported in the earlier chapter the researcher is in a position to state the problem, its significance, objectives, hypotheses and variables clearly.

3.1 SIGNIFICANCE OF THE STUDY

"Of all the different factors which influence the quality of education and its contribution to national development, the quality, competence and character of teachers are undoubtedly the most significant. Nothing is more important than securing a sufficient supply of high quality recruits to the teaching profession, providing them with the best possible professional preparation and creating satisfactory conditions of work in which they can be fully effective."

—*Indian Education Commission, 1966, (p.46)*

"A sound programme of professional education of teachers is essential for the qualitative improvement of education. Investment in teacher education can yield very rich dividends because the financial resources required are small when measured against the resulting improvements in the education of millions".

—*Indian Education Commission (1964-66)*

The teacher occupies a pivotal position in the system of education. With good leadership and appropriate teaching aids, the teacher's effectiveness can be enhanced but the most ingenious plans of inspired administrators and the best array of instructional devices are of little avail if the teacher is ignorant, unskilled or indifferent. Thus, the success of any educational reform depends upon the quality of teachers and in turn the quality of teachers depends to a large extent on the quality of teacher education.

The pace and magnitude of socio-economic development of any nation is basically determined by the level of education of its citizens. Education has been recognised as a fundamental right and it is viewed as a process of human resource development where the knowledge, skills and capabilities are sharpened to achieve a wide range of objectives. The success of democracy, developed programmes, community involvement, utilisation of physical and human resources, national integration, cultural emancipation, etc., are influenced by the education of the massess. There is no meaning in aiming for development without playing emphasis on education. India has a glorious history but it could not keep up its momentum due to several reasons and one of the major reasons is the neglect of education. Several Commissions like Macaulay Minutes (1835), Wood's Despatch (1854), Hunter Commission (1882), Indian University Act (Lord Curzon Act) 1904, Sadler Commission (1918), Sarvepalli Radhakrishnan Commission (1948), Mudaliar Commission (1952), Kothari Commission (1964-66), National Policy on Education (1986), etc., and a good number of social reformers like Swami Vivekananda, Mahatma Gandhi, Rabindranath Tagore, Jawaharlal Nehru, Raja Ram Mohan Roy have unanimously endorsed their strong concern about the need for extending educational opportunities to all sections of the community.

Education is a nation building activity and teachers are the pillars of the educational system. A good number of inputs like school buildings, community support, physical facilities, finances, administrative support and teachers are needed for a good educational system. But, it is basically the quality teachers who occupy a pivotal and frontline position and all other inputs are only secondary. With the development of science and technology our educational system is getting modernised and even then the role of a teacher in the academic system can never be under-estimated. The success of the school system especially a country like in India, which is rural and backward in its nature is basically determined by the level of commitment and concern on the part of the teachers to contribute their mite to the cause of primary education. A teacher requires a wide range of skills like communicative skills, skill of reinforcement, reasoning, questioning and especially the exploratory skill. These skills are essential as the teacher works amidst several deficiencies like lack of school building, lack of community participation, lack of teaching-learning materials, hard-ware equipment, etc. The teacher is expected to perform his functions in the best possible manner by the authorities and here comes the ability of the teacher to tap and utilise the local resources for education at the grass-root levels. Teaching profession is a noble profession and the word and deed of the teacher leaves a permanent mark in the hearts of the little children at the primary level.

Hence, the teacher has to be a good model, he is expected to be a good scholar, an ideal social worker and committed to improve the lot of the poor and downtrodden by extending to them educational opportunities and there by sensitizing them to claim their basic fundamental rights in the country. The role of the teacher is not merely limited to the four walls but it extends to outer world as well.

Teaching is an art and many are to be trained in this art. Anybody can become a teacher but everybody cannot become an effective teacher. In olden days the requirements in terms of teacher education were limited but the present system requires only well trained teachers. A comprehensive teacher education programme may help in producing quality teachers. At present the DIETs are given the responsibility of providing pre-service training. Hence, there is every need to look into the status of DIETs from various angles and to study the situation on the basis of perceptions of students, staff, principals, etc., who form a part and parcel of the total training programme at the DIET level. So the present study is an ardent effort in this direction.

3.2 STATEMENT OF THE PROBLEM

The title of the problem is precisely as follows: "AN EVALUATIVE STUDY OF PRIMARY SCHOOL TEACHER EDUCATION PROGRAMME IN ANDHRA PRADESH".

3.3 OBJECTIVES OF THE STUDY

The main objectives of the study are :

1. To study the perceptions of the student teachers of DIETs about different aspects of their training.
2. To study the attitude of the student teachers towards teaching profession.
3. To note the variation in the perceptions and attitudes of student teachers due to different personal and demographic variables.
4. To study the perceptions of the teacher educators about different aspects of the DIETs.
5. To study the attitudes of the teacher educators towards existing teacher education programme.
6. To identify the differences in the perceptions and attitudes of teacher educators depending upon their personal and demographic variables.
7. To study the perceptions of the principals about different aspects of the DIETs.
8. To record the physical and academic facilities available in the DIETs.
9. To observe and notice the specific deficiencies in the DIETs.
10. To suggest remedial measures to nullify the deficiencies in the existing primary level teacher education proramme.

3.4 HYPOTHESES

On the basis of the above objectives the following hypotheses were formulated. The hypotheses were set up in a 'null-form' as this form of hypotheses is akin to the legal principle that a man is innocent until he is proved guilty (Guilford and Fruchter, 1978; Garrett and Woodworth, 1966).

3.4.1 THE STUDENT TEACHERS IN GENERAL DONOT POSSESS POSITIVE PERCEPTION ON DIFFERENT ASPECTS OF DIETs.

3.4.2 THE STUDENT TEACHERS ARE NOT FAVOURABLE TO TEACHING PROFESSION.

3.4.3 THE PERSONAL AND DEMOGRAPHIC VARIABLES OF STUDENT TEACHERS WOULD NOT INFLUENCE THEIR LEVEL OF PERCEPTIONS ON DIFFERENT ASPECTS OF DIETs AND THEIR ATTTITUDE TOWARDS TEACHING PROFESSION. THIS MAJOR HYPOTHESIS IS SPLIT INTO DIFFERENT MINOR HYPOTHESES AS FOLLOWS FOR THE PURPOSE OF TESTING EACH VARIABLE SEPARATELY.

3.4.3.1 Male and female student teachers do not differ significantly with regard to their perceptions on various aspects of their teacher education programme.

3.4.3.2 Male and female student teachers do not differ significantly with regard to their attitudes towards teaching profession.

3.4.3.3 The student teachers of different age groups do not differ significantly on their perceptions.

3.4.3.4 The student teachers of different age groups do not differ significantly in their attitude towards teaching profession.

3.4.3.5 The qualifications of student teachers do not have any significant bearing on their perceptions.

3.4.3.6 The qualifications of student teachers do not have any significant bearing on their attitude towards teaching profession.

3.4.3.7 The locality from which the student teachers hail would not indicate any significant difference in their perceptions.

3.4.3.8 The locality from which the student teachers hail would not indicate any significant difference in their attitude towards teaching profession.

3.4.3.9 The methodology subject of the student teachers would not indicate any significant difference in their perceptions.

3.4.3.10 The methodology subject of the student teachers would not indicate any significant difference in their attitude towards teaching profession.

3.4.3.11 The methodology in language of the student teachers would not indicate any significant difference in their perceptions.

3.4.3.12 The methodology in language of the student teachers would not indicate any significant difference in their attitude towards teaching profession.

3.4.3.13 The literacy index would not significantly influence the perceptions of the student teachers.

3.4.3.14 The literacy index of the student teachers would not significantly influence the attitudes of student teachers towards teaching profession.

3.4.3.15 Father's occupation of student teachers would not significantly influence their perceptions.

3.4.3.16 Father's occupation of student teachers would not significantly influence their attitude towards teaching profession.

3.4.3.17 Mother's occupation would not significantly influence the perceptions of the student teachers.

3.4.3.18 Mother's occupation of student teachers would not significantly influence their attitude towards teaching profession.

3.4.3.19 Family annual income of student teachers would not significantly influence their perceptions.

3.4.3.20 Family annual income would not significantly influence the attitude of student teachers.

3.4.4 THE TEACHER EDUCATORS, IN GENERAL, DONOT POSSESS POSITIVE PERCEPTIONS ON DIFFERENT ASPECTS OF DIETs.

3.4.5 THE ATTITUDE OF TEACHER EDUCATORS TOWARDS THE EXISTING PRE-SERVICE TRAINING PROGRAMME IS NOT FAVOURABLE.

3.4.6 THE PERSONAL AND DEMOGRAPHIC VARIABLES OF TEACHER EDUCATORS DONOT INFLUENCE THEIR PERCEPTIONS ON DIFFERENT ASPECTS OF DIETs AND ATTITUDES. THIS MAJOR HYPOTHESIS IS SPLIT IN TO DIFFERENT MINOR HYPOTHESES AS FOLLOWS FOR THE PURPOSE OF TESTING EACH VARIABLE SEPARATELY.

3.4.6.1 Male and female lecturers do not differ significantly with regard to their perceptions on various aspects of teacher education programme.

3.4.6.2 Male and female lecturers do not differ significantly with regard to their attitude towards teacher education programme.

3.4.6.3 Age of the lecturers would not significantly influence their perception of various activities of teacher education programme.

3.4.6.4 Age of the lecturers would not significantly influence their attitude towards teacher education programme.

3.4.6.5 Educational qualifications of lecturers would not significantly influence their perceptions.

3.4.6.6 Educational qualifications of lecturers would not significantly influence their attitudes towards teacher education programme.

3.4.6.7 Designation of lecturers would not significantly influence their perceptions of the various activities of the DIET.

3.4.6.8 Designation of lecturers would not significantly influence their attitude towards teacher education programme.

3.4.6.9 Lecturers experience as primary school teacher would not significantly influence the perceptions of the various activities of the DIET.

3.4.6.10 Experience as primary school teacher would not significantly influence the attitudes of lecturers towards teacher education programme.

3.4.7 THE PRINCIPALS IN GENERAL, DONOT POSSESS POSITIVE PERCEPTION ON DIFFERENT ASPECTS of DIETs.

3.4.8 THE PHYSICAL FACILITIES AVAILABLE IN DIETs ARE NOT SATISFACTORY.

3.4.9 THE SPECIFIC OBSERVATIONS NOTICED BY THE INVESTIGATOR ARE NOT SERIOUS AND DO NOT FORM AS OBSTACLES FOR PRODUCING QUALITY TEACHERS.

3.5 VARIABLES INCLUDED IN THE STUDY

As the present study envisages an evaluation of the primary school teacher education programme in Andhra Pradesh on the basis of the perceptions and attitudes of student teachers, teacher educators and principals, the dependent variables are as follows:

1. Perception of student teachers on different aspects of DIET.

2. Attitude of student teachers towards teaching profession.

3. Perception of teacher educators on different aspects of DIET.

4. Attitude of teacher educators toward the existing teacher training programme.

5. Perception of principals on different aspects of DIET, and

6. Availability of material and infrastructural facilities.

INDEPENDENT VARIABLES

The independent variables considered in the investigation are of two kinds, namely, student teacher related personal and demographic variables and teacher educator related personal and demographic variables. The student teacher related independent variables are sex, age, educational qualifications, locality, methodology in subject, methodology in language, family literacy index, father's occupation, mother's occupation and family annual income. The teacher educator's related independent variables are sex, age, educational qualifications, designation and experience as primary school teacher.

3.6 OPERATIONAL DEFINITIONS OF TERMS

The following operational definitions and descriptions are operationalised for the purpose of measuring the variables in the study.

Perception

A person's perception may be defined as to cognize or perceive other physical and psychological characteristics, their intentions, feelings, activities, emotions, motives and attitudes.

Perception, refers to the process whereby sensory stimulation is translated into organised experience.

That experience on percept is the joint product of the stimulation and of the process itself. Keeping in view the explanation given to the word 'perception' an attempt has been made in the present research to study perception of student teachers, teacher educators and principals with regard to various aspects of teacher education programme.

Attitude

Guilford (1954) defined attitude as a "personal disposition common to individual but possessed to different degrees which impels to react to object situations or positions in ways that can be called favourable or unfavourable".

Evaluation

Evaluation can be defined as a process of assigning units of measurement to phenomena in order to characterise their worth or value, usually with reference to some social, cultural or scientific standard. (In the present study the investigator has chosen to evaluate the pre-service teacher education programme by taking the opinions of student teachers, teacher educators and principals on the various aspects of DIETs in Andhra Pradesh).

Teacher Education

It has been defined as "all formal and informal activities and experiences that help to qualify a person to assume the responsibilities as a member of the educational profession and to discharge his responsibilities more effectively".

Training

It is defined as a process of helping others to acquire skill and knowledge without reference to any great meaning for the individual's learning to perform the skills or to verbalise the knowledge, this being performed at the instance of conditioned course.

Physical Facilities

Generally it includes a variety of aspects such as institution, plant-locations and buildings, accomodation and furniture for staff and students, well established library and laboratories, aeriation and ventilation, water and sanitation, play-ground, electricity, sports and games equipment and teaching aids.

Academic Amenities

Learning takes place only in the motivating learning environment. Academic amenities pertain to the institution. Mostly the requirement begins with the well organised seating arrangement for students in the classroom, availability of library facilities for developing good reading habits, laboratory facilities for experimentation by the student teachers to develop scientific attitudes and temperament and proper use of audio-visual equipments to supplement the classroom instructions, apart from the educational tours, games, puzzles and projects. All these things determine the academic climate of the institutions.

Finance and Management

The main source of income for any institution is the grant-in-aid which is provided by the state government. Besides the grants-in aids, special fee is also collected from the student teachers in all government institutions. There is also the provision of recurring cost and contingent expenditure in all government managed institutions.

Interpersonal Relationships

It denotes the pattern of social interaction that characterizes an organisation. The positive human interactions within the school organisation among student teachers, student teachers and lecturers, student teachers and principals, lecturers and principals and also with the non-teaching staff and outside the school with students, parents and community are of utmost value to promote more cohesive and caring environment which has direct impact on student learning.

METHODS OF INVESTIGATION

This chapter deals with the different procedures followed in the construction and development of data gathering instruments on different variables which are included in the study and the methods adapted in selection of sample, collection of data, method of scoring and analysis.

4.1 THE DESIGN OF THE STUDY

The present study is essentially an explorative and descriptive in nature. On the basis of the general survey the design of the study may be called as a survey type of research.

4.2 MEASUREMENT OF THE VARIABLES AND DEVELOPMENT OF THE TOOLS

As it has been described earlier it is proposed to study the perceptions of student teachers, teacher educators and principals on different physical, academic and administrative aspects of DIETs, three perception scales meant for the above three groups are to be developed. Apart from these three tools and attitude scale to measure the attitude of the student teachers towards teaching profession, another attitude scale to measure the teacher educators disposition on the existing teacher education programme in DIETs and a check-list for principals to identify the non-availability of requirements of DIETs are also to be developed. Of course, to collect data pertinent to personal and demographic variables of student teachers and teacher educators are also to be developed. The development of each one of the above tools is described in the following pages.

4.2.1 PERCEPTIONS OF STUDENT TEACHERS

It is by the organising process that we come to know objects in their appropriate identity. It is the immediate result of environmental input and the state of brain, perception pertaining to reaction to objects. Psychologists use the term "perception" to denote the cognitive process which stems from sensory stimulation. Sense organs have been considered the door ways of knowledge. As a result, Ellis (1965) defined perception as the interpretation of sensory stimuli and interpretation is the process of associating the stimulus with the past experiences that make it meaningful.

Likewise, Barber and Legge (1976) have opined that perception is about receiving, selecting, acquiring, transforming and organising the information supplied through our senses. Young (1957) is of the view that perception refers to the activity of sensing, interpreting and appreciating objects both physical and social.

To sum up these definitions—a person's perception may be defined as the ability to cognize or perceive other physical and psychological characteristics, their intentions, feelings, activities, emotions, motives and attitudes.

The present investigation is a study of the perceptions of the student teachers towards various aspects of their academic programme. DIETs are located almost outside the main towns/cities and most of the student teachers come from other places travelling daily. A few of them may be residing in the hostels or may be making their own arrangements till the completion of their course which is of one year duration. Not many attempts have been made to study the perceptions of the student teachers regarding physical facilities, organizational aspects, etc., (vide review of related literature). It is only action researchers that peep into the existing situations to suggest remedial measures, alternatives, new approaches, variety of programmes, changes in policies, evaluation techniques and organizational and administrative arrangements. The situations need to be modified according to the requirements of the student teachers at times who are going to be the main beneficiaries from the DIETs. Viewed from this perspective the perceptions of student teachers have to be studied pertaining to the several aspects like entrance test, qualifications prescribed for Teacher Training Course intake, physical facilities provided, duration of the course, classroom aspects like teaching-learning process, teachers influence, lecturers influence, helpfulness of academic and non-academic staff, physical accommodation available for class-rooms, lesson planning, model lessons to be taught, methods of teaching adapted, utility of the methods taught during the course in future cooperation of co-teachers, internship, laboratory, library and hostel facilities, quantum of record work, discipline, congenial environment available for smooth continuation of the course in the locality, etc., in order to bring in suitable changes for the effective organisation of the course. The investigator proposes to develop a perception scale for the student teachers.

4.2.1.1 Preparation of the Preliminary Form

To start with the nature and scope of the items that are to be included in the perception scale have been examined. Items that could be possibly included under the headings listed above have been collected and pooled together from the available literature. To supplement the list, 5 principals, 40 senior lecturers and 60 student teachers have been contacted and requested to suggest several items that could be included under the perception scale meant for student teachers. Thus the item pool consists of 60 items relating to physical facilities, 40 items relating to academic matters, 20 items from interpersonal relations, 20 items from financial aspects and 20 items from administrative aspects.

A panel of 10 experts comprising of 5 university level teachers and 5 senior faculty members of DIETs has been constituted for finalization of the scale and they have been requested to suggest omissions and modifications wherever necessary and to categorise the items under different aspects namely, physical, academic, administrative, financial, interpersonal, etc. They have also been requested to suggest whether the items should be presented under statement form or question form and also the nature of response pattern. Based on their suggestions the items have been presented in the form of questions with three alternative responses, namely, to the maximum extent, to the moderate extent and to the least extent. On the whole a total of 86 good items have been included in the pilot form of the perception scale. To establish the criterion validity of the scale an item is added at the end to measure the overall perception of the student teachers with two alternatives namely, Yes/No.

4.2.1.2 Pilot Study

The pilot form of the perception scale has been administered on a sample of 180 student teachers from three DIETs, one from each region—Coastal Andhra, Telengana and Rayalaseema, selected at random. The responses are as explained below:

S.No.	*Nature of Response*	*Numerical value assigned*	
		Positive statement	*Negative statement*
1.	Maximum extent	3	1
2.	Moderate extent	2	2
3.	Least extent	1	3

The total scores have been obtained for each subject. On the basis of the total score the top 27 per cent and the bottom 27 per cent scorers have been identified as the criterion groups. The mean scores on each item for both the criterion groups are calculated. The difference between the mean scores on each item is called as the discrimination value as suggested by Edwards (1969). The detailed discrimination index table is presented in Appendix—A_1.

4.2.1.3 Preparation of the Final Form

Those items whose discrimination value is greater than or equal to 0.3 have been selected as valid items to be included in the final form of the scale. Out of 86 items 11 items are found to be not having the required level of discrimination and thus 75 items are included in the final form of the scale. The English version of the final form is appended in Appendix—A_2.

4.2.1.4 Reliability of the Scale

Any scale developed to study the perceptions of individuals representing specific categories will be effective only when its reliability is established. For this purpose, the test-retest reliability of the scale has been examined by obtaining the responses of the scale with an interval of three weeks between the first and second administration of the tool to the same set of 60 student teachers. The correlation co-efficient between the two sets of the scores is 0.89 and is significant at 0.01 level. Hence the perception scale may be considered to have high reliability.

4.2.1.5 Validity of the Scale

The student teachers perception scale is established with (i) Content Validity (ii) Item Validity (iii) Criterion Validity, and (iv) Intrinsic Validity.

(i) *Content Validity*

Content validity is established for the perception scale meant for the student teachers. The present scale has been developed on the basis of review of literature, discussions with a good number of principals, senior staff members who are likely to become principals and student teachers and personal observation of the DIETs by the investigator. Every item chosen is a perfect respresentative of different aspects of DIETs. Thus it can be fairly assumed that the perception scale meant for student-teachers developed on the above lines possesses satisfactory content validity.

(ii) *Item Validity*

Item validity is established for the scale. In order to determine the discriminative power and usefulness of statements chosen for the scale, the mean difference of criterion groups on each item is established. Therefore, it could be concluded that each item included in the final form has high discrimination value. In other words each item has item validity.

(iii) *Criterion Validity*

On the basis of the responses obtained for the 87th item in the pilot form the entire group of 180 subjects has been divided into two groups—those who respond as 'Yes' and those who respond as 'No'. The mean scores obtained by these two groups and the respective standard deviations have been calculated. Critical ratio ('t' - test) is employed to see whether the two groups differ significantly from each other. The obtained critical ratio value, 4.34 is found to be far greater than the table value even at 0.01 level of probability for 178 df (degrees of freedom). In other words the mean of 'Yes' group is significantly greater than the mean of 'No' group. Thus, the instrument to measure the perception of student teachers may be said to have criterion validity.

(iv) *Intrinsic Validity*

The degree to which a test measures what it purports to measure (Guilford, 1954) is indicated by its intrinsic validity. In other words it means an indication of how well the obtained scores measure the test's true score component. Square root of its reliability value of the scale means its intrinsic validity. Hence the intrinsic validity of the developed scale is $\sqrt{0.89} = 0.95$ which can safely be assumed as satisfactory intrinsic validity.

4.2.1.6 A Brief Description of the Final Form of the Student-Teachers' Perception Scale

The final form of the student-teachers perception scale developed in the lines described above, consisted of 75 items of which 43 were negative and 32 were positive items. Each item can be rated on any of the three response categories namely, maximum extent, moderate extent and least extent which carry numerical values 3, 2 and 1 for positive items and numerical values 1,2 and 3 respectively for negative items. The score for a subject on the scale can be obtained by summing up the weights of the individual responses. The score of a student teacher on the scale will range between 75 to 225 points.

4.2.2 ATTITUDE OF THE STUDENT-TEACHERS TOWARDS TEACHING PROFESSION

"Attitude" is a familiar word and is used freely to express one's way of thinking, feeling or behaving. The term 'attitude' has been used by psychologists in several connotations and there are a number of agreed definitions of the term. Allport (1929) defined it "as a mental or neural state of readiness, organised through experiences exerting a directive or dynamic influence upon the individual response to all the objects and situations with which it is related".

In the dictionary of philosophy and psychology Baldwin (1901) defined attitude as "readiness for attention or action of a definite sort".

By attitude we understand "a process of individual consciousness which determines real or possible activity of the individual counterpart of the social value, activity in whatever form, is the bond between them".

—Thomas and Znamiecki, 1981, p.27.

This definition stresses that attitude is a generalized pattern of perception or action which is a result of integration of various experiences.

In the words of Lundberg (1929) "an attitude denotes the general set of the organism as a whole toward an object or situation which calls for adjustment".

Kohler (1929) remarked that "an attitude involves a definite psychological stress exerted upon the sensory field by processes originating in other parts of the nervous system".

"Attitude is a tendency to act toward or against something in the environment which becomes there by, a positive or a negative value".

—Bogardus, 1931

Droba (1933) opined that "an attitude is a mental disposition of the human individual to act for or against a definite object".

Attitude are literally mental postures, guides for conduct which each new experience is referred before a response is made.

—Morgan, 1936

In the dictionary of Psychology attitude is defined as "the specific mental disposition in coming experience where by that experience is modified or a condition of readiness for certain type of activities".

—Warren, 1934.

Guilford (1954) defined attitude as a personal disposition common to individuals but possessed in different degrees which impels to react to object situations or positions in ways that can be called favourable or unfavourable.

According to Freeman (1968) an attitude is a dispositional readiness to respond to certain situations, persons, or objects in a constant manner which has been learned and has become one's typical mode of response.

All the definitions cited above give importance to the degree of liking or disliking towards a psychological object and in line with above. Thurstone (1944) defined attitude as the degree of positive or negative affect associated with some psychological object.

Though attitude and opinion are allied terms they are not synonyms. Attitude denotes the inner feelings or belief of a person towards a psychological phenomenon. Opinion is therefore a verbal expression of attitude.

4.2.2.1 Different Methods of Measuring Attitude

Attitude can be measured in several ways. Attitudes are revealed in the behaviour of an individual. So, attitudes can be measured by direct observation of overt behaviour of the individual. This has all the defects of observation in addition to the difficulty of experimentally creating a real situation, where in behaviour can be observed.

Projective techniques can also be used to assess an individual's attitude. The basis for the use of projective techniques to measure attitude is that attitude can be inferred by one's unconscious responses to certain stimuli like photographs, cartoons, etc. This method also has the disadvantages of observation techniques like difficulty in administration, scoring, low inter scorer reliability, etc.

The most common method of estimating a person's attitude is through a questionnaire where, the individual expresses his opinion on several controversial statements on some psychological object. The logic behind the use of opinion to measure attitude is that the positive correlation between what people say about a subject and what they will do about it. To the extent people's actions correlates with their expressed opinion we can predict the former from the latter. Any single action however will be extremely unreliable from the point of view of treatment. A person's particular actions cannot be predicted with a high degree of accuracy yet one's position of an attitude scale can be assessed.

This method of assessing attitude from expressed opinion is also subject to some limitations like faking of responses by the individual where he tends to give socially acceptable response there by concealing his real attitude. But this could be overcome in several ways like making the questionnaire anonymous.

The two most well known methods of measuring attitude directly by attitude scale are :

A. Thurstone's method of equal appearing intervals, and

B. Likert's method of summated ratings.

A. Thurstone's method of equal appearing intervals

Thurstone's proposal to measure the attitude by statements scaled by the method of equal-appearing intervals would apply. A large number of favourable and unfavourable statements on the issue under investigation are written and given to a number of judges (subject experts) to sort them at their face value. The items which bring disagreement among the judges have been discarded. For the remaining items scaled values have been found out with the help of ogives. The respondent is to give his reaction to each statement by accepting or rejecting it. The medium values of the statement that he checks establishes his scores or quantifies his attitude.

B. Likert's method of Summated Ratings

It is considered an improvement over Thurstone's method. The first step in his method is collection of a number of items. They must express definite favourableness or unfavourableness to a particular view point and their number should be approximately equal. A trial test would be administered to a number of subjects and only those items that correlate with the total test should be retained. Five alternative responses, strongly agree and strongly disagree are given and a scaled value is given to each of the five responses. For positive items it is from 5 to 1 and for negative items it is from 1 to 5. The total of these scores on all items measures a respondent's favourableness or unfavourableness towards the subject in question.

Thus, the attitude of any person towards any subject can be estimated or measured by any of these methods. In the present study of measuring the attitude of student teachers towards teaching profession and attitude of teacher educators towards teacher education programme Likert's method of summated ratings is used.

4.2.2.2 Preparation of the Preliminary Form

There is no suitable standardized test to measure the attitude of the student teachers towards teaching profession. In view of this the investigator has to develop an attitude scale to suit his purpose. For the purpose of preparing the preliminary form first the nature and scope of the statements that have to be included in the proposed attitude scale have been examined in the light of the operational definition of the concept of student-teachers attitude towards teaching profession. All the favourable and unfavourable statements that are likely to indicate the attitude of student teachers towards teaching profession are pooled together from the available literature. The statements have been further supplemented by interviews with a good number of lecturers, senior lecturers, principals, administrators and student teachers. They have been asked to list either favourable and unfavourable statements that are supposed to indicate attitude towards teaching profession. The statements thus obtained have been scrutinised and the relevant one's are chosen and adapted to the list. After this, in order to avoid ambiguity and overlapping all the statements have been reviewed and re-written. The preliminary form thus prepared constitutes 68 statements of which 35 are supposed to represent positive attitude and the remaining 33 statements negative attitude of teacher trainees towards teaching profession. This has been presented to a panel of 20 experts (comprising of 5 lecturers, 5 principals and 10 student teachers) with a request to suggest improvements wherever necessary and the suggestions of the experts have been duly carried out. In all 57 statements have been selected for pilot form of which 27 statements are positive and the remaining are negative statements. An overall item to test whether the student teachers possess a favourable or unfavourable attitude towards teaching profession is included as 58th item for the purpose of establishing criterion validity.

4.2.2.3 Pilot Study

The pilot form of the attitude scale thus formulated has been administered to 180 student teachers from three DIETs, one from each region—Coastal Andhra, Telengana and Rayalaseema selected at random in order to examine whether the statements are easily understood by them or not and to know whether they possess clarity or not. The responses are scored by giving appropriate weightage as described below : For the purpose of scoring of the statements, numerical values are assigned to the five categories of responses (weightages) against each statement.

S.No.	*Nature of Response*	*Numerical value assigned*	
		Positive statement	*Negative statement*
1.	Strongly Agree	5	1
2.	Agree	4	2
3.	Un-decided	3	3
4.	Disagree	2	4
5.	Strongly Disagree	1	5

On the basis of weightages total scores have been obtained on the scale to all the 180 subjects. The top 27 per cent and bottom 27 per cent of the subjects have been identified as criterion groups and the mean scores obtained by these two groups on each item have been calculated. The difference between the mean scores is discrimination value or Item Validity Index, (Edward, 1969). The detailed table showing discrimination index is presented in Appendix —B_1.

4.2.2.4 Preparation of the Final Form

Out of 57 items in the final form only 45 (19 positive and 26 negative) have been selected for the inclusion in the final form of the attitude scale meant for student teachers depending upon the discrimination value of each item. Those items whose discrimination index is 0.3 and above have been selected for the final form. The English version of the final form of the attitude scale is presented in Appendix—B_2.

4.2.2.5 Reliability of the Measure

An attitude scale has been developed to measure the attitude of specific group of individuals representing a specific category. In order to find out effectiveness of the attitude scale developed, its test-retest reliability has been examined by obtaining scores for the tool with an interval of three weeks between the first and the second administration of the scale to the same set of 60 teacher trainees. The correlation co-efficient between the two sets of scores is 0.845 which is significant at 0.01 level. Hence the scale may be considered as having high reliability.

4.2.2.6 Validity of the Scale

Validity is another criteria considered to estimate the appropriateness of any tool developed to examine a particular aspect of an individual's attitude. The attitude scale of the present study developed on the lines described above indicates satisfying content validity, item (statement) validity, criterion validity and intrinsic validity. The details relating to them are as described.

(i) *Content Validity*

Content validity refers to the establishment and evaluation of the significance of the test items individually and as a whole. Every item should be a sampling of that aspect which the test purports to measure. In addition, items should collectively constitute a representative sample of the variable that is measured.

As already described, items for measure have been collected from different sources viz., review of literature, principals, lecturers, senior lecturers, student teachers and university teachers. In addition it has also been supplemented by interviewing select learners and experts to make sure that all possible items are covered. Thus it can be reasonably assumed that the attitude scale developed possesses satisfactory content validity.

(ii) *Item Validity*

Item validity stresses the number of discriminations of the desired sort that the item is capable of making. It stresses the extent to which the item predicts segregation of respondents into those with high versus those with low criterion scores. The discriminative power of each item of the present scale has been established as explained earlier. Thus the items chosen for the scale have been found to be satisfactorily valid.

(iii) *Criterion Validity*

On the basis of the responses obtained for the 58th item in the pilot form the entire group of 180 subjects has been divided into two groups—those who responded as 'Yes' and those who responded as 'No'. The mean scores obtained by these two groups and the respective standard deviations have been calculated. Critical ratio ('t' - test) has been employed to see whether the two groups differ significantly from each other. The obtained critical ratio value, 4.12 is far greater than the table value even at 0.01 level of probability for 178 df (degrees of freedom). In other words the mean of 'Yes' group is significantly greater than the mean of 'No' group. Thus, the instrument to measure the attitude of teacher trainees is said to have criterion validity.

(iv) *Intrinsic Validity*

According to Guilford (1954), intrinsic validity indicates the degree to which the test measures what it purports to measure. In other words this means verification of how well the obtained scores measure the test true score component. Intrinsic validity of a test is expressed in terms of square root of its reliability value. Thus the intrinsic validity of the attitude scale developed is $\sqrt{0.845} = 0.919$ and it can be assumed as a highly satisfactory intrinsic validity.

4.2.2.7 A Brief Description of the Final Form of the Attitude Scale

The final form of the attitude scale in the lines described above consists of 45 items of which 19 items are positive and 26 are negative. Each item can be rated on any of the five response categories viz., strongly agree, agree, undecided, disagree and strongly disagree which carry numerical values 5, 4, 3, 2 and 1 for positive statements and 1, 2, 3, 4 and 5 respectively for negative statements. The score for a respondent on the scale can be obtained by summing up the weights of the individual item responses which vary from 45 to 225.

4.2.3 PERCEPTIONS OF THE LECTURERS

The present investigation studies the perceptions of lecturers towards DIETs physical, academic, administrative, financial and interpersonal aspects. From the review of related literature it is clear that there are no standardized instruments to measure the perceptions of teacher educators on the aspects mentioned above. In view of this the investigator had to develop a perception scale for teacher educators to suit the purpose of the study.

4.2.3.1 Preparation of the Preliminary Form

To start with, the nature and scope of questions that are to be included in the perception scale have been examined. Items that could be possibly included under the headings namely, physical facilities, academic, administrative, financial and interpersonal aspects have been collected and pooled together from the available literature. To supplement the list 20 principals, 40 senior staff members who could become principals have been contacted. They have been requested to indicate several items that could be included under the perception scale meant for teacher educators. As many as 150 statements have been collected and written without overlapping and ambiguity. A form thus prepared consisted of 60 items relating to physical facilities, 50 items relating to academic matters and 20 items each relating to administrative and interpersonal aspects. A panel of 20 experts comprising of 10 principals, 5 university level teachers and 5 senior faculty members of DIETs has been constituted for finalization of the scale and they have been requested to suggest omissions and modifications wherever necessary. They have also been requested to categorise the items under different aspects and to suggest whether the items should be presented under statement form or question form and also the number of response categories. Based on their suggestions it has been decided to present the items in the form of questions with three alternative responses namely, to the maximum extent, to the moderate extent and to the least extent. On the whole a total of 107 good items have been identified to be included in the pilot form of the perception scale. To establish the criterion validity of the scale an item has been added at the end to measure the overall perception of the teacher educators with two alternatives namely Yes/No.

4.2.3.2 Pilot Study

The pilot form of the perception scale has been administered on a sample of 45 teacher educators from three DIETs one from each region—Coastal Andhra, Telengana and Rayalaseema selected at random. The responses are scored as explained below:

S.No.	*Nature of Response*	*Numerical value assigned*	
		Positive statement	*Negative statement*
1.	Maximum extent	3	1
2.	Moderate extent	2	2
3.	Least extent	1	3

The total scores for each subject has been obtained and on its basis the top 27 per cent and the bottom 27 per cent have been identified as the criterion groups. The mean scores on each item for both the criterion groups have been calculated. The difference between the mean scores on each item is called as the discrimination value as suggested by Edwards (1969). The detailed discrimination index table is presented in Appendix—C_1.

4.2.3.3 Preparation of the Final Form

Those items whose discrimination value is greater than or equal to 0.3 have been selected as valid items to be included in the final form of the scale. Out of 107 items 18 items are found to be not having the required level of discrimination and thus 89 items are included in the final form of the scale. The English version of the final form is appended in Appendix—C_2.

4.2.3.4 Reliability of the Scale

Any scale developed to study the perceptions of individuals representing specific categories will be effective only when its reliability is established. For this purpose, the test-retest reliability of the scale has been examined by obtaining the responses of the scale with an interval of three weeks between the first and second administration of the tool to the same set of 20 principals and senior lecturers likely to become principals. The correlation co-efficient between the two sets of the scores is 0.89 and is significant at 0.01 level. Hence the perception scale may be considered to be of high reliability.

4.2.3.5 Validity of the Scale

The teacher educators perception scale has been established with (i) Content Validity (ii) Item Validity (iii) Criterion Validity, and (iv) Intrinsic Validity.

(i) *Content Validity*

Content validity has been established for the perception

scale meant for the teacher educators. The present scale has been developed on the basis of review of literature, discussions with a good number of principals and senior staff members who are likely to become principals and personal observations of the DIETs by the investigator. Every item included in the pilot form is a sampling of many items and all the items put together form a representative sample of total possible items covering all the aspects of the variable. Thus, it can be fairly assumed that the perception scale meant for teacher educators developed on the above lines possesses satisfactory content validity.

(ii) *Item Validity*

Item validity has been established for the scale. In order to determine the discriminative power and usefulness of statements chosen, the mean difference of criterion groups on each item was established. Therefore, it could be concluded that each item included in the final form possesses high discrimination value, that is item validity.

(iii) *Criterion Validity*

On the basis of the responses obtained for 108th item in the pilot form the entire group of 45 subjects has been divided into two groups—those who respond as 'Yes' and those who respond as 'No'. The mean scores obtained by these two groups and the respective standard deviations have been calculated. Critical ratio ('t' - test) has been employed to see whether the two groups differ significantly from each other. The obtained critical ratio value, 5.61 is far greater than the table value even at 0.01 level of probability for 178 df (degrees of freedom). In other words the mean of 'Yes' group is significantly greater than the mean of 'No' group. Thus, the instrument to measure the perception of teacher educators is said to have criterion validity.

(iv) *Intrinsic Validity*

The degree to which a test measures what it purports

to measure (Guilford, 1954) is indicated by its intrinsic validity. In other words it means indication of how well the obtained scores measure the test's true score component. Square root of its reliability value of the scale means its intrinsic validity. Hence the intrinsic validity of the developed scale is $\sqrt{0.89} = 0.95$ which can be safely be assumed as satisfactory intrinsic validity.

4.2.3.6 A Brief Description of the Final Form of Teacher Educators' Perception Scale

The final form of the teacher's perception scale has been developed on the lines stated above consists of 89 items of which 16 are negative and 73 are positive items. Each item can be rated on any of the three categories namely maximum extent, moderate extent and least extent which carry numerical values 3, 2 and 1 for positive items and numerical values 1, 2 and 3 for negative items respectively. The score for a subject on the scale can be obtained by summing up the weights on all the items. The score of a teacher educator on the scale ranges between 89 to 267 points.

4.2.4 ATTITUDE OF THE TEACHER EDUCATORS TOWARDS TEACHER EDUCATION PROGRAMME

Attitude of teacher educators towards teacher education programme is one of the important areas of research in the current times. The effective organisation of teacher education programme lies in the hands of teacher educators who are entrusted with it. They are supposed to possess a very strong positive attitude towards teaching profession without which they will not be able to do justice for their jobs. Positive attitude towards various aspects associated with teacher education programmes like admission procedure, classroom interaction, teaching methods, maintenance of academic standards, qualitative organisation of pre-service and in-service programmes, organisation and participation in workshops, seminars, interest in designing innovative methods of teaching, social adjustment, studying the psychology of teacher trainees and providing academic and technical guidance, concern for achieving the objectives of teacher education programme, desire to update one's own knowledge in current trends in the profession and developing integrated personality of the teacher trainees, etc., is the need of the hour. It is the attitude of the teacher educators that decides the luck or fate of the would-be teacher trainees. Teachers are sculptors who carve raw material of teacher trainees with regard to knowledge and skills into a fine and smooth finished product. Excellence in the teaching profession is a gradual and continuous process. Commitment to the profession and the zeal, and motivation on the part of the teacher educators to give the best to the teacher trainees are a boon not only to the teacher trainees but also to the student community at large. Any amount of negative attitude will seriously affect the future of the nation. Many seem to think that teaching in DIETs is very easy and the purpose is limited to simply handling of classes by way of writing some notes or by touching upon a few important points from the examination point of view. The responsibility of teacher educators pervades beyond the classroom situation. It is not a quantum of salary that a teacher receives but it is his accountability, scholarship and wisdom that is passed on to the teacher trainees. It is also necessary at this juncture to think about the attitude of teachers towards their co-teachers, principals, physical facilities, administrative matters, academic matters, professional organisations, career matters which are going to affect their involvement in the profession in one form or the other. Hence, the study of teachers towards teacher education programme cannot be underestimated but should be studied scientifically and objectively to make it more and more systematic and purposeful.

4.2.4.1 Development of Attitude Scale

All the steps involved in the scientific procedure of constructing and developing an attitude scale are followed in the development of attitude scale for teacher educators to measure their attitude towards the teacher training programme exising at present in DIETs. Statements have been collected on different aspects on T.T.C. programme from all possible sources—review of literature, discussions with teacher educators and principals and personal observations by the investigator. In total 90 items have been prepared as item pool and circulated to an expert committee for their comment on the suggestions made by the members of the committee. 48 items have been selected for the preparation of pilot form of the attitude scale. Pilot study has been conducted on 45 faculty members of DIETs and the item-wise analysis has been carried out to establish item validity (item discrimination value). The results of item analysis are presented in Appendix—D_1.

35 items have been selected for the inclusion of in the final form of the scale on the basis of the item discrimination value. The English version of the final form is shown in Appendix—D_2. The scale has also been established with content validity, item validity, criterion validity and intrinsic validity in the same manner as explained for the earlier tools. The test-retest reliability of the tool has also been established and found as statistically significant.

4.2.5 MEASUREMENT OF PERCEPTIONS OF PRINCIPALS

For the purpose of the present study a scale that can measure the perceptions of principals regarding physical, academic, administrative, financial and interpersonal aspects is necessary. From the review of related literature it is clear that there are no standardized instruments to measure the perceptions of principals. So the investigator has developed a perception scale for principals to suit the purpose of the study.

4.2.5.1 Preparation of the Preliminary Form

In the light of the experience in collecting items for the perception scales meant for student teachers and teacher educators on different aspects of DIETs the items have been written confidently by the investigator and given to the experts. In the light of their suggestions, 97 items have been finalised for inclusion in the principals' perception scale. The sample of principals employed in the investigation is very small. Only on the judgement of the experts committee the final form of the tool with 97 items has been considered and taken as reliable. The final form of the tool in English version is presented in Appendix—E.

4.2.6 PRINCIPALS CHECK-LIST

It has been widely accepted that physical and infrastructural facilities exert their influence in work situations as well as in areas associated with education and training. The higher the level of physical facilities the better will be its influence on training of the participants. Physical facilities are often related to buildings, equipment, rooms, library, furniture, hardware equipment, audio-visual aids, play-ground, etc. The present investigation requires a measure that can effectively estimate the availability of different physical facilities in DIETs. An examination of the available literature indicated that there are no specific tools to assess the availability of different physical facilities in DIETs. Hence, the investigator has design a tool for the purpose. To start with the investigator has collected the type of items that come under physical facilities, by visiting different DIETs and by having discussions with principals, teaching and non-teaching staff. In order to develop the tool first the broad areas that come under availability of physical facilities in DIETs have been identified. The broad headings include DIET plant, furniture, teaching-aids, play-ground, equipment, sports, games facilities and others. After this the various items that are to be covered under each area have been examined under 'DIET Plant'. Items like buildings, lighting facilities, air and ventilation, environment, surroundings of DIET, principal's room, classrooms available, library, laboratory, museum, seminar hall, canteen, computer room, training hall, trainees residence accommodation, toilets, gymnasium, fire extinguishers, approach roads, electricity availability, bulbs, generator, place of location of the DIET, etc., have been included. Under the area 'furniture' items like chairs, benches, almirahs, telephone facility, vernier calipers, screw-gauge, meter scale, spring balance, beakers, chemicals, etc., have been covered. The area 'teaching aids' includes items like film projector, slide projector, overhead projector, epidiascope, microscope, television, record player, radio, globe, comics, diagrams, black board, bulletin board, peg board, magnetic boards different types of charts, pictures, models and the like. The area 'play-ground' equipment includes the availability of play-ground, physical education teachers, courts for games and sports as well as equipment and material for different games and sports. Under the area 'others' items like yoga, first-aid material, facilities for health check-ups, etc. Thus a list of items that comes under the measure of physical facilities in DIETs have been finalized. Often questionnaires or check-list has been used to find out the availability of different facilities. Then a panel of experts has been contacted with a request. (a) to suggest omissions and additions wherever necessary (b) to check the appropriateness of the items under particular broad area (c) to suggest the better way of presentation of items if any in order to elicit information. Their suggestions have been carried out. All the items were rewritten incorporating the suggestions offered by the experts and again calculated for their scrutiny about clarity, simplicity and coverage of each item. The suggestions given by the experts have been incorporated wherever necessary. A check-list was felt appropriate to elicit the information with regard to the availability of various physical facilities in DIETs under Yes/No form for the measure as endorsed by the investigator is duly supported by the panel of experts.

Content validity has been established for the check-list. It refers to the establishment and evaluation of the significance of the test items individually and as a whole. In addition, items that collectively constitute representative sample of the variable that is measured as already described items for the check-list have been collected from different sources namely review of literature, direct observations of DIETs by the investigator, discussions with DIET principals, teaching and non-teaching staff members. In addition the items have been supplemented by noting the versions of academicians working at the university level to make sure that all the possible items have been covered. Thus, it can be reasonably assumed that the check-list meant for principals on DIETs physical facilities possess satisfactory content validity. The final format of the check list is shown in the Appendix—F.

4.2.7 PERSONAL DATA SHEET

The personal information regarding the student teachers and the teacher educators of DIETs has collected through a well planned personal data sheet meant for the two types of subjects separately. A carefully worded personal data sheets have been added at the end to the tools meant for the two categories of subjects. Hence, those sheets could be seen in B_2 and D_2 Appendices.

4.3 SELECTION OF THE SAMPLE

As stated earlier the present investigation is essentially a survey type of research aimed at evaluating the existing pre-service training of primary school teachers conducted by the DIETs in Andhra Pradesh. Hence, the population covers the 23 DIETs situated in 23 districts of Andhra Pradesh. As the investigator considered three categories of subjects namely, student teachers, teacher educators and principals of DIETs, three sub samples have been selected at random.

At the first stage the sampling unit is a DIET. The 23 DIETs have been divided into three strata based on the three regions of the state of Andhra Pradesh, viz., Coastal Andhra, Telengana and Rayalaseema. 10 DIETs have been selected from the three strata.

At the second stage the sampling units are student teachers, teacher educators and principals. 50 student teachers have been selected at random from each one of the DIETs selected in the first stage so as to make the first sub-sample of the student teachers as 500. The second sub-sample of teacher educators has been identified by following cluster sampling technique which means considering all the available teacher educators from each one of the DIETs selected at the first stage. Thus, a total of 101 teacher educators have formed the second sub sample of the survey. The third sub-sample consists of 10 principals from 10 DIETs. Thus, the sampling teachniques employed in the investigation may be called two stage stratified random sampling technique.

4.4 COLLECTION OF THE DATA

The investigator personally visited all the DIETs included in the sample (10 DIETs). A good rapport has been developed with the head of the institution and he has given permission to administer the tools on himself, teacher educators and on the student teachers. The student teachers have been made to sit in a seperate room where no teacher would observe what they do. Then the self explanatory instruments developed by the investigator have been administered on 50 student teachers selected at random from each one of the 10 DIETs. The procedure of scaling has been explained with the help of an example to make them understand clearly what they should do. They have been provided with a copy of perception and attitude scale questionnaires and requested to respond to all the items in the tools. They have been asked to put a tick mark in one of the brackets, against each item, which suits their feelings. At the end of the tool, to collect information about personal and demographic variables, various items have been given and the subjects have been instructed to fill those items properly. Thus the data collected from the student teachers in a pleasant approach.

The teacher educators have been given the two instruments meant for them, viz., perception and attitude scales and also personal data sheet to collect personal and demographic variables and requested to respond to all parts of the booklets of instruments to all questions without leaving any single question.

The principals have also been given the copies of all the instruments meant for them, viz., perception scale, check-list and requested to respond to all parts of the booklets of instruments without leaving any single question.

Thus, the data has been collected from the student teachers, teacher educators and principals in a pleasant way. Apart from this the investigator has studied different aspects of DIETs and noted down the important points while interacting with different individuals during the period of his stay in each DIET.

4.5 SCORING OF THE RESPONSES

As the instruments used in this investigation are perception scale, attitude scale and check-list, they have been scored by giving following weightages.

Perception scales have scored on a three-point scale by giving weights 3,2 and 1 in the case of positive items and 1,2 and 3 in the case of negative items to the three alternatives, viz., maximum extent, moderate extent and least extent respectively. The grand total on the entire scale has been obtained by adding the weights on all the items to each individual.

The Likert type of attitude scales have been scored on a five-point scale by giving weights 5,4,3,2 and 1 in the case of positive items and 1,2,3,4 and 5 in the case of negative items respectively. The grand total to each individual on the entire scale has been obtained by adding the weights on all the statements.

As the items in the Check-list are Yes/No type, the items available in the DIET are coded as '1' and the items not available in the DIET are coded as 'O'.

The information provided by the respondents in the personal data sheet is also numerically coded to suit the computer analysis.

4.6 ANALYSIS OF DATA

As the data collected through different statements in the tools from different subjects is qualitative in nature, item-wise analysis has been carried out to identify the specific deficiencies in different aspects of DIETs. Statistics such as frequencies, percentages and Chi-square have been employed to make the qualitative description more precise.

The total scores obtained by all subjects on all the variables have been computed. The data has been carefully analysed employing appropriate statistical techniques. Descriptive statistics such as mean, median, mode, quartile deviation, standard deviation, skewness and kurtosis have been used to describe the distribution of scores. Graphical representations are also made suitably to test different hypothesis. The inferential statistical techniques such as 't'-test. (Critical-ratio) and 'F' test have been employed to test different hypotheses. The obtained numerical results have been interpreted meaningfully.

The detailed analysis of the data and discussion on the results are presented in the succeeding chapter.

ANALYSIS OF THE DATA AND DISCUSSION

As explained earlier both qualitative and quantitative methods of data analysis are employed to realize the different objectives through testing various hypotheses that have been formulated. This chapter is divided into three parts. The first part deals with item-wise analysis on the six tools administered. The qualitative analysis was also made on the personal observations made by the investigator. In second part, the influence of personal and demographic variables related to student teachers and teacher educators on their perceptions and attitudes is described. Part three presents the correlational aspects and the differences on different issues between more and less effective institutions.

5.1 ITEM-WISE ANALYSIS OF DIFFERENT TOOLS EMPLOYED

The first step in the item-wise analysis has been to record the number of responses to each of the three alternatives of each question in the perception scale meant for student teachers. To test whether the response pattern is different from the equal probability hypothesis (due to chance) Chi-square test has been employed. The frequencies of responses to each item and the results of Chi-square are shown in the form of table in Appendix—G_1. Out of 75 items only on 7 items the responses do not reveal any indication of either positive or negative perception. On all other items the divergency in the responses is significant.

On the basis of the item total it has been identified that on only 26 items the student teachers have expressed their negative perception and thereby they are unhappy with those aspects in the DIETs. On the remaining items the student teachers have reacted positively. A detailed discussion on each one of the negatively perceived aspects presented hereunder may help to improve the quality of pre-service teacher education at primary level.

5.1.1 RESPONSES OF THE STUDENT TEACHERS

5.1.1.1 Perceptions of the Student Teachers

Encouragement by Physical Education Instructor

Out of 500 student-teachers 353 are of the opinion that they have not been encouraged to participate in physical education activities by their respective physical education instructors. We, all know that the primary school does not have a physical instructor's post to provide physical education to the children. So it is necessory that all the teachers appointed should be exposed to the required physical training activities which in turn may be useful for them to conduct physical education programmes. But unfortunately such training has not been given in the DIETs. Appropriate steps should be taken in this regard by the State Department of School Education.

Non-Availability of Sports Material

More than 50 per cent respondents among student teachers reacted negatively to the statements that there is sufficient sports material in their DIET. It is true that most of the educational institutions now-a-days do not have even a minimum extent of place for the play ground. But it is fortunate that almost all the DIETs in the state possess sufficient land for both net games and field events. Physical education being an integral part of any educational programme, sufficient attention is to be paid to provide a well trained physical education master and sufficient funds to purchase games and sports material and to maintain the play-fields congenially. Then only the trainees (prospective teachers) would become proficient in playing games and encourage the school children to participate in all games and sports.

Failure of Existing Examination System

Majority of the student teachers have perceived that the present system of examinations has failed in assessing the teaching skills that are developed among student teachers during the period of their training. In a way, it indicates that sufficient care is not shown on the practical aspects of teacher training programme. In other words, undue importance is given to theoretical aspects of teacher education while testing the abilities of the student teachers. This is one of the most important deficiencies in the present teacher education programmes as has identified by the core group of National Council for Teacher Education (NCTE) team appointed for the study of the existing curricula in the country. To overcome such deficiencies the NCTE has been trying to convince the teacher educators to make the duration of the course two years instead of one year.

Teaching Practice at far away places

Almost 50 per cent of the subjects have expressed a feeling of difficulty to go to far away places from their institute (DIETs) for practice teaching sessions. This is true as most of the DIETs are established away from the thickly populated towns (almost in the remote rural areas) where the concentration of primary schools is thin. The 150 student teachers, naturally, find it difficult to have the teaching practice in the nearby schools by getting guidance from their teacher educators instantly.

Lack of Laboratory Facilities

About 60 per cent of the sample of student teachers have perceived that the laboratory facilities are very poor in their training institution. Especially to teach science subjects demonstration method of teaching claims its supremacy over other methods of teaching. If the required equipment and instruments are not available to practise the most appropriate teaching method of science, the purpose of teacher education programme is defeated. Similarly, the educational technology laboratory provides opportunity to the trainees to develop different low cost improvised teaching aids with locally available material. A well equipped psychology laboratory creates an opportunity to the student teachers to gain the practical knowledge about different psychological variables of the individual which in turn helps better understanding of the children. Thus all kinds of laboratories related to the course are very essential for the conduct of effective training programme.

Lack of Furniture in the Hostel

With regard to the furniture in the hostels roughly about 60 per cent of the student teachers are of the opinion that the problem of furniture is very severe and roughly about 25 per cent feel that the problem is moderate. This indicates the poor conditions of the hostels maintained by DIETs. On the recommendations of 1986 National Policy on Educaiton the DIETs have been established throughout the country with a special assistance by Minstry of Human Resource Development (MHRD). Still the condition of most of DIETs with regard to their physical facilities appears to be poor, which indicates that the State Department of Education is, undoubtedly, not taking appropriate steps to improve the quality of teacher education in the state.

The Impact of Demonstration Lessons on Learning to Teach

Except 1/5th of the sample of 500 student teachers all others are of the opinion that the demonstration lessons given by teacher educators alone would not improve teaching abilities among student teachers. It may be due to poor quality of demonstration lessons limited in nature and that too on selected topics which are easy for teaching. Therefore, the teacher educators should select the topics for demonstration lessons in such a way that they cover all types of lessons—concept teaching, abstract issues where lot of imagination is required to understand the most difficult appplication aspects.

Guidance to use Library

All except 153 out of 500 student teachers are unhappy with the non-availability of suitable guidance and advice to utilise library facilities effectively. It is true that most of the institutional libraries are not effectively used by users and DIET libraries are not an exception. This trend may be due to lack of physical facilities, insufficient staff, non-availability of required books, lack of commitment on the part of library staff in particular and teaching faculty in general. The situation should be improved by the government taking appropriate steps in this regard.

Surroundings of the Hostel

The student teachers have stated that they are unhappy about the sorry state of their hostel premises. The observations of the investigator reveal that the DIETs are not able to maintain the standards in terms of accommodation, lighting, ventilation, hygiene, mess maintenance, cleanliness of surroundings, etc. It is difficult to expect healthy surroundings when the DIETs and their hostels are unhygienic and not up to the mark. Hence, the first and foremost suggestion of the study is that the hostel premises should be kept clean and hygienic.

Lack of Entertainment

70 per cent of the subjects in the sample are unhappy with the lack of sufficient amenities in the DIETs for entertainment. As teacher trainees they are to be exposed to different cultural activities, sports, games, etc. In the context of the inadequate library, sports and games facilities

it is necessary that a variety of co-curricular and extra-curricular activities are included in the curriculum so as to promote the aesthetic values among the student teachers.

Paid-Apprenticeship

What the student teachers acquire in the DIETs in terms of their theoretical and practical experiences needs to be strengthened and reinforced through paid-apprenticeship for a period of atleast two years. This will help the student teachers to gain perfection, mastery and resourcefulness in becoming efficient teachers. If this is followed naturally the existing low standards at the primary level can be improved and after the completion of the paid-apprenticeship the trainees of the DIETs can be positioned in school without further entrance test, selections, etc. The sample of the student teachers have felt that the compulsory apprenticeship would strengthen the qualitative improvement in teacher preparation.

Overcrowded Classrooms in DIETs

The annual intake in DIETs is 150. While dealing with general papers such as philosophical and sociological foundations and principles of educational psychology, the entire group of 150 may be divided into two sections each consisting of 75 students or at many time all the 150 students may be in a single class. This has been creating lot of dissatisfaction among the trainees. The National Council for Teacher Education insists on smaller groups for the purpose of providing training in general and developing specific skills in particular to improve the quality in teacher education. Therefore, the DIETs may think of making three sections atleast to teach general papers and even when the methodology papers are dealt with the size of the class should not exceed 50 at any time. Probably then the DIET teacher trainees may develop a positive outlook towards teacher training programme.

Insufficient Water Facility in the Hostels

Out of 500 subjects in the sample, 247 strongly

perceived and 103 moderately perceived that there is no sufficient water facility in the hostels. The investigator has observed that most of the DIETs do not provide proper hostel facilities to the student teachers. The reasons are obvious. In a very few DIETs the hostel facilities are available but the conditions are very very poor. When basic training schools provided teacher education two decades ago hostel management was one of the most important components of teacher training. The student teachers maintained their own hostel on rotation basis. The best team which managed the hostel effectively was suitably rewarded at the end of the training programme. But all such experiences disappeared in the present day training and unfortunately a large number of social welfare hostels are under the management of the ill-equipped trained teachers.

No Lessons on Nutrition and Health Habits

Our economy being a developing one a large number of primary school children of illiterate parents and poor families face the problem of mal-nutrition and lack of good health habits. The primary school teacher is supposed to have a thorough knowledge of these problems, detect such problems at early stages and provide suitable remedial measures. Unfortunately, more than 50 per cent of the subjects feel that the knowledge required on these issues has not been provided during their training period.

Lecturers' Disinterest to use Audio-Visual Equipment

It is very sad to note that the teacher educators seem to be disinterested in using audio-visual aids in the course of their teaching. Being 'models' before the trainees they are supposed to innovate different situations where one can employ the teaching aids as a natural phenomena of effective teaching. Unfortunately, 'poor models' are exhibited in our DIETs. This kind of lethargic attitude may be eliminated by conducting in-service programmes, and by exposing the student teachers to national and international workshops, seminars, etc. In this connection the NCTE has opined that there is need to create a separate special training programme for the purpose of producing teacher educators.

No Need to Increase the Number of Records

At present the trainees in DIETs have to write a number of records, viz., work experience record, educational technology record, art and music record, scout record, evaluation record, physical education record, observation record, demonstration record, criticism record, etc.

Within 180 working days the trainees have to attend four theory papers, 40 practice teaching classes in six subjects, observation classes, demonstration classes, educational tours apart from preparing different teaching aids. It appears that the trainees are over-loaded with different curricular and co-curricular activities during the one year period of their training and therefore, they have reacted strongly against the increase in the number of records during their training. It is one of the reasons to increase the duration of the T.T.C. from one year to two years. However, the student teachers are not interested in the increase of the duration of the course and also in the increase of the number of records.

Out-dated Curriculum

About 70 per cent of the sample trainees have perceived that the present curriculum of T.T.C. is outdated. It is true that the existing curriculum is not able to provide all the skills required for an effective teacher. Hence, the NCTE wants to bring radical changes in the existing curriculum.

Lack of the Conduct of Subject Associations

Even in high schools different co-curricular activities such as literary association, science club, maths quiz, mock -parliament, etc., are conducted to create interest among the school children in various school subjects. In teacher preparation programme subject specialised activities do play a significant role in qualitative improvement of teaching a school subject. For example, students belonging to Mathematics methodology may start Maths Student Teachers Association which may undertake different activities to promote interest in teaching Mathematics. By conducting such subject-wise special programmes in all school subjects the training programme can become more effective.

5.1.1.2 Attitudes of the Student Teachers

In order to know whether there is any divergence in terms of responses of student teachers with regard to attitude towards teaching profession Chi-square has been employed and the results are presented in Appendix—G_2. Out of 45 attitudinal statements where the Chi-square values have been found to be statistically significant at 0.05 level and 0.01 level, the following items deserve attention and some of the reasons for difference in their attitude are given below:

Society is responsible for the miseries of the teachers;

Using teachers for activities other than teaching bothers me;

Now-a-days students are not obedient to the teachers;

Teaching profession has no recognition in the society; and

Many students do not respect teachers.

The responses of student teachers reveal that society is responsible for the unhappiness and dissatisfaction of the teachers. It is often observed that the teachers are not cared for by major sections at the village level and in some cases they are treated as low due to their poor economic status. Further, the teachers have often been found outside the school premises entrusted with the works of Census collection, Literacy Programmes, Pulse-Polio, Janmabhoomi, etc.

A few sarpanchs by virtue of their being unofficial members on various committees expect the teachers to carry out whatever work they assign at the village level. As the parents have no respect for the teacher, their influence in one form or the other makes the children not to care for the teacher. All these aspects have strengthened the teachers' view that the society is responsible for the miseries of the teachers.

Of course, it is quite natural that people blame others whenever they fail in performing their duties efficiently. Similarly, the prospective teachers are of the opinion that the society—the community, parents, students and authority—is responsible for their failure in realising their goals. If one looks at the positive side, the school teacher is supposed to rise to the level of a social leader and command respect from all sections of the society, instead of demanding respect. There are many examples where a village teacher has become a true friend, philosopher and guide to the community in which he lives. The training given to the prospective teachers should eliminate this type of negative attitude towards teaching profession among them.

5.1.2 RESPONSES OF THE TEACHER EDUCATORS

5.1.2.1 Perceptions of the Lecturers

There are 89 items in the perception scale meant for teacher educators. Most of these items are similar to the items in the perception scale meant for student teachers. To test the divergency in their responses Chi-square has been employed and item-wise analysis carried out. The results of Chi-square and the frequency of responses to each item are presented in Appendix—G_3.

25 out of 89 responses have not revealed any trend and in the remaining 64 items 51 items have indicated negative perception. The detailed discussion on these 51 items may help to identify the deficiencies in the DIET programme and the solutions to bring qualitative improvement in the pre-service training programme conducted by DIETs.

Need for Increasing Demonstration Classes

About 40 per cent of the samples have strongly perceived that the number of demonstration classes are insufficient and the same idea has also been expressed by the student teachers. Hence, there is every need to increase the number of demonstration classes.

Inadequate Furniture in Reading Room

It has already been pointed out that the DIETs are ill-equipped. About 85 per cent of the samples have felt that the reading room attached to the library is not furnished well. As all the DIETs are governed by the State Department of Education, it should pay more attention to eliminate such deficiencies.

Insufficient Duration for Internship

Majority of the teacher educators are of the opinion that the existing period of internship is insufficient. The same has been expressed by the student teachers. Consequently the duration of T.T.C. has been increased to two years so as to provide longer periods of teaching practice by the trainees.

Promotional Opportunities

Roughly about 1/3rd of the subjects have felt that the promotional opportunities are meagre for the faculty members of DIETs. The other 1/3rd of the sample have perceived this need as moderate and the remaining 1/3rd have bothered least about this need. Thus, 2/3rds of the samples are unhappy for want of promotional opportunities. The Andhra Pradesh State Government does not provide a cadre to the staff of DIETs. It is unfortunate and it should be set right atleast in the near future.

Need for Curriculum Change

84 out of 101 teacher educators and the student teachers have perceived that the existing curriculum needs to be changed. The NCTE has prepared a draft curriculum

frame work for the purpose of bringing radical changes in the curriculum for teacher educators at all levels.

Use of Teaching Aids by Student Teachers

More than 50 per cent of teacher educators are of the opinion that the student teachers have not been using the necessary teaching aids in their internship. The student teachers have expressed that they have been facing hardship during internship as they have to go to distant places for teaching practice. This might be one of the reasons for not using teaching aids as and when necessary. As student teachers have not been supervised by their teacher educators regularly there might have been lethargy among student teachers.

Ill-equipped Physical Science Laboratory

More than 80 per cent of the teacher educators accept that the physical science laboratories are not properly equipped. Similar condition has been observed with educational technology and biological science laboratories. Therefore, there is every need to modernise the laboratories in DIETs.

Inadequate Laboratory Buildings

Almost equal number of respondents were seen under three alternative responses to this item. In our words 2/3rds of sample were of the opinion that the building facility for different kinds of laboratories was insufficient.

Need for an Effective Recruiting Agency

The present policy is to appoint 70 per cent of lecturers from among the school teachers who have put in experience at secondary educational level. Only once i.e., during 1989 after the establishment of the DIETs, 30 per cent were recruited by direct appointment. Further, with regard to promotions a lecturer can become a senior lecturer after putting in around 5 years of service and one can have a ray of hope to become a principal based upon the existing vacancy position. The chances of promotion are meagre, the services are not regularised and the humble appeals of the lecturers for promotion as District Educational Officers have not been cared for at all. Further, the requests of lecturers to work in affiliated colleges in the same cadre where there is scope for some more financial support and promotional chances in future have also been not considered by the government authorities. This sorry state of affairs of the lecturers in DIETs needs to be remedied promptly. Hence, it is suggested that there should be an effective recruiting agency for the appointment of lecturers in DIETs and to look into their service matters and promotions.

Lack of Technical Staff in Laboratories

The entire sample teachers except five are of the opinion that the laboratories do not have technical staff such as technicians, lab assistants etc. In such a situation the maintenance of equipment becomes a problem and moreover most of the equipment items have not been put to use. Therefore, technical staff to the laboratories may be provided for maximum utilisation of different equipment items.

Financial Soundness of the Institution

33 out of the 101 teacher educators feel that the financial position of the DIETs is not sound where as 52 feel that it is moderate. This indicates that the State Department of Education is unable to provide necessary funds to DIETs even after the first 10 years of their establishment during which period these institutions have managed with the central aid. It is unfortunate that the State Department does not bestow the required attention on producing quality teachers.

Inadequate Drinking Water Facility

Almost two thirds of the sample teacher educators have perceived difficulty regarding drinking water facility in DIETs to the maximum extent or to the moderate extent and the remaining one-third perceive it to the least extent. Although the chi-square value on this item is not significant, the problem is alarming. Drinking water facility is a bare minimum facility in any organisation and if such need is also not met by DIETs what can be achieved by such institutions?

Co-operative Book-Banks

About 75 per cent of the subjects have perceived that the co-operative book-banks maintained by the DIET libraries are useful neither to the students nor to the staff members. Probably the co-operative book-bank system may not be functioning effectively in most of the DIET libraries. It has been pointed out earlier that the libraries are poorly furnished and have not been provided with sufficient staff to assist the librarian. If so how can the co-operative book-banks be effectively maintained?

The Role of Local Philanthropists in Institutional Development

As many as 76 teacher educators out of 101 have perceived to the maximum extent that the local philanthropists have not at all been participating in the institutional development. The DIETs have been established by the State Governments. The students admitted into DIETs are from the entire district or at times from the region (Rayalaseema or Coastal Andhra or Telengana). So the local people may not evince any interest in these institutions. Special schemes such as naming the specific buildings, play-grounds, laboratories, etc., after the donars may help in attracting the local philanthropists to participate in the developmental activities of the DIETs.

Inadequate Furniture in Staff Rooms

About 90 per cent of the teachers are unhappy with the inadequate fruniture in the staff rooms. Effective participation of workers in any production activity or service is possible only, when there is congenial atmosphere. Comfortable seating and accomodation are minimum requirements. The management has to take the necessary steps in this direction.

Availability of Institutional Buildings for Common People

It is expected that the public institutions should be useful to the local community for a variety of social activities so that the attachment between the institution and local community can increase. But in the case of DIETs such affinity between the institution and society has not been existing as perceived by the teacher educators working in DIETs.

Lack of Clearly Defined Service Conditions

Roughly 2/3rds of the sample are unhappy with the service conditions of the teaching staff of the DIETs. Their cadre is not included in the hierarchy of different categories of people working in education department of the state government. This is one of the major bottlenecks in providing promotional opportunities too. As has been pointed out the state government should take necessary steps in preparing clear cut service conditions for them.

Lack of Initiation by the Principal in Organising Parent's meet

95 per cent of the teacher educators are of the opinion that their principal is not interested in convening the parents' meet to interact with them about their children. Most of the teacher educators also may not take any initiative to inform the parents about their wards. But they do not hesitate to find fault with their principal. This tendency is to be corrected by conducting special theme based orientation programmes to the teacher educators.

Principal's Role in Establishing Institutional Climate

Most of the sample teachers think that the principal does not enforce discipline and maintain proper academic climate in the institution. Of course if the principal is strict, the staff may dub him an autocrat. This kind of unhealthy criticism should be avoided.

Inadequate Teaching-Learning Material

As many as 62 teacher educators have perceived that the DIETs possess with the required teaching-learning material only to the moderate extent whereas 20 per cent have perceived it to the maximum extent. This trend indicates that the DIETs should procure adequate teaching -learning material.

Involvement of Unemployed Youth in Institutional Activities

To a great extent more than 50 per cent and to a moderate extent 1/3 of the teacher educators admit that they have not been able to involve the unemployed youth in the institutional activities. In the context of District Primary Education Project (DPEP) it is very essential to make the community a party to achieve cent per cent literacy atleast by 2010.

A special training appears to be necessary to all the teacher educators, especially at the primary level in utilizing the services of the unemployed youth in a variety of institutional activities related to community development.

Water Facility for Gardening

Roughly about 70 per cent of the teachers working in the DIETs have perceived that there is no sufficient water facility for gardening in the DIETs. It has already been pointed out that the drinking water facility is also meagre. When such is the case expecting water facility for gardening appears to be more ambitious. The government should take necessary steps in fulfilling atleast such basic requirements.

Need for Technical Staff Participation in Preparing Teaching Aids

Roughly about 50 per cent of the DIET lecturers have opined that the required teaching aids can be prepared by them with the help of technically qualified and experienced persons if such people are appointed in the DIETs. Although an instructor's post is created no properly trained person is posted and thereby the teaching faculty feel it difficult to prepare needed teaching aids many a time. It is necessary that the DIET lecturers should be exposed to different kinds of workshops where they will be trained to prepare various kinds of teaching aids as they have to train in return, the pupil teachers in this regard.

Encouragement by Principal in Preparing Teaching Aids by Student Teachers

It appears that the principals do not show much interest and provide sufficient encouragement to the students of DIETs in preparing teaching aids. 50 per cent of the subjects are unhappy with the situation. Preparing good teachers is no doubt a difficult task. But a little effort and commitment to their job on the part of DIET principals and lecturers will definitely bring about a radical change in the pupil teachers.

Inadequate Furniture in DIET Office

Although the MHRD has provided huge grants to establish DIETs on the recommendations of NPE-1986, the State Government has not been able to implement the scheme with necessary vision. Most of the DIETs are lack either buildings, furniture, library, laboratories, hostels or the required staff. This is because of sheer negligence on the part of the state government in establishing ideal institutions of teacher education at the primary level.

Inadequate Copies of Education Commission Reports in the Library

96 out of 101 DIET lecturers have perceived that their institutional library has not procured sufficient copies of reports of various Education Commissions. As explained above the state department of education did not have proper vision while establishing the model teacher education institutions. Hence, more than 50 per cent of the DIETs are Ill-equipped and under-staffed. Of course, with the World Bank assistance for District Primary Education Project (DPEP), the State Department of Education is strengthening the DIETs at present and it is believed that in the near future the DIETs will become fulfledged.

Lack of Extension Lectures on Health and Moral Education

Almost all lecturers working in DIETs are of the opinion that there have been no sufficient number of extension lectures by experts on either health education or moral education. It will be an inspiration to both student teachers and teacher educators if they are exposed to such inspiring lectures. Necessary steps should be taken by the principal of DIETs in this regard.

Curriculum is not Meeting the Local Needs

Majority of the subjects have perceived that the curriculum offered in DIETs has not been able to meet the local needs of the community. Therefore, there is an urgent need to change the existing curriculum. The NCTE has prepared a draft curriculum for two years course and the state department of education has readily accepted it and it will be implemented from the academic year of 1999-2000.

Library Facility Outside the Normal Working Hours

More than 75 per cent of the teachers are dissatisfied that the institutional library has not been kept open beyond working hours of the institution. Therefore, the principal is advised to reschedule the library working hours which will meet the demands of both teaching staff and student teachers as far as the library facility is concerned.

Inadequate Hostel Staff

As many as 71 lecturers have perceived to the maximum extent and 23 to the moderate extent that the DIET hostels are under staffed. Elsewhere it has been observed that most of the DIETs do not provide hostel facility at all. Thus, the entire scenario discloses that there are very poor or no hostel facilities in the DIETs. The government should take necessary steps to correct the situation.

Ideal Principal

Roughly about one-third of the lecturers have perceived

to the maximum extent and a little more than one-third have perceived to the moderate extent and a little more than one-third have perceived to the least extent that their principal is not regarded as an ideal administrator. Probably, most of the principals do not have suitable training in the area of personal management and are not exposed to leadership qualities. Educational leadership has become a rare good in the present circumstances.

Inadequate Books on Teaching Methods

Majority of the lecturers have perceived that their institution's libraries do not have sufficient number of books on methods of teaching. As explained earlier the libraries are poorly equipped in allways lack of sufficient books of different kinds, furniture and staff. This situation should be immediately corrected.

Need for Changing the Curriculum of Teacher Education

More than 80 per cent of the lecturers are of the opinion that the existing curriculum for pre-service training programme should be thoroughly changed. As has been already explained steps are under way to bring total change in the existing teacher education curriculum by the NCTE and the State Department of Education.

Principal's Suggestions to Rectify the Mistakes Committed by Lecturers

Roughly about 2/3 of the sample teachers feel that their principal has not been able to correct their mistakes and give valuable suggestions. This means, the principals are not able to come up to the expectations of their staff members. Directly or indirectly, the situtation reveals that the principals of DIETs are not resourceful.

Inspiring and Hardworking Principal

From the perception of the teacher educators it is observed that the principals are not ideal and hard working and thereby not able to inspire them. Hence, it is suggested that there should be a comprehensive training programme to all the principals to make them dynamic in their job performance.

Inadequate Furniture in Hostels

Majority of the sample have perceived that the hostels are poorly furnished. This situation is also in line with the earlier statements that many things required for the effective running of the institute are either not available or inadequate. The government should take appropriate steps to provide atleast minimum requirements in the DIETs.

Principal's Help to Lecturers in Utilising their Full Potentialities

Almost equal number of lecturers have responded to the three alternatives to the maximum extent, moderate extent and to the least extent to the item which indicates that the principal is unable to tap the potentialities of the lecturers in different activities of the DIET. Weak organisational climate in the DIETs may be the reason for this. Suitable programmes such as orientation courses and extension lectures may be planned as corrective measures to improve the situation.

Constructive Criticism by the Principal

On the basis of the responses obtained to the above statement it appears that the principal resorts to negative approach and destructive criticism. This may be due to lack of appropriate training as administrator. It is one of the fundamental principles that any administrator, to obtain good results in any organisation, should be positive in his approach and constructive in his criticism.

Lack of Furniture in Seminar-Hall

It is yet another statement which reveals that the DIETs are poorly equipped. Some of the DIETs, as observed by the investigator, do not have a seminar-hall and some others have seminar halls without adequate furniture.

Principal's Help in Solving the Differences among the Staff

Majority of the subjects are of the opinion that their principal has not been able to help in solving the issues which create differences among the staff members. This is a clear case of inefficient interpersonal relationships. This can be set right only with expertise in personal management. Among the areas of material, financial and personal managements educational management mainly revolves around the efficient personal management-dealing with students, staff, management, administrators and community. Hence, the principals should be exposed to appropriate training in personal management.

Principals' Supervision

More than 50 per cent of the lecturers have perceived that their principal does not have active supervision over the lecturers and enthuse them to work better. Of course, if principals supervise the work done by the lecturers regularly some may feel it inconvenient and react negatively. As it is a sensitive issue a very wise decision has to be taken by the principal to follow the golden mean more suitable to his circumstances.

Ineffective Library Advisory Committee

Majority of the lecturers working in DIETs think that the Library Advisory Committees have been ineffective. When there are no sufficient funds to purchase the required books, educational committee reports, journals, magazines, etc., it is but quite natural that these committees are ineffective.

Inadequate Sports and Games Material

It is yet another statement which reveals the poor status of physical education in the DIETs. When there is non-availability of sports and games material the question of proper utilisation of play-ground does not arise as perceived by the staff earlier. The investigator has also observed that the post of physical education teacher has been vacant for years in most of the institutions.

5.1.2.2 Attitude of the Lecturers towards Teacher Education Programme

In order to know whether there is any divergence in the responses of teacher educators with regard to attitude towards teacher education programme Chi-square has been employed and the results are presented in Appendix—G_4. Out of 35 attitudinal statements where the chi-square values have been found to be statistically significant at 0.01 level the following items deserve attention.

Standards in Teacher Education are Rapidly Deteriorating Day by Day

The responses of the lecturers reveal that standards not only in teacher education but also in all types of educational activities have been deteriorating. The reasons are obvious.

This state of affairs may be due to quantitative expansion and the principle of equity (social justice). In an over populated developing country like ours these things are inevitable resulting in poor management and low quality in the output. In the recent times many conscious efforts have been made to increase the efficiency in all sectors of the economy. The National Policy on Education (1986) is an attempt in this direction. The qualitative improvement in teacher education at all levels by establishing DIETs (primary level), IASEs and CTEs (secondary level) and ASCs (higher/university level) is one of the significant recommendations of the policy. But the teacher educators working in DIETs are of the opinion that the programme conducted by them is not upto the mark. What a pitiable situation! The steps taken by National Council for Teacher Education alone should bring change in the existing teacher education programmes.

Physical Education is Allotted Very Little Time in the Time-Table

Physical education is an important co-curricular activity and only two periods are allotted for it in the time-table. A very limited number of institutions that can be counted on fingers in Andhra Pradesh have been devoting about four hours for physical education. The attitude of lecturers reveal that physical education has been accorded less priority in the student teacher time-table of DIETs. This may be due to lack of physical education teachers, lack of equipment, lack of adequate norms from the government and management's preference to other subjects in relation to physical education.

The Quality of Teacher Education is not Able to Maintain its Standards Due to Lack of Strict Adherence to the Administrative Rules

It is often observed that the administrative and academic matters have not been strictly implemented in DIETs. Lack of proper supervision over DIET programmes, time to time changes in DIETs curriculum, entrance, admission matters, adherence to time-table, coordination with University Education Departments, District Educational Officers, utilisation of funds, provision of buildings, hostels, etc., are not given attention in DIETs, which are affecting the quality of teacher education programme. No doubt our plans are extremely good but their implementation is weak. The same thing may be said about the functioning of DIETs. The DIETs are Comprehensive Institutions solely incharge of primary teacher education programme in the district established on the recommendations of NPE-1986. The implementation of various policies relating to their effective functioning should be given top priority to achieve qualitative improvement of teacher education. Necessary steps should be taken by the government in this direction.

There is No Correlation Between Theoretical and Practical Aspects of Training

Out of 101 teacher educators slightly more than 50 per cent have revealed that the theoretical aspects in the training programme do not have any practical implications.

It means there is an urgent need to modernise the curriculum of pre-service training programme for primary teachers. The mechanical way of writing lesson plans, preparing teaching aids, block teaching, etc., are to be converted into more committed and creative activities. The realistic situations existing in our primary schools, namely, multigrade teaching, composition of extreme groups in the same class, large classrooms, disinterested parents, lack of non-availability of minimum requirements, etc., should be taken into account while educating and training the primary school teachers.

Student Teachers During their Training Period have Less Chances to Participate in Social Activities

The student teachers should be exposed to the society in which they live and which they have to serve in the future. Participation in community works like pulse polio, census surveys, literacy programmes, cleanliness of surroundings, awareness generation in rural masses on developmental issues, etc., should be duly emphasised. However, student teachers are not given sufficient margin to participate in these activities. Curriculum matters and block-teaching followed by examinations are the normal procedure which is emphasised for different batches of student teachers in the DIETs. The primary reason for this is the short duration of the course i.e., one year. Practically, this one year is reduced to six to eight months due to statewide common entrance test, delayed admissions, etc. Within the short duration the more ambitious curriculum cannot be implemented effectively and therefore, the curricular activities will get their priority over co-curricular activities and social activities. From the discussions on this item and earlier items it is obvious that the one year duration of the training programme is insufficient. The A.P. Government made this T.T.C. programme as a two year course on the recommendation of the NCTE. The investigator is hopeful that the realistic objectives of pre-service primary teacher education programme will be fulfilled.

To Improve the Teaching Skills, In-service Training Programme Lacks the Needed Dynamism

Different in-service programmes of the DIETs meant for primary school teachers, non-formal instructors, community workers, etc., has not been effectively organised in DIETs resulting in the loss of financial, physical and human resources. The programmes are organised per se to be formally completed during the calendar year. There is no identification of the learning needs, training needs, evaluation and follow-up for the different programmes. These are possibly the reasons for unfavourable responses of the lecturers of the sample towards the programme.

Though the Practicals are More Important than Theory in Teacher Training they are not Given Much Importance

Micro-teaching and block-teaching followed by demonstration lessons in DIETs need to be highly emphasised. When practice in teaching is given, the student teachers can become effective teachers. Practice makes man perfect, so goes the proverb. This is true in the field of teaching too. However, practice teaching is given less importance in relation to theory and record work. That is why teachers basically lack in the skill of communication.

Non Participation in Co-curricular Activities Due to Lack of Leisure

As it has been pointed out in the earlier discussions the one year duration of the course and the more ambitious curriculum have made the student teachers restless in the training programme and there by they are not able to participate in co-curricular activities. About 75 per cent of teacher educators support this statement. Hence, the government's decision of making the course duration as two years is justifiable. In the two years course probably the student teachers may find leisure and the teacher educators may utilise it for inculcating in student teachers healthy practices such as participation in games, sports, cultural and social activities.

Even though DIET is Spending More Money to Impart Primary Teacher Education, it is Unable to Achieve the Desired Goals

The DIETs have been investing a lot on training the student teachers with a view to strengthening the primary education system. But the laudable objectives of 100 per cent school enrolment, coverage of street children, organisatin of non-formal education programmes, checking drop-outs and absenteeism, back to school drive programmes, play-way method of teaching, etc., have not been achieved. Further, poor socio-economic conditions of parents, lack of school buildings, supervision, community participation in primary school activities, etc., have been impeding the progress of school education system. Keeping these things in view probably the lecturers of the sample would have expressed that the efforts of DIET have not been born fruits at the primary level.

Supervision in Teaching Practice is Nothing but an Eye-Wash

Most of the DIETs are located away from the towns and it is difficult to provide and supervise practice teaching classes to the student teachers in the towns. The student teachers may not have number of schools within the radius of ten to fifteen kilometres and so they have been given freedom to choose the place and school for their teaching practice in any corner of the district. Even if a lecturer wishes to supervise the teaching practice it is practically very difficult to visit the different places due to time and distance constraints. Further, the teachers in the schools who are expected to supervise the teaching practice of student teachers are very passive in the matter. Ultimately a certificate of teaching practice is submitted without any effective supervision. Probably because of this the lecturers have perceived that supervision in teaching practice is merely an eye-wash.

Teacher Education is not Attracting the Attention of the Best Brains in Our Country

Teaching profession requires intellectuals who can grasp quickly and execute their ideas intelligently keeping in view the circumstances at the village level in the best direction possible. Intelligent students possess will, calibre, judgement and articulation skills and with a little bit of patience they can rise to higher levels in the profession starting with their entrance as a student teacher at the DIET level. Unfortunately, the cream of the intermediate students has not been attracted to this profession. This may be due to low salaries, poor recognition, poor facilities at the village level and bright career opportunities in other fields. But the trend is slowly changing. As there are more employment opportunities for teachers, bright students are attracted towards this profession. Every year more than one lakh aspirants take the common entrance test and only 8,500 meritorious candidates are selected and admitted to DIETs.

The Present Day Teacher Education Curriculum is Outdated for the Modern Society

The existing curriculum of teacher education programme is outdated and obsolete. Current topics are not found in the DIETs teacher education programme though they are found in the text books every year. A five year old curriculum or ten year old curriculum in vogue in DIETs teacher education programme cannot serve the purpose. Again the NCTE has prepared the curriculum framework for the purpose of modernising teacher education suited to the present day needs.

5.1.3 RESPONSES OF THE PRINCIPALS

5.1.3.1 Perceptions of the Principals

There are 97 items in the perceptionl scale meant for principals. Most of these items are similar to those in the scale meant for teacher educators. To test the divergency in the responses made by principals item-wise analysis has been carried out. Responses to each item are presented in Appendix—G_5.

28 out of 97 items have revealed their negative perception on principals. A detailed discussion of these 28 items may help in identifying the deficiencies in the DIET

programme and in identify solutions to bring qualitative improvement in the pre-service training programme. The central idea of these items has been presented as follows: (1) Improper utilisation of institution's play-ground. (5) Insufficient teaching-learning material. (10) No scope to conduct sufficient workshops to develop primary school curriculum. (12) No scope to increase the number of demonstration classes. (25) Lack of adequate maps in the institution. (30) Inadequate electric bulbs in the classrooms. (34) Failure of lecturers in guiding the student teachers to use library effectively. (35) Insufficient technical staff in the laboratories. (40) Inadequate equipment in educational technology laboratory. (43) No conduct of parents' meetings. (48) Technical staff are not available to prepare the teaching aids. (51) Local people are not helpful in solving personal problems. (54) No help from local philanthropists in institute's development. (55) Lack of extension lectures on health and moral education. (60) Insufficient hostel staff. (65) Inadequate sports material. (66) Inadequate furniture in DIET office. (73) Library facility outside the normal working hours. (74) No effective recruiting agency for appointing DIET lecturers. (75) Lack of financial soundness of the institution. (82) No help from local peoples in the institutional development. (83) Inadequate furniture in hostels. (84) Inadequate text books in library. (86) Non availability of institutional buildings for common people. (87) Inadequate books on teaching methods. (88) Insufficient play-grounds to play different types of field games. (91) No well defined service rules. (94) Lack of furniture in seminar hall.

Most of these items have also been negatively perceived either by lecturers or by student teachers and in certain cases by both. Therefore, it can be safely concluded that the DIETs are weak in general in the following aspects : Lack of furniture, insufficient teaching-learning material, ill-equipped laboratories, poor library, poor status of physical education, poorly managed hostels and weak linkages between the DIETs and local community.

However, the DIET lecturers have felt that there is greater need for more number of in-service training programmes in improving the curriculum of T.T.C. But the principals opposed it. This may be due to their negative perception in managing the institution without staff members. Similarly on the issue of a separate recruitment board also the perceptions of principals and lecturers are mutually contradictory.

The common features that have been identified in the perceptions of lecturers and student teachers are more interesting to note. Both the groups have felt that the curriculum of pre-service training programme ought to be changed thoroughly, the duration of the course should be increased, there should be more number of demonstration lessons, observation lessons and criticism lessons, and there should be more number of days for internship.

5.1.3.2 Principals' Check-List of DIETs Physical Facilities

One of the important aspects relating to the quality of the activities of the DIETs is associated with the availability of physical facilities like DIET plant, furniture, teaching-aids, sports and games equipment, etc. The present study peeps into the availability of several of these aspects which are essential conditions as per the norms stipulated by the MHRD in the DIET guidelines. Responses to each item are presented in Appendix—G_6.

Out of 179 items of physical facilities, the following 69 items are available in all the 10 DIETs included in the study. They are: (1) own buildings suitable for the DIET purpose, (2) air and ventilation, (3) separate principal's room, (4) sufficient number of classrooms, (5) separate staff rooms, (6) separate office rooms, (7) store room, (8) seminar hall, (9) fire extinguishers, (10) path-ways, (11) approach roads, (12) power, (13) chairs with hands, (14) iron safes, (15) telephone facility, (16) screw-guage, (17) vernier callipers, (18) metre-scale, (19) simple pendulum, (20) micro-balance, (21) beakers, (22) measuring jars, (23) liquid measuring jars, (24) microscope, (25) electrodes, (26) pippets, (27) burettes, (28) spirit lamps, (29) spring balances, (30) test tubes, (31) vaccum tubes, (32) rubber tubes, (33) mirrors, (34) lenses, (35) dissection boxes, (36) science models, (37) chemicals, (38) slide projector, (39) radio, (40) public address system, (41) slides, (42) transparencies, (43) globes, (44) cartoons, (45) posters, (46) folding cards, (47) flash cards, (48) picture's of national leaders and scientists, (49) models, (50) objects, (51) study kits, (52) black boards, (53) chalk boards, (54) flow charts, (55) stream charts, (56) timeline charts, (57) strip charts, (58) line graphs, (59) bar graphs, (60) circle graphs, (61) district, (62) state, (63) national, (64) world maps, (65) uniform, (66) volley ball court, (67) kabbaddi court, (68) throw ball equipment, and (69) volley ball equipment.

The following items namely (1) reading room, (2) separate biological science, (3) physical science laboratories, (4) library room, (5) girls lavatories, (6) boys toilets, (7) fire buckets, (8) hostel, (9) compound wall, (10) meadow, (11) drinking water facility, (12) sufficient shelves in the library, (13) news letters, (14) books on teaching methodology, (15) sufficient number of text books, (16) sufficient number of tables with drawers, (17) sufficient number of benches in the class rooms, (18) kipps apparatus, (19) overhead projector, (20) television, (21) audio tape recorder, (22) filmstrips, (23) still pictures, (24) comics, (25) bulletin boards, (26) flannel boards, (27) pictorial graphs, (28) contemporary maps, (29) historical maps, (30) survey maps, (31) political maps, (32) weather maps, (33) badminton court, (34) tennis court, (35) throw ball court, (36) kho-kho court, (37) badminton, (38) basket ball, (39) foot ball, (40) ring tennis, (41) gymnasium equipment, and (42) first aid box are available in about 70 per cent of the DIETs. It means out of 10 DIETs included in this study the above items of physical facilities are available in 7 DIETs.

The third category of items listed below are available only in 4 out of the 10 DIETs studied. They are : (1) psychology, (2) social studies laboratories, (3) computer room, (4) garden, (5) water facility for garden, (6) sufficient tables in library, (7) sufficient chairs in library, (8) film-strip projector, (9) projection screen, (10) record player, (11) diagrams, (12) topographical maps, and (13) yoga are available.

The fourth category of items listed below are available only in 3 out of the 10 DIETs. They are (1) educational technology laboratory, (2) staff quarters, (3) non-teaching staff quarters, (4) canteen, (5) sports training building, (6) co-operative book-bank, (7) educational commission reports, (8) 16 m.m. film projector, (9) opaque projector, (10) micro-projector, (11) still photograph camera, (12) photo darkroom equipment, (13) puppets, (14) mobiles, (15) magnetic boards, (16) peg boards, (17) micro-teaching facility, (18) flannel graphs, (19) outline maps, (20) cricket equipment, and (21) asanas.

The fifth category of items listed below are not at all available in the DIETs covered under investigation. They are (1) gymnasium, (2) electric generator, (3) epidiascope, (4) closed circuit-television, (5) vedio tape-recorder, (6) letter press, off-set and other printing equipment, (7) slide and filmstrip making equipment, (8) slide and filmstrip copying equipment, (9) gramophone records, (10) 16 m.m. sound films, (11) 16 m.m. silent films, (12) mock-ups, (13) diorama, (14) museum, (15) rented buildings, (16) girls toilets, (17) boys lavatories, (18) garden care, (19) journals, (20) gramophone records, (21) tree charts, (22) pictorial maps, (23) hockey court, (24) basket ball court, (25) foot ball court, (26) cricket court, (27) soft ball court, (28) base ball court, (29) circle game court, (30) deep frog court, (31) hockey equipment, (32) soft ball equipment, (33) base-ball equipment, and (34) tennis equipment.

Thus, out of 179 items about 1/3 of the items are available in all the DIETs and the remaining 2/3 items are not available in all the DIETs. This pathetic situation has also been revealed by student teachers, lecturers and principals through the perception scale meant for them.

5.1.4 INVESTIGATOR'S PERSONAL OBSERVATIONS

The investigator personally visited all the 10 DIETs to collect data from the student teachers, lecturers and principals. He stayed for a day or two in each of the ten DIETs and studied the physical, academic, administrative, financial, interpersonal aspects of the teacher education programme and student's attitude towards teaching profession. His significant observations are as follows :

1. The investigator has interacted with many student teachers while staying with them. Most of the student teachers have expressed that they are unhappy as their institution is situated for away from the district headquarters. It is true that very few DIETs are situated in the district headquarters. The student teachers are unhappy as they have been asked to go to far off places for teaching practice because of non-availability of sufficient number of schools nearer to their DIETs.

2. During discussion with student teachers on different issues some have expressed that the DIET principal has been mismanaging institutes finances. It seems in some of the institutions money is pooled up through collections for a variety of activities such as student tours, citizenship camps, uniform records, celebration of literacy and cultural activities, etc. However, some students may not be interested in such activities and they feel dissatisfied with such unhealthy practices.

3. As explained earlier on the basis of perceptions of student teachers, lecturers and principals the libraries in DIET are in very poor status for want of books, journals, committee reports, spacious room, furniture and staff. While collecting data the investigator has raised different issues related to library facilities. The comments noticed are in line with the perceptions recorded earlier when

the investigator actually visited the library room and found the condition to be horrible.

4. The investigator in his observations has found that majority of the DIETs are not well equipped with sports and games material. In some DIETs student teachers have expressed that they have never seen their physical director. During the collection of data the investigator while interacting with the student teachers has raised questions on different aspects related to play-grounds, sports and games equipment, number of physical education periods, etc. The response for his queries are mostly negative and they are in line with the perceptions of student teachers, lecturers and principals.

5. As explained earlier on thc basis of perceptions of student teachers, lecturers and principals, the laboratories in DIETs are in dire need of buildings, equipment, teaching aids, furniture and staff. While collecting data the investigator has raised several queries related to the laboratory facilities. The comments noticed concur with the perceptions recorded earlier. Majority of the student teachers have expressed that they are unhappy as their institution's laboratories are in bad condition.

6. The investigator in his observation has found that majority of the DIETs have inadequate audio-visual equipment. Even the existing audio-visual equipment has not been properly maintained due to lack of technical staff. The lecturers are not interested in using the available audio-visual equipment effectively. Most of the student teachers have expressed their unhappiness for not using audio-visual equipment in their classes. The observations noticed agree with the perceptions sof student teachers, lecturers and principals.

7. The investigator in his observation has come to know that there is a little coordination among

DIETs, NCERT, SCERT and RIEs in developing and implementing innovative activities to achieve qualitative improvement in teacher education. The comments noticed at the time of investigator's personal observations and the perceptions of the student teachers, lecturers and principals are the same.

8. To his surprise the investigator has observed that there has been insufficient teaching staff in most of the DIETs. The student teachers have expressed their dissatisfaction with this phenomena. It is true that majority of the DIETs have insufficient teaching staff. The student teachers are unhappy as some of the subjects have been taught by non specialised lecturers. Thus, we may conclude that the comments noticed concur with the perceptions recorded earlier by the student teachers, lecturers and principals.

9. During the investigator's discussion with student teachers some of them have expressed that the DIET principal has been mismanaging the student-teachers' scholarships. The student teachers have complained that they have been denied scholarships due to them. The comments noticed here are in agreement with the perceptions recorded earlier.

10. The investigator has interacted with many student teachers while staying with them. Majority of the student teachers have expressed that they are unhappy as their institution is far away from the practicing schools. It is true that very few schools are situated nearer to the DIETs. The student teachers are asked to go to far off places for teaching practice. Even lecturers are unable to visit schools to supervise the teaching practice classes effectively. Under these conditions we may conclude that supervision on teaching practice in majority of the DIETs has become an eye wash.

11. The student teachers have expressed that the present day teacher education curriculum is outdated and that it should be restructured and reorganised keeping in view the present day needs and aspirations of the young trainees. The comments noticed are in line with the perceptions recorded earlier by the student teachers, lecturers and principals.

12. Majority of the student teachers feel that undue delay in admissions to DIET on the basis of State wide common entrance test has resulted in the loss of one academic year. Therefore, it is essential that DIET academic year is set right to be on par with other educational institutions.

13. The investigator has found that majority of the student teachers have not been able to acquire any teaching skills during the brief span of one month teaching practice. They feel that the time is insufficient for improving teaching skills. Barring a few majority of them have completed their course without acquiring any skills. The comments noticed are in agreement with the perceptions recorded earlier.

14. Based on the perceptions of student teachers, lecturers and principals it has been pointed out that the DIET lecturers still follow the age old lecture method. The student teachers are unhappy that they are not taught other methods such as lecture-cum-discussion method, inductive-deductive approach, analytical-synthetical approach, enquiry approach, etc. Seminars, symposia, workshops, etc., should also be conducted to help the student teachers acquire teaching skills. The most prominent training method namely, micro-teaching has almost been neglected. Hence, it is high time modifications were made both in the curriculum and the methods employed in its transaction.

15. The investigator has observed that majority of the DIET lecturers do not have clear cut idea about their duties, functions and responsibilities in their respective branches. Lack of periodical orientation training programmes is one of the reasons for this sorry state of affair. The comments noticed are in line with the perceptions recorded earlier.

16. It has also come to the notice of the investigator that the DIET lecturers are not granted T.A. & D.A. for visiting teaching practice centres, mandal offices, etc. It is true that very few DIETs have been providing T.A & D.A. to lecturers. The lecturers are unhappy as they are asked to go to far off places for supervising teaching practice without any T.A. & D.A. Thus, the comments noticed are in line with the perceptions of the lecturers recorded earlier.

17. During his interaction with the lecturers the investigator has observed that some of the DIET lecturers have no commitment to their profession. It is not surprising that the majority of the teachers choose teaching as a means of livelihood. The comments noticed are in line with the perceptions recorded earlier.

18. The investigator has found that 80 per cent of DIETs lack staff quarters. The National Policy on Education (1986) emphasizes through the DIET Guidelines that every DIET must have staff quarters. Being residential in nature DIET without staff quarters is incomplete. Majority of lecturers have expressed their unhappiness in this regard. The comments noticed agree with the perceptions recorded earlier by the lecturers and principals.

19. During his interaction with the student teachers he has come to know that the DIET lecturers are not punctual to their classes. It is true that lack of supervision makes the lecturers unaccountable.

This observation is akin to the perceptions recorded earlier.

20. It has also been found by the investigator that majority of lecturers are not confined to teaching alone. They have been forcibly involved in programmes like literacy programmes, census surveys, state wide common examinations besides teaching. This leads to deterioration of teaching skills and quality of teaching. Majority of the lecturers are unhappy with this additional burden.

21. Majority of the lecturers and student teachers have expressed that their institution has no attached model school. It is true that very few DIETs have attached model schools. The student teachers have been asked to go to far off places for demonstration classes, observation classes, criticism classes and teaching practice classes. Thus, the comments noticed are in line with the perceptions recorded earlier by the student teachers, lecturers and principals.

5.2 DESCRIPTION OF THE DISTRIBUTION OF SCORES OF PERCEPTIONS AND ATTITUDES AND THE INFLUENCE OF PERSONAL AND DEMOGRAPHIC VARIABLES OF THE STUDENT TEACHERS AND LECTURERS

The description of perception scores, attitude scores of the student teachers and the influence of personal and demographic variables on their perceptions and attitudes are presented in this unit.

5.2.1 ABOUT STUDENT TEACHERS

(i) Description of the Distribution of Student Teachers' Perception Scores

The perception scores obtained through the administration of the perception scale to the student teachers have been arranged in a systematic manner by grouping them into classes and tabulating them into frequency distribution. It may be noted that the perception scale of student teachers includes aspects relating to physical facilities, academic, administrative, financial, interpersonal aspects, admission procedure, duration of the course, minimum qualification for entrance test, curriculum, theory, practicals, etc. The analysis is carried out to know the kind of average, range and scatteredness. The perception scores obtained by 500 student teaches are tabulated into frequency distribution and various descriptive statistics such as mean, median, mode, range, quartile deviation, standard deviation, skewness and kurtosis are calculated to understand the nature of distribution. The frequency distribution and the values of descriptive statistics are presented in Table—1.

Table—1 : Table showing the description of the distribution of perception scores of student teachers

Class Interval	*Mid values*	*Frequency*	*Smoothed Frequency*	*Cumulative Frequencies*
110-119	114.5	2	4.67	2
120-129	124.5	12	15.67	14
130-139	134.5	33	42.67	47
140-149	144.5	83	77.00	130
150-159	154.5	115	103.00	245
160-169	164.5	111	106.00	356
170-179	174.5	92	79.33	448
180-189	184.5	35	46.00	483
190-199	194.5	11	17.33	494
200-209	204.5	6	5.67	500
		N = 500		

Mean	=	160.109	Q.D.	=	11.305
Median	=	159.905	S.D.	=	16.216
Mode	=	159.499	Sk.	=	0.038
Range	=	97.000	Ku.	=	0.281

Fig. 1 : Frequency Polygon and Smoothed Frequency Curve of Perception Scores of Student Teachers

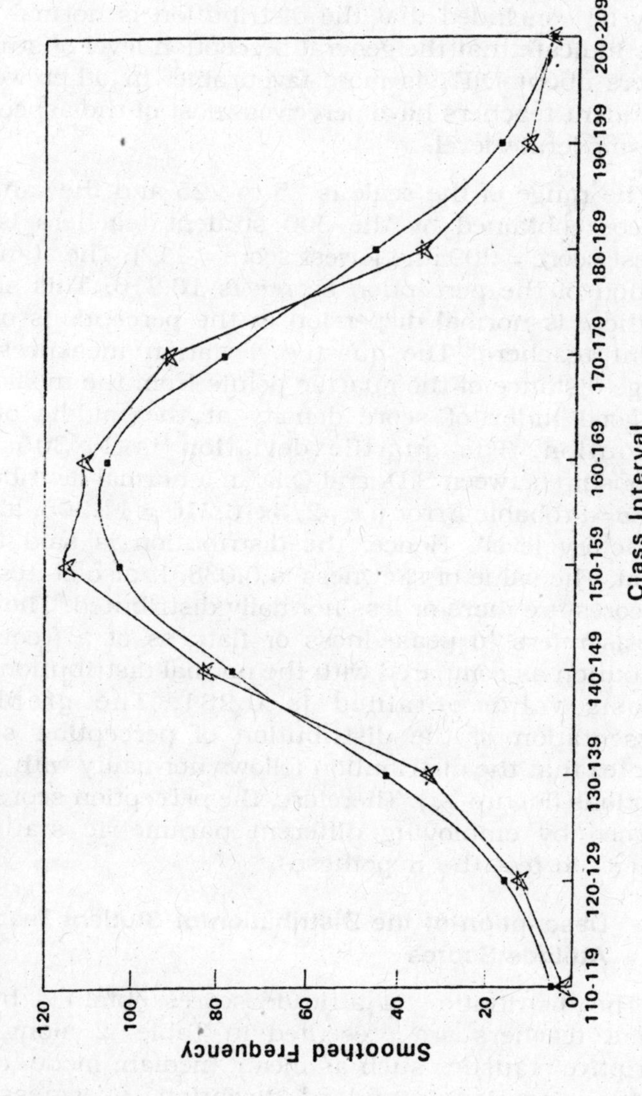

The mean perception scores of student teachers on different aspects of DIET is 160.109. The values of median and mode are 159.905 and 159.499 respectively. All the measures of central tendency are almost equal and therefore it may be concluded that the distribution is normal. The values indicate that the general perception level of student teachers about DIET is more favourable. In other words, the student teachers have perceived most of the aspects at above moderate level.

The range of the scale is 75 to 225 and the range of the score obtained by the 500 student teachers is 97. (highest score = 209 and lowest score = 112). The standard deviation of the perception scores is 16.216. This shows that there is normal dispersion in the perceptions of the student teachers. The quartile deviation measures the average distance of the quartile points from the median. It is a good index of score density at the middle of the distribution. The quartile deviation is 11.305. The relationship between S.D. and Q.D. in a normal distribution is $2/3\sigma$= Probable Error (i.e., 2/3x16.216 = 11.305, almost satisfactory level). Hence, the distribution is said to be normal. The value of skewness is 0.038. It also states that the scores are more or less normally distributed. The term kurtosis refers to peakedness or flatness of a frequency distribution as compared with the normal distribution. The kurtosis value obtained is 0.281. The graphical representation of the distribution of perception scores indicates that the distribution follows normality with slight exceptions (Figure—1). Therefore, the perception scores are analysed by employing different parametric statistical methods to test the hypotheses.

(ii) Description of the Distribution of Student Teachers' Attitude Scores

The distribution of attitude scores obtained by the student teachers are presented in Table—2 along with descriptive statistics such as mean, median, mode, range, quartile deviation, standard deviation, skewness and kurtosis.

Table—2 : Table showing the description of the distribution of attitude scores of student teachers

Class Interval	*Mid values*	*Frequency*	*Smoothed Frequency*	*Cumulative Frequencies*
110-119	114.5	1	1.00	1
120-129	124.5	2	3.33	3
130-139	134.5	7	9.00	10
140-149	144.5	18	20.67	28
150-159	154.5	37	44.33	65
160-169	164.5	78	83.67	143
170-179	174.5	136	112.33	279
180-189	184.5	123	108.00	402
190-199	194.5	65	71.33	467
200-209	204.5	26	32.67	493
210-219	214.5	7	11.00	500
		N = 500		

Mean	=	176.676	Q.D.	=	10.030
Median	=	177.347	S.D.	=	16.054
Mode	=	178.689	Sk.	=	-0.125
Range	=	97.000	Ku.	=	0.242

The mean scores obtained by the sample is 176.676, which means the general level of attitude among student-teachers is much higher than the average point (45 x 3 = 135) on the scale. The values of median and mode 177.347 and 178.689 respectively have confirmed that the general level of attitude towards teaching profession among the sample of subjects is greater than $M+\frac{1}{2}\sigma$ and hence it may be concluded that the student-teachers have a favourable attitude towards teaching profession. As the measures of central tendency are in the ascending order, the value of mean is less than median, median is lesser than mode and mode is the highest, the distribution is said to be negatively skewed to a little extent. Of course it is evident from the calculated value of skewness (-0.125). The value

Fig. 2 : Frequency Polygon and Smoothed Frequency Curve of Attitude Scores of Student Teachers

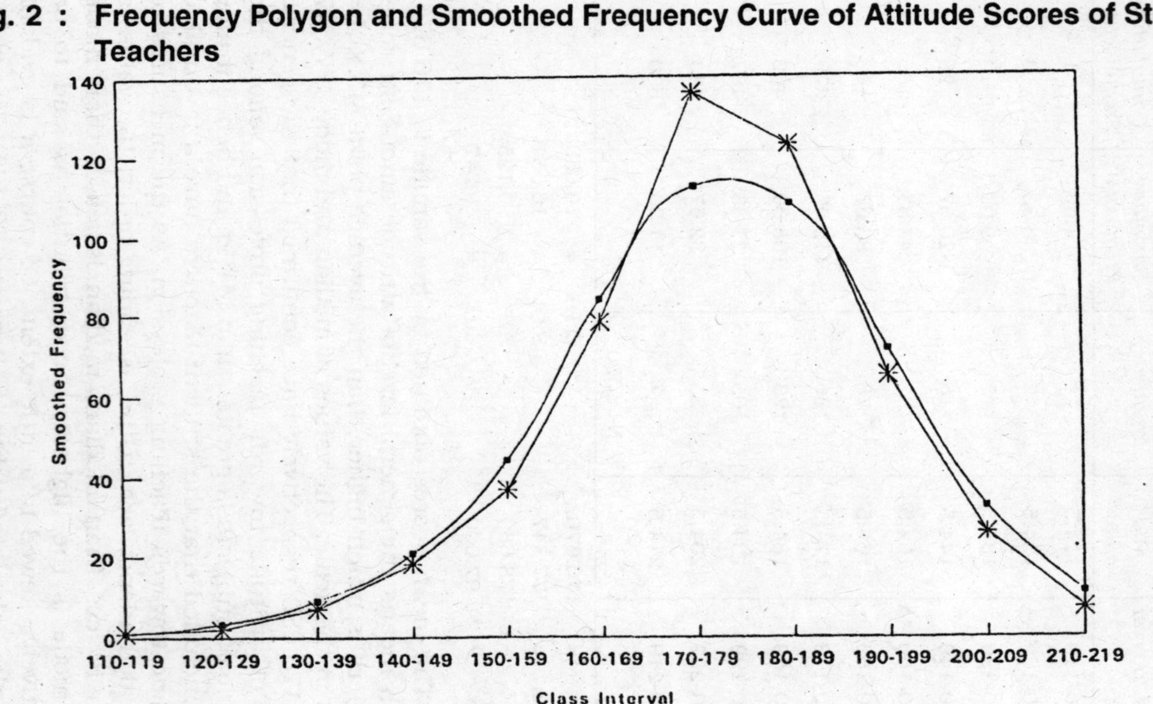

of kurtosis 0.242 discloses that the distribution is slightly lepto kurtic.

The range of the distribution of scores is 97. (highest score = 214 and lowest score = 117). The Q.D. and S.D. are 10.030 and 16.054 respectively. These measures of dispersion reveal that the spread in the distribution is normal. The relationship between standard deviation and quartile deviation as exists in the normal probability curve is S.D. x 2/3 = Q.D. (i.e., 16.054 x 2/3 = 10.030) is observed in the distribution, with a negligible difference of 0.673. So it can be said that the distribution belongs to the family of normal curves. Thus, the null hypotheses formulated that "the student teachers are not favourable to teaching profession", is rejected. The graphical respresentation of the distribution of attitude scores indicates that the distribution follows normality with slight exceptions (Figure—2).

As the distribution of attitude scores follows normality it is feasible to apply all parametric statistics in the analysis of the data obtained and test the different hypotheses formulated.

(iii) The Influence of Personal and Demographic Variables on Student Teachers' Perceptions and Attitudes

Sex : The influence of sex on the perceptions and attitudes of student teachers is as presented in Table—3.

Table—3 : Table showing the influence of sex on perceptions and attitudes of student teachers

S.No.	*Variables*	*Groups*	*N*	*M*	*S.D.*	*'t'*
1.	Perceptions	Men	264	158.64	14.86	2.21 *
		Women	236	161.81	17.18	
2.	Attitudes	Men	264	175.23	15.43	2.38 *
		Women	236	178.62	16.43	

Note : @ Not significant
* Significant at 0.05 level
** Significant at 0.01 level

(These symbols are followed throughout the thesis).

An observation of the table reveals that women student teachers have secured a better mean score on perceptions when compared to their counterparts. The observed difference between the means is found to be statistically significant since the obtained 't' value of 2.21 is found to be significant at 0.05 level. Therefore, the null hypothesis that men and women student teachers do not differ significantly with regard to their perception is rejected.

In a similar fashion an observation of the attitude scores obtained by men and women student teachers also reveal that women teachers have scored a better mean when compared to men students and 't' value obtained to test the significance of difference is found to be statistically significant at 0.05 level. Hence, it can be assumed that women student teachers have a better attitude towards teaching profession. The null hypothesis that men and women student teachers do not differ significantly with regard to their attitude towards teaching profession is rejected.

Age

In the present study an attempt has been made to know the influence of age on the perceptions of student teachers on different aspects of their training programme and their attitude towards teaching profession. On the basis of the age the subjects are divided into three groups namely, the subject in the 17 to 19 years age group, 20 to 22 years age group and 23 years and above age group. Their mean perception scores, standard deviations along with 'F' values on perceptions and attitudes are as presented in Table—4.

Table—4 : Table showing the influence of age on perceptions and attitudes of student teachers

S.No.	*Variables*	*Groups*	*N*	*M*	*S.D.*	*'F'*
1.	Perceptions	17 - 19	173	161.10	16.44	
		20 - 22	190	159.46	15.18	0.507 @
		23 and above	137	159.85	16.80	
2.	Attitudes	17 - 19	173	175.76	16.32	
		20 - 22	190	176.48	15.94	1.350 @
		23 and above	137	178.67	15.57	

An observation of the above table reveals that the subjects with lower age (17-19 years) have secured a better mean score compared to the other two age groups. As there are more than two groups and only one classification variables, analysis of variance, one way classification technique is felt to be the appropriate statistical technique that can be employed in the situation. From the table it can be noticed that the 'F' value is 0.507 at 2, and 498 degrees of freedom and the value is not statistically significant even at 0.05 level. Therefore, the null hypothesis that the perceptions of student teachers of different age groups do not differ significantly in their perceptions is accepted.

When the attitude scores of different age groups of student teachers are considered there is no significant difference between the mean scores and the calculated 'F' value of 1.350 is far below than the table value at 0.05 level of significance. However, when the means are considered the student teachers representing 23 years and above age group have secured a better mean when compared to that of the other age groups may be due to sampling fluctuations. Hence, the null hypothesis that student teachers representing different age groups do not differ significantly in their attitude towards teaching profession is accepted.

Educational Qualifications

Often educational level is viewed as an important variable that influences the performance of the subjects in several investigations and more so with regard to academic performance. Therefore, the sample of the student-teachers included in the study is divided into two groups, viz., suitably qualified with intermediate qualification and over qualified i.e., graduation and above. The Means and S.Ds of both perception and attitude scores of the above two groups are calculated and 't' test is employed to test whether there is any significant difference in the perceptions and the attitudes of the two groups. The results are presented in Table—5.

Table—5 : Table showing the influence of educational qualifications on perceptions and attitudes of student teachers

S.No.	*Variables*	*Groups*	*N*	*M*	*S.D.*	*'t'*
1.	Perceptions	Intermediate	216	162.26	17.31	2.60 **
		Degree	284	158.52	14.86	
2.	Attitudes	Intermediate	216	177.25	16.47	0.52 @
		Degree	284	176.51	15.62	

A glance at the table denotes that subjects with intermediate qualification have secured a better mean score than their counterparts with regard to perceptions. There is a difference of 3.74 mean points between the two groups of subjects and the 't' value of 2.60 is statistically significant at 0.01 level. Hence, the null hypothesis that the qualifications of student teachers do not have any significant bearing on their perceptions is rejected.

A peep into the table with regard to attitudes of the subjects reveals that the mean scores of subjects of intermediate and degree qualifications is almost nearer (177.25 and 176.51) and the 't' value of 0.52 is found to be not statistically significant. Hence, the null hypothesis that the qualifications of student teachers do not have any significant bearing on their attitude towards teaching profession is accepted.

Locality

The influence of locality on the perceptions of student teachers and attitudes is as presented in Table—6.

Table—6 : Table showing the influence of locality on perceptions and attitudes of student teachers

S.No.	*Variables*	*Groups*	*N*	*M*	*S.D.*	*'t'*
1.	Perceptions	Rural	329	159.60	16.05	1.03 @
		Urban	171	161.16	16.06	
2.	Attitudes	Rural	329	177.25	15.57	20.81 @
		Urban	171	176.02	16.77	

A glance of the table denotes that the student teachers of urban areas have secured a mean score of 161.16 and the standard deviation is 16.06. Similarly, the rural student teachers have secured a mean score of 159.60 and the standard deviation is 16.05 with regard to perception. In order to test whether there exists any significant difference between the mean scores of rural and urban student teachers 't' test is employed. The calculated 't' value of 1.03 is not statistically significant at 0.05 level of significance and the null hypothesis that the locality from which the student teachers hail would not indicate any significant difference in their perceptions is accepted.

The analysis relating to the attitude of student teachers with regard to locality reveals that the subjects hailing from rural areas have secured a mean score of 177.25 where as the subjects representing urban areas have secured a mean score of 176.02 and the means are almost nearer. The calculated 't' value of 0.81 is statistically not significant at 0.05 level and the null hypothesis that the locality from which the student teachers hail would not indicate any significant difference in their attitude towards teaching profession is accepted.

Methodology in subject

In the present investigation an attempt is made to know the influence of methodology in subject of the student teachers of the sample on their perceptions and attitudes. The results are as presented in Table—7.

Table—7 : Table showing the influence of methodology in subject on the perceptions and attitudes of student teachers

S.No.	*Variables*	*Groups*	*N*	*M*	*S.D.*	*'t'*
1.	Perceptions	Mathematics	162	160.56	16.11	0.14 @
		Physical Sciences	76	159.17	18.10	
		Biological Sciences	109	159.93	16.26	
		Social Sciences	153	160.30	14.88	
2.	Attitudes	Mathematics	162	175.69	15.96	0.43 @
		Physical Sciences	76	177.07	15.01	
		Biological Sciences	109	177.29	15.28	
		Social Sciences	153	177.59	17.02	

The table shows that there are four categories of subjects in methodology namely Mathematics, Physical Sciences, Biological Sciences and Social Sciences. When perceptions of the sample are considered there is not much variation in the mean scores of different subject groups. The calculated 'F' value to test the significance of difference among the mean scores of the student teachers based upon the subject in methodology is only 0.14 which is not statistically significant even at 0.05 level. Hence, the null hypothesis that the methodology in subject of the student teachers would not indicate any significant difference in their perceptions is accepted.

A glance at the mean scores secured by the sample based upon the methodology in subject with regard to their attitude towards teaching profession also indicates very limited differences of mean scores. The calculated 'F' value to test the difference in the mean scores is 0.43. This value is not significant at 0.05 level of probability. Hence, the null hypothesis that the methodology in subject of the student teachers would not indicate any significant difference in their attitude towards teaching profession is accepted.

Methodology in language

The means and standard deviations of perception scores and attitude scores along with 't' values of the two language groups are presented in Table—8.

Table—8 : Table showing the influence of methodology in language on the perceptions and attitudes of student teachers

S.No.	*Variables*	*Groups*	*N*	*M*	*S.D.*	*'t'*
1.	Perceptions	Telugu	417	160.03	15.60	0.32 @
		English	83	160.64	18.28	
2.	Attitudes	Telugu	417	176.73	15.91	0.31 @
		English	83	177.34	16.41	

It is clear from the table that the two groups of sample representing Telugu and English languages have scored mostly the same means (160.03 and 160.64). The 't' value of 0.32 is far below the table value at 0.05 level of significance. Hence, the null hypothesis that the methodology in language of the student teachers would not indicate any significant difference in their perceptions is accepted.

The attitude scores of the subjects representing Telugu and English methodology groups indicate that the Telugu methodology group have secured a mean score of 176.73 with a standard deviation 15.91 where as the subjects representing English methodology student teachers have secured a mean score of 177.34 with a standard deviation of 16.41. The 't' value obtained to test the significance of difference between the two mean scores is 0.31 and this value is not statistically significant at 0.05 level. Hence, the null hypothesis that the methodology in language of the student teachers would not indicate any significant difference in their attitude towards teaching profession is accepted.

Family literacy index

In the present study it is presumed that literacy index of the family of student teachers may influence their perceptions and attitudes. Therefore, the sample is divided into two groups, viz., low literacy index of the family and high literacy index of the family. The means and S.Ds of perception and attitude scores for both the groups are calculated and 't' test is employed. The results are presented in Table—9.

Table—9 : Table showing the influence of family literacy index on the perceptions and attitudes of student teachers

S.No.	*Variables*	*Groups*	*N*	*M*	*S.D.*	*'t'*
1.	Perceptions	Low literacy index	253	160.29	15.32	0.22 @
		High literacy index	247	159.97	16.81	
2.	Attitudes	Low literacy index	253	176.94	15.13	0.17 @
		High literacy index	247	176.71	16.85	

A glance at the table denotes that there is no much difference in the perception and attitude mean scores. Even the 't' values of 0.22 and 0.17 respectively for perceptions and attitude scores are not statistically significant. Hence, the null hypothesis that literacy index would not significantly influence the perceptions of the student teachers and the attitude towards teaching profession of the student teachers was accepted.

Father's occupation

The details pertaining to the influence of father's

occupation on the perceptions and attitudes of student teachers are presented in Table—10.

Table—10 : Table showing the influence of father's occupation on the perceptions and attitudes of student teachers

S.No.	*Variables*	*Groups*	*N*	*M*	*S.D.*	*'F'*
1.	Perceptions	Coolies/Daily wagers	62	160.05	13.90	0.06 @
		Cultivators/ Businessmen	287	159.95	15.45	
		Secured job holders	151	160.51	17.95	
2.	Attitudes	Coolies/Daily wagers	62	177.94	15.21	0.18 @
		Cultivators/ Businessmen	287	176.60	15.14	
		Secured job holders	151	176.81	17.84	

A glance at the table indicates that the three occupational groups namely, coolies/daily wagers, cultivators/businessmen, secured job holders have obtained more or less similar means and the 'F' value obtained is also found to be not statistically significant at 0.05 level. Hence, the null hypothesis that the father's occupation of student teachers does not significantly influence their perceptions is accepted. The table further shows that there is no significant influence of the father's occupation on the attitude of student teachers. The mean attitude scores obtained by the different groups of the sample are more or less the same. The calculated 'F' value is statistically not significant. Hence, the null hypothesis that father's occupation of student teachers does not significantly influence their attitude towards teaching profession is accepted.

Mother's occupation

The information relating to the influence of mother's occupation on the perceptions and attitudes of student teachers is shown in Table—11.

Table—11 : Table showing the influence of mother's occupation on the perceptions and attitudes of student teachers

S.No.	*Variables*	*Groups*	*N*	*M*	*S.D.*	*'t'*
1.	Perceptions	Working women	279	158.44	15.71	2.67 **
		Housewives	221	162.28	16.27	
2.	Attitudes	Working women	279	176.76	16.62	0.11 @
		Housewives	221	176.91	15.17	

It may be observed from the table that the group representing working women has obtained a mean of 158.44, whereas that of housewives a mean of 162.28. There is a mean difference of 3.84 points between the two groups. The 't' value of 2.67 obtained to test the significance of the difference between the two means is significant at 0.05 level. Hence, the null hypothesis that the mother's occupation does not significantly influence the perceptions of the student teachers is rejected. The children of housewives possessed significantly higher positive perceptions than the other groups.

The details relating to the influence of mother's occupation on the attitude of student teachers indicate that the means of the two groups are almost equal. Further, the 't' value of 0.11 to test the significance of the difference between the means of the two groups is statistically not significant. Hence, the null hypothesis that mother's occupation of student teachers does not significantly influence their attitude towards the teaching profession is accepted.

Family Annual Income

The means and standard deviations of perception and attitude scores of student teachers along with 'F' values of the three income groups are presented in Table—12.

Table—12 : Table showing the influence of family annual income on the perceptions and attitudes of student teachers

S.No.	*Variables*	*Income Groups*	*N*	*M*	*S.D.*	*'F'*
1.	Perceptions	Upto Rs. 12,000/-	177	161.33	14.75	
		Rs. 12,001/- to Rs. 36,000/-	155	159.96	15.75	0.91 @
		Rs. 36,001 and above	168	159.02	17.60	
2.	Attitudes	Upto Rs. 12,000/-	177	177.74	15.50	
		Rs. 12,001/-to Rs. 36,000/-	155	175.37	16.61	0.99 @
		Rs. 36,001 and above	168	177.21	15.90	

On the basis of the total annual income of the family the sample is divided into three groups 1.with family income upto Rs. 12,000/- per year, 2.with income between Rs. 12,001/- and Rs. 36,000/- per year, and 3.with income of Rs. 36,001/- and above. The three student teacher groups based upon their family income have obtained the mean and standard deviation scores of 161.33 and 14.75, 159.96 and 15.75 and 159.02 and 17.60 respectively. 'F' test was employed to test the significance of the differences among the three groups. The 'F' value of 0.91 obtained is not statistically significant even at 0.05 level. Hence, the null hypothesis that 'the family income of student teachers does not significantly influence their perceptions' is accepted.

The details relating to the influence of the family income on the attitude of the student teachers are also on similar lines. There is not much variation in the mean scores representing the three groups and the 'F' value of 0.99 is also not statistically significant at 0.05 level. Hence, the null hypothesis that the family income does not significantly influence the attitude of student teachers is accepted.

To sum up, the variables namely sex, educational qualifications,and mother's occupation have significantly influenced the perceptions of student teachers whereas the variable of sex alone has a significant influence on the attitude of the student teachers towards the teaching profession.

5.2.2 ABOUT LECTURERS

(i) Description of the Distribution of Lecturers' Perception Scores

The perception scores obtained through the administration of the perception scale to the lecturers have been arranged in a systematic manner by grouping them into classes and tabulating them into frequency distribution. It may be noted that the perception scale of lecturers includes the aspects relating to physical facilities, academic, administrative, financial, interpersonal aspects, admission procedure, duration of the course, minimum qualification for the entrance test, curriculum, theory, practicals, students' behaviours and activities of co-lecturers and principals, etc. The analysis has been carried out to know the kind of average, range and scatterdness. The perception scores obtained from 101 lecturers have been tabulated into frequency distribution and various descriptive statistics such as mean, median, mode, range, quartile deviation, standard deviation, skewness and kurtosis have been calculated to understand the nature of distribution. The frequency distribution and the values of descriptive statistics are presented in Table—13.

Table—13 : Table showing the description of the distribution of perception scores of lecturers

Class Interval	*Mid values*	*Frequency*	*Smoothed Frequency*	*Cumulative Frequencies*
130-139	134.5	2	3.67	2
140-149	144.5	9	8.00	11
150-159	154.5	13	12.00	24
160-169	164.5	14	15.00	38
170-179	174.5	18	16.00	56
180-189	184.5	16	16.00	72
190-199	194.5	14	12.67	86
200-209	204.5	8	9.00	94
210-219	214.5	5	4.67	99
220-229	224.5	1	2.33	100
230-239	234.5	1	0.67	101
		N = 101		

Mean	=	176.876	Q.D.	=	15.893
Median	=	176.444	S.D.	=	21.302
Mode	=	175.580	Sk.	=	0.061
Range	=	106.000	Ku.	=	0.278

The mean perception scores of lecturers on different aspects of the DIET is 176.876. The values of median and mode are 176.444 and 175.580 respectively. All the measures of central tendency are almost equal and therefore it could be concluded that the distribution is normal. The values indicate that the general perception level of lecturers about the DIET is very favourable.

The range of the scale is 89 to 267 and the range of the scores obtained from 101 lecturers is 106 (the highest score = 237 and the lowest score = 131). The standard deviation of the perception scores is 21.302. This shows that there is normal dispersion in the perceptions of the lecturers. The quartile deviation measures the average distance of the quartile points from the median. It is a

Fig. 3 : Frequency Polygon and Smoothed Frequency Curve of Perception Scores of Teacher Educators

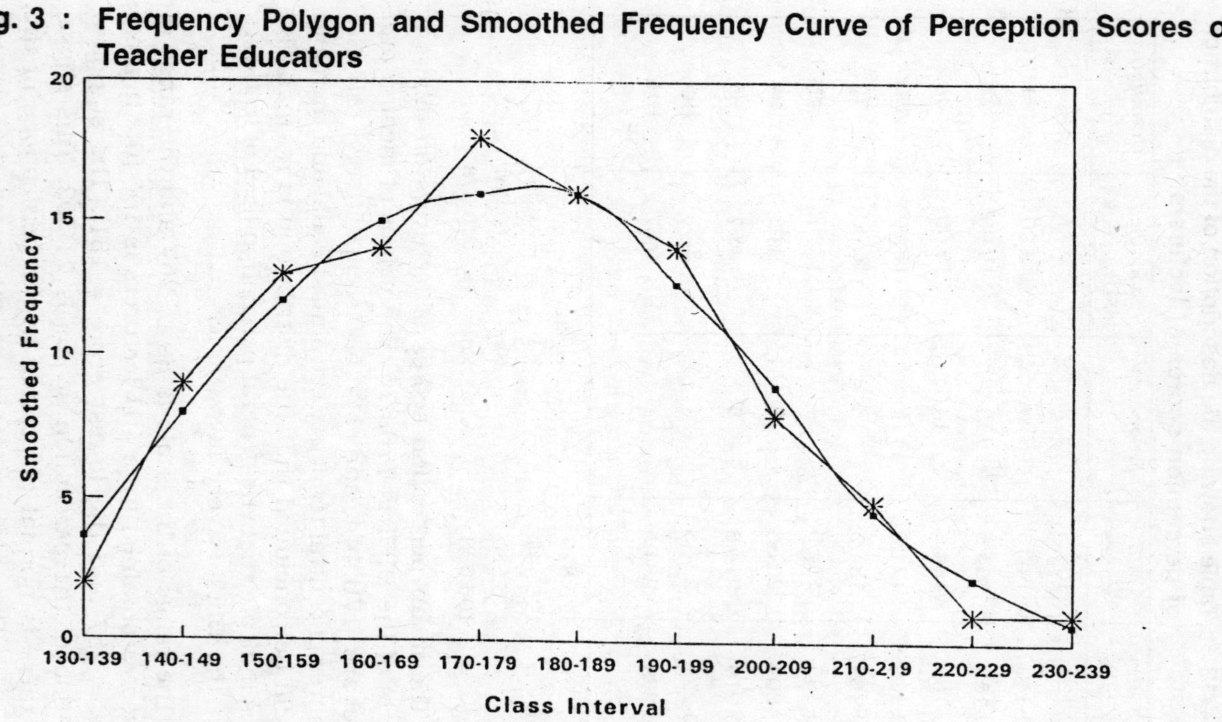

good index of score density at the middle of the distribution. The quartile deviation is 15.893. The relationship between S.D. and Q.D. in a normal distribution is 2/3σ= Probable Error or Q.D. (i.e., 2/3 x 21.302 = 15.893, almost satisfactory level). Hence, the distribution is said to be normal. The value of skewness is 0.061. It also states that the scores are more or less normally distributed. The term kurtosis refers to peakedness or flatness of a frequency distribution as compared with the normal distribution. The kurtosis value obtained is 0.278. The graphical representation of the distribution of perception scores indicates that the distribution follows normality with slight exceptions. Therefore, the perception scores are analysed by employing different parametric statistical methods to test the hypotheses. (Figure—3).

(ii) Description of the Distribution of Lecturers' Attitude Scores

The distribution of attitude scores obtained from the lecturers are presented in table—14, along with descriptive statistics such as mean, median, mode, range, quartile deviation, standard deviation, skewness and kurtosis.

Table—14 : Table showing the description of the distribution of attitude scores of lecturers.

Class Interval	*Mid values*	*Frequency*	*Smoothed Frequency*	*Cumulative Frequencies*
70-79	74.5	2	2.33	2
80-89	84.5	5	9.00	7
90-99	94.5	20	16.33	27
100-109	104.5	24	20.00	51
110-119	114.5	16	18.67	67
120-129	124.5	16	13.67	83
130-139	134.5	9	11.00	92
140-149	144.5	8	6.00	100
150-159	154.5	1	3.00	101
		N=101		

Mean	=	112.025	Q.D.	=	13.172
Median	=	109.292	S.D.	=	17.650
Mode	=	103.820	Sk.	=	0.465
Range	=	84.000	Ku.	=	0.279

The mean scores obtained by the sample is 112.025, which means the general level of attitude among lecturers is slightly higher than the average point (35x3=105) on the scale. The values of median and mode 109.292 and 103.820 respectively indicate that the general level of attitude towards the existing teacher education programme among the samples of the subjects is almost at the average level. As the measures of the central tendency are in the descending order, the value of mean is more than median, median is also more than mode and mode is the lowest, the distribution is said to be positively skewed. Of course it is evident from the calculated value of skewness (0.465). The value of kurtosis 0.279 discloses that the distribution is meso kurtic, i.e, normal.

The range of the distribution of scores is 84 (the highest score = 154 and the lowest score = 70). The Q.D. and S.D. are 13.172 and 17.650 respectively. These measures of dispersion reveal that the spread in the distribution is not normal. The relationship between standard deviation and quartile deviation as it exists in the normal probability curve of SD x 2/3 = Q.D. (i.e., 17.650 X 2/3 = 13.172) is not observed in the distribution. However, it can be said that the distribution belongs to the family of normal curves. Thus, the null hypotheses that "the attitude of lecturers towards the existing pre-service training programme is not favourable", may be accepted. The graphical representation of the distribution of attitude scores indicates that the distribution follows normality with slight divergencies. (Figure—4).

As the distribution of lecturers' attitude scores follows normality with marginal exceptions it is feasible to apply all the parametric statistics in the analysis of the data obtained and test the different hypotheses formulated.

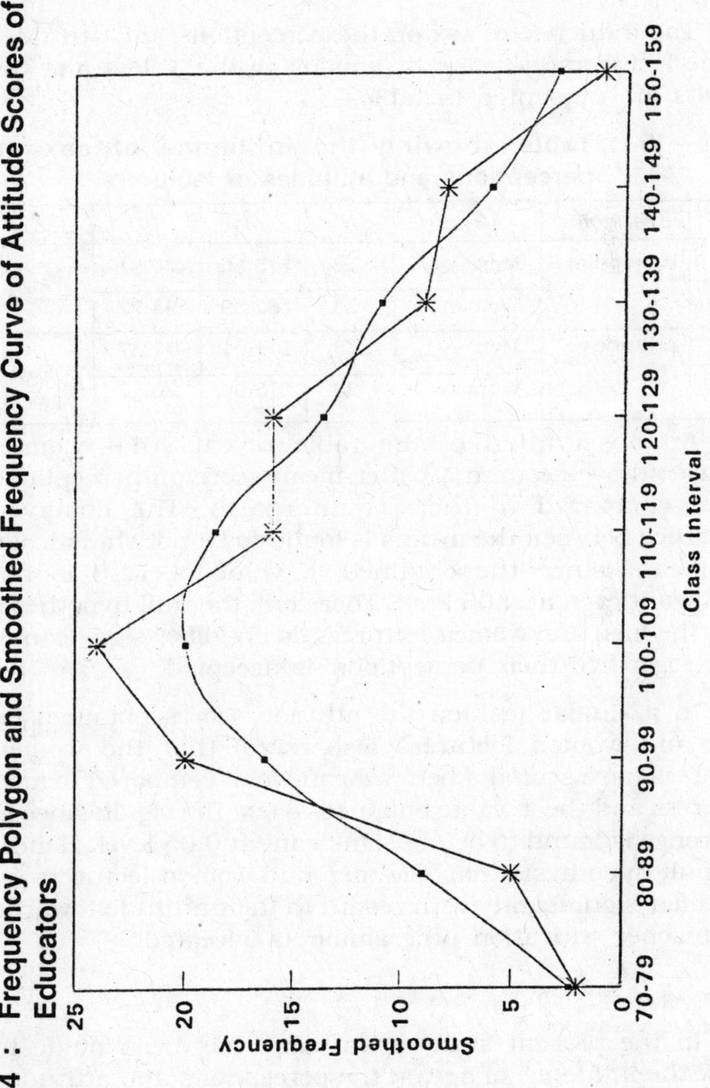

Fig. 4 : Frequency Polygon and Smoothed Frequency Curve of Attitude Scores of Teacher Educators

(iii) The Influence of Personal and Demographic Variables on Lecturers' Perceptions and Attitudes

Sex

The influence of sex on the perceptions and attitudes of the lecturers is tested by employing the 't' test and the results are presented in table—15.

Table—15 : Table showing the influence of sex on perceptions and attitudes of lecturers.

S.No.	*Variables*	*Groups*	*N*	*M*	*S.D.*	*'t'*
1.	Perceptions	Men	78	175.86	20.51	1.28@
		Women	23	182.39	24.77	
2.	Attitudes	Men	78	111.01	17.37	1.15@
		Women	23	115.96	20.47	

An observation of the table reveals that women lecturers have secured a better mean score on perceptions when compared to their counterparts. The observed difference between the means is found to be not statistically significant since the obtained 't' value of 1.28 is not significant even at 0.05 level. Therefore, the null hypothesis that 'the men and women lecturers do not differ significantly with regard to their perceptions' is accepted.

In a similar fashion the attitude scores obtained by men and women lecturers also reveal that the women lecturers have scored a better mean when compared to men lecturers and the 't' value obtained to test the significance of difference is found to be not significant at 0.05 level. Hence, the null hypothesis that 'the men and women lecturers do not differ significantly with regard to their attitude towards the teacher education programme' is accepted.

Age

In the present study an attempt has been made to know the influence of age on the perceptions and attitudes of lecturers. On the basis of the age the subjects are divided into two groups, namely, those whose age is in between

32-44 years and those who are above 45 years of age. Their mean perception scores, standard deviations along with 't' values are presented in table—16.

Table—16 : Table showing the influence of age on perceptions and attitudes of lecturers.

S.No.	*Variables*	*Groups*	*N*	*M*	*S.D.*	*'t'*
1.	Perceptions	32-44 years	47	174.89	21.37	1.07@
		45 years and above	54	179.48	21.78	
2.	Attitudes	32-44 years	47	110.11	19.10	1.05@
		45 years and above	54	113.91	17.24	

The above table reveals that the lecturers of the higher age group have secured a mean score of 179.48 in relation to the lecturers of the lower age group. The 't' test has been employed to know the significance of the difference between the two means. The calculated 't' value of 1.07 is found to be statistically not significant. Hence, the null hypothesis that 'the age of the lecturers does not significantly influence their perception of various activities of the teacher education programme' is accepted.

Similarly, the attitude scores of the lecturers denote that the lecturers belonging to higher age group have secured a better mean score than their counterparts (113.91 > 110.11). However, the calculated 't' value of 1.05 is not statistically significant at 0.01 level. Therefore, the null hypothesis that 'the age of the lecturers does not significantly influence their attitude towards the existing teacher education programme' is accepted.

Educational Qualification

In the present study the mean and standard deviations of perception scores and attitude scores of lecturers possessing varied qualifications are compared with the 't' test and the results are presented in table—17.

Table—17 : Table showing the influence of educational qualifications on perceptions and attitudes of lecturers.

S.No.	*Variables*	*Groups*	*N*	*M*	*S.D.*	*'t'*
1.	Perceptions	M.A., M.Ed.,	77	175.69	20.28	1.39@
		M.A., M.Ed., and above	24	182.67	25.13	
2.	Attitudes	M.A., M.Ed.,	77	110.74	18.03	1.39@
		M.A., M.Ed., and above	24	116.63	18.12	

The sample of the lecturers included in the study have been divided into two groups, viz., those possessing M.A., M.Ed., qualifications and those having M.A., M.Ed., and other higher qualifications. The above table indicates that the second category of lecturers possess a better perception about various facilities meant for the teacher education programme since their mean perception value is higher than their counterparts (182.67>175.69). However, the calculated 't' value of 1.39 is not statistically significant even at 0.05 level. Hence, the null hypothesis that 'the educational qualifications of lecturers does not significantly influence their perceptions' is accepted.

The details pertaining to the influence of the educational qualifications on the attitude of lecturers also indicate the same trend as in case of perceptions. The lecturers who have better educational qualifications have secured a better mean score than those with minimum level of educational qualifications prescribed for the lecturers of the DIETs (116.63 > 110.74). However,the calculated 't' value of 1.39 is found to be statistically not significant at 0.05 level. Hence, the null hypothesis that 'the educational qualifications of lecturers does not significantly influence their attitudes' is accepted.

Designation

There are two categories of lecturers covered in the sample, namely, lecturers and senior lecturers. An attempt has been made to know the influence of designation on their perceptions and attitudes. The results relating to the same are presented in table—18.

Table—18 : Table showing the influence of designation on the perceptions and attitudes of lecturers.

S.No.	*Variables*	*Groups*	*N*	*M*	*S.D.*	*'t'*
1.	Perceptions	Lecturers	51	175.37	20.63	0.93@
		Sr.Lecturers	50	179.36	22.58	
2.	Attitudes	Lecturers	51	113.86	21.42	0.96@
		Sr. Lecturers	50	110.38	14.04	

With regard to perceptions the senior lecturers have secured a mean and standard deviation of 179.36 and 22.58 whereas the lecturers have secured a mean and standard deviation of 175.37 and 20.63. It appears that there is a significant difference between the mean scores of lecturers and those of the senior lecturers. However, the calculated 't' value of 0.93 is statistically not significant even at 0.05 level. Hence, the null hypothesis 'that the designation of lecturers does not significantly influence their perceptions' is accepted. With regard to the attitude scores also lecturers and those of the senior lecturers do not differ much. The mean difference is only 3.48. The 't' value of 0.96 which is obtained for attitudes is not significant even at 0.05 level. Hence, the null hypothesis that 'the designation of lecturers does not significantly influence their attitudes' is accepted.

Experience as Primary School Teacher

The sample of the lecturers included in the study has been divided into two groups, namely, lecturers without experience as primary school teacher and lecturers with experience as primary school teachers. The details relating to the influence of experience as primary school teacher on the perceptions and attitudes of lecturers is presented in table—19.

Table—19 : Table showing the influence of experience as primary school teacher on the perceptions and attitudes of lecturers.

S.No.	*Variables*	*Groups*	*N*	*M*	*S.D.*	*'t'*
1.	Perceptions	Without experience as primary school teacher	46	178.17	22.26	0.35@
		With experience as primary school teacher	55	176.65	21.22	
2.	Attitudes	Without experience as primary school teacher	46	112.57	18.13	0.22@
		With experience as primary school teacher	55	111.78	18.30	

The table indicates that the lecturers without experience as primary school teachers have scored a better mean on perceptions than those with experience (178.17 > 176.65). In order to test the significance of the difference between the two means the 't' test is employed. The 't' value of 0.35 obtained is statistically not significant. Hence, the null hypothesis that 'the experience as primary school teacher does not significantly influence the perceptions of lecturers' is accepted.

The details relating to the attitudes of lecturers is in line with their scores of perceptions and the 't' value of 0.22 is also not significant even at 0.05 level. Hence, the null hypothesis that 'the experience as primary school teacher does not significantly influence the attitude of lecturers towards the existing teacher education programme' is accepted.

Thus, the five independent variables, namely, age, sex, educational qualifications, designation and experience as primary school teacher could not bring any significant difference in the perceptions and attitudes of lecturers.

5.3. DIFFERENCES AMONG MORE AND LESS EFFECTIVE INSTITUTIONS (ITEM-WISE ANALYSIS)

Keeping in view the perception scores obtained from student teachers, lecturers and principals the two most effective DIETs and the two least effective DIETs have been identified. The two positively perceived DIETs are at Warangal and Mynampadu and the two negatively perceived DIETs are at Kurnool and Mahaboobnagar. To identify the differences between them further analysis has been carried out and it has been found that on 23 items, both student teachers and lecturers have been significantly different perceptions. A detailed discussion on the 23 items appears to be more meaningful in the light of the improvement in the prevailing conditions of the DIETs in Andhra Pradesh.

The student teachers of the most effective DIETs (N=100) and the less effective DIETs (N=100) could show significant difference in their perceptions on the following items : (1) Do you think that the student teachers face unnecessary problems in the institution? (2) Do you think that there are insufficient number of classrooms in your institution? (3) Do you feel that there is sufficient sports material in your institution? (4) Do you feel that your institute is a 'model institute' in terms of institutional climate and clean campus? (5) Do you think that too much of record work in the training programme makes you unpleasant? (6) Do you feel that the principal of your institute is cooperative ? (7) Do you think that there is no need to increase the teaching practice period? (8) Do you feel that the lecturers give adequate advice and guidance for teaching practice ? (9) Do you feel that the authorities of the institution do not show concern for the requirements of the student teachers ? (10) Are you unhappy with the unhygienic surroundings of the hostel ? (11) Do you think that the model lessons taken by your lecturers are helpful in your teaching practice? (12) Do you accept that the student teachers have enough facilities for recreation in the institute? (13) Do you like to write lesson plans? (14) Do you feel that there is cordial relationship between the principal and the student teachers? (15) Is there adequate water facility in your hostel? (16) Do you think that the student teachers are not provided with sufficient opportunities to exhibit their talent in cultural activities? (17) Do you feel that the lecturers are impartial in awarding internal assessment marks? (18) Do you feel that the teachers in the respective schools are very happy during the teaching practice period ? (19) Do you think that the lecturers do not give sufficient demonstration classes ? (20) Do you feel that there are inadequate facilities for reading in the library? (21) Do you teach the lesson by drawing good figures on the black board during the teaching practice period? (22) Do you feel that the present curriculum offered in the teacher training is outdated ? (23) Do you feel that the DIET curriculum should be restructured and reorganised ?

A close study of the above 23 items discloses that the deficiencies or inadequacies in different aspects of the DIETs are alarming. These 23 aspects can be conveniently classified under different heads as interpersonal relations, physical facilities and academic aspects, viz., curriculum, evaluation, practical work, etc.

With regard to interpersonal relations it appears that the principal and staff are unable to develop personal rapport with student teachers. As per the norms of the NCTE the teacher-pupil ratio in teacher education institutions should be at 1:10. This ratio helps individual attention in developing teaching skills among the trainees. A close association between the teacher educators and the student teachers is necessary. There is no need to maintain distance between the two groups. If such healthy and friendly atmosphere existed in the institute the students would not have reported that they were bothered about unnecessary problems. Special orientation programmes are to be designed for the DIET lecturers to nullify the above deficiency.

Similarly it appears that the principals of the DIETs keep themselves aloof from student teachers in the less effective institutions. The head of the institution is supposed to create a feeling of oneness among all the individuals associated with the organisation and he should be dynamic and humane in his approach for effective administration. But unfortunately seniority is the only criterion followed in the appointment of the principals. Moreover, there are no special training inputs to the principals for making their administrative styles more acceptable and at the same time more effective.

Unfortunately it has become the fashion of the day to find fault with the inadequate facilities in the educational institutions of the country. There is some truth that some of the DIETs are poorly equipped. On the recommendation of the 1986 National Policy on Education, the DIETs have been established with full financial assistance from the central government but the state government could not visualise the importance of the teacher education and thereby mechanically attended to the activity of establishing the DIETs only to satisfy the conditions stipulated by the central government without concentrating on the quality of teacher preparation. This has led to the poor status of the DIETs as far as their physical facilities are concerned.

With regard to the practical activities of the teacher training programme there was significant difference between more and less effective institutions on (1) lot of record work (2) number of teaching practice classes (3) less impact of model lessons (4) laborious process of writing lesson plans (5) inadequate demonstration classes, etc. After all, the pre-service training programme has been designed to develop teaching skills in the trainees. The theoretical component should not dominate the practical component but the theory taught should be the basis for much more important practical activity. However, in practice the practical work is given less priority than theory. Keeping this in view the NCTE has proposed to bring about radical shift in the curriculum of the teacher education at all levels from theory to practice.

The student teachers of the more and the less effective DIETs could exhibit significant differences in their perceptions on outdated curriculum and desire for restructured curriculum. These differences could also get nullified if the suggested curriculum frame by NCTE comes into vogue in the institutions of the teacher education.

The lecturers of the most effective DIETs (N=21) and the less effective DIETs (N=22) could show significant difference in their perceptions on the following items : (1) Do you agree that there is comfortable furniture in your classrooms ? (2) Do you accept that there is a beautiful campus for your institution? (3) Do you agree that your principal is overburdened in your DIET? (4) Does your institution have a play-ground to play different field games ? (5) Do you think that there are adequate reference books in your library ? (6) Is your campus clean and green? (7) Do you think that there are sufficient buildings for laboratories in your institution? (8) Do you feel that there is need for an effective recruiting agency for appointing the DIET lecturers ? (9) Do you think that there are sufficient technical staff members in your laboratories ? (10) Do you have adequate drinking water facility in your DIET? (11) Do you think that there is adequate space for office use? (12) Do you accept that the principal of your institution follows strict administrative rules to maintain good atmosphere in your institution? (13) Do you think that there is a spacious building for seminar-hall? (14) Do you have adequate water supply in the garden of your institution? (15) Do you think that your principal always observes the behaviour of the lecturers in your institution? (16) Do you feel that there is need for complete overhaul of the present day PSTE curriculum? (17) Do you feel that your principals' criticism is always constructive ? (18) Do you feel that there are sufficient chairs and tables in your seminar-hall? (19) Do you feel that the student teachers fail to use the teaching aids in their teaching practice ? (20) Do you feel that the principal of your institution makes the lecturers more alert and work minded through effective supervision? (21) Do you have a sufficient play-ground ? (22) Do you utilise your institution's play-ground optimally ? (23) Do you feel that there are sufficient almirahs and racks in your institution's library ?

As in the case of student teachers' perceptions, the lecturers' perceptions can also be categorized under interpersonal relations, physical facilities and academic activities.

The perceptions of the lecturers working in the more effective institutions are significantly different from those of the lecturers working in the less effective institutions on the principals' style of administration, involvement, constructive criticism and the encouragement provided. All these issues relate to interpersonal relationships which are the backbone for a congenial climate in the organisation. A healthy climate promoted by the principal certainly helps in the effective functioning of the institution. This requires a specialist or specially trained personnel. The academic staff colleges have been conducting workshops for the principals of degree colleges but no such training programme/workshop is there to improve the efficiency of principals in the DIETs in creating congenial academic climate.

With regard to the physical facilities as perceived by the lecturers of more and less effective institutions, the same logic can be applied as it has been stated earlier in the case of the student teachers' perceptions.

The academic aspects on which the two groups of teachers differ significantly are inability of the student teachers in using teaching aids, need for complete overhaul of the pre-service teacher education curriculum, insufficient teaching staff in the DIETs and need for an effective recruiting agency of lecturers for the DIETs.

The student teachers fail to use the teaching aids in teaching practice as it involves financial commitment on the part of the student teachers who are mostly from poor/lower middle class families. To overcome this the lecturers should train them in improvising the available material in the surroundings for use as teaching aids. Low cost or no cost approaches should be practiced in our society. Accordingly the curricular activities should also be changed.

Till recently there has been no cadre for the lecturers working in the DIETs. Similarly an independent agency to recruit lecturers has also not been established. The Directorate of School Education selects and appoints lecturers in the DIETs from among the qualified school teachers. Of course, a strong agency such as the Andhra Pradesh Public Service Commission (APPSC) and the Andhra Pradesh College Service Commission (APCSC) may be kept incharge for selection and appointment of the lecturers in the DIETs.

5.3.1 THE RELATIONSHIP BETWEEN PERCEPTIONS AND ATTITUDES

The data relating to the perceptions of student teachers on different aspects of DIET and their attitude towards teaching profession have been collected. It is interesting to note that the student teachers who were more favourable to the teaching profession also perceived different aspects of the DIET positively and vice-versa.

On the basis of the scores of attitude towards the teaching profession the sample of 500 student teachers is divided into three groups, namely, those who possess more favourable attitude towards the teaching profession ($> M+\frac{1}{2}\sigma$), those who possess moderate favourable attitude towards the teaching profession (between $M+\frac{1}{2}\sigma$ and $M-\frac{1}{2}\sigma$) and those who possess less favourable attitude towards the teaching profession ($< M-\frac{1}{2}\sigma$). The mean and standard deviations on perceptions of these three groups and the value of 'F' ratio are presented in Table—20.

Table—20 : Table showing the means and standard deviations of perception scores of three groups of student teachers whose attitude towards the teaching profession varies and the results of the 'F' test.

S.No.	*Variables*	*Groups*	*N*	*M*	*S.D.*	*'F'*
1.	Perceptions	Less favourable Attitude	133	156.92	14.36	
		Moderate favourable Attitude	200	159.02	14.99	8.25**
		More favourable Attitudes	167	164.00	17.79	

From the table one can observe that the level of perception varies proportionately with the favourableness manifested through their attitude towards the teaching profession. The mean difference between the two extreme groups is about seven units and the calculated 'F' ratio, 8.252 is statistically significant at 0.01 level of probability for 2,498 df. Hence, it may be concluded that the attitude of the student teachers towards the teaching profession could significantly influence their perceptions on different aspects of the DIETs. The correlation between the two variables, viz., attitude towards the teaching profession and the perception on various aspects of the DIETs is found to be 0.204 which is statistically significant at 0.01 level of probability for 500 df.

In the case of the lecturers also (N=101), it is found that their attitude towards the existing teacher education programme at the primary level positively influenced their perceptions on different aspects of the DIETs. The mean and the standard deviations of perception scores of the three groups of lecturers with more favourable attitude, moderate favourable attitude and less favourable attitude are presented in Table—21.

Table—21 : Table showing the means and standard deviations of perception scores of the three groups of lecturers whose attitude towards the pre-service training programme varies and the results of the 'F' test.

S.No.	*Variables*	*Groups*	*N*	*M*	*S.D.*	*'F'*
1.	Perceptions	Less favourable Attitude	35	168.40	18.74	
		Moderate favourable Attitude	33	178.06	22.12	6.36**
		More favourable Attitudes	33	186.12	20.70	

The table discloses that there exists a wide gap in the mean perception scores of the three groups. The calculated 'F' ratio of 6.358 is statistically significant at 0.01 level of probability for 2,97 df. Therefore, it may be said that the lecturers' attitudes towards the existing teacher education programme significantly influenced their perceptions on the various aspects of the DIETs. To support this the simple correlational value between the two variables is also significant at 0.01 level of probability for 99 df.

Summary, Conclusions, Recommendations And Suggestions

6.1 SUMMARY

Education is the main instrument of change, which can greatly engineer national development through self sufficiency in food, economic growth and full employment, political development, social and national integration. Any revolution in the field of education needs to be related to life, needs and aspirations of the people. Of all the different factors which influence the quality of education the quality, competence and character of the teachers are undoubtedly the most significant.

The pace and magnitude of the socio-economic development of any nation is basically determined by the level of the education of its citizens. Education has been recognised as a fundamental right and a process of human resource development where the knowledge, skills and capabilities are sharpened to achieve a wide range of objectives. The success of democracy, development programmes, community involvement, utilisation of physical and human resources, national integration, cultural emancipation, etc., are influenced by the education of the masses. There is no meaning in aiming at development without giving due importance to education. India has a glorious history but it has not able to keep up its momentum due to several reasons and one of it is the neglect of education. Several Commissions like Macaulay Minutes (1835), Wood's Despatch (1854), Hunter Commission (1882), Indian University Act (Lord Curzon Act) 1904, Sadler Commission (1918), Sarvepalli Radhakrishnan Commission (1948), Mudaliar Commission (1952), Kothari Commission (1964-66), National Policy on Education (1986) and a good number of social reformers like Swami Vivekananda, Mahatma Gandhi, Rabindranath Tagore, Jawaharlal Nehru, Raja Ram Mohan Roy have all endorsed the need for extending educational opportunities to all sections of the community.

Education is a nation building activity and teachers are the pillars of the educational system. A good number of inputs like school buildings, community support, physical facilities, finances, administrative support and quality teachers are needed for a good educational system. But it is basically the teachers who occupy a pivotal and frontline position and all other inputs are only secondary. With the growth and development of science and technology our educational system has been modernised and even then the role of the teacher in the academic system can never be underestimated. The success of the school system especially in a country like India, which is rural and developing in its nature is basically determined by the level of the commitment and concern on the part of the teachers to contribute their mite to the cause of primary education. A teacher requires a wide range of skills like communicative skills, skill of reinforcement, reasoning, questioning and especially the exploratory skill. This skill deserves its attention by the teachers due to the fact that amidst several deficiencies like lack of school buildings, lack of community participation, lack of teaching-learning materials, hardware equipment, etc., the teacher is expected to perform his functions to perfection by the authorities and here comes the ability of the teacher to tap and utilise the resources for education at the grass-root levels. Teaching profession is a noble profession and the word and the deed of the teacher leave a permanent imprint on the hearts of the little children at the primary level.

Hence, the teacher has to be a good model, a good scholar, an ideal social worker and a committed person who can help to improve the lot of the poor and downtrodden by extending to them educational opportunities and there by sensitizing them to claim their basic fundamental rights in the country. The role of the teacher is not merely limited to the four walls of the class room but it extends to the outer world as well.

Teaching is an art and many are to be trained in this art of teaching. Lakhs of school buildings and thousands of teachers are required in our primary education system and especially the number and quality of the teacher trainees has to be borne in mind. Adequate finances are to be allocated. Good teacher training facilities are also desired and the teacher trainees also need to have a positive and healthy attitude towards the profession. Anybody can become a teacher but everybody cannot become an effective teacher. In olden days the requirements in terms of teacher education were limited but the present system requires only the trained teachers. The facilities are open to all those who wish to become teachers after obtaining general level of education upto S.S.L.C./Intermediate and who wish to continue in the profession. At present the responsibility of training the teachers especially at the primary level is given to the DIETs. The quality of these teacher trainees depends upon the norms of admission, course duration, content, facilities available, internship and procedure of evaluation.

It has been observed that, although nomenclatures have changed, such as "Education" instead of "Training", the system in practice has, by and large, remained unchanged. The existing system appears to be too static and rigid to cope with the new national goals. It provides the student-teacher very little awareness of the role that education can play in transforming the present Indian society into a truly democratic, socialistic and secular one that we cherish. As the Education Commission (1964-66) remarked, vitality and realism are lacking in the curricula, and the programmes of work continue to be largely traditional. Even in a limited area like methods of teaching, the teacher educator fails to impress upon the trainee their usefulness and applicability, as the teacher educator himself rarely uses any method other than the "talk-and-chalk" method. Set patterns of lesson planning and rigid techniques of teaching are followed in practice-teaching, regardless of the nature of the subject-matter and the objectives to be achieved in terms of behavioural changes. Evaluation procedures, specially those followed for assessing the competencies of the would-be teachers, are, by and large, subjective and unscientific seeking to find out mainly how successfully the factual knowledge has been memorised. In general really competent people are not attracted to the teacher training institutions, nor do the staff attached to those institutions make sufficient and substantial efforts to raise the image of "Education" as a discipline in the eyes of their counterparts working in other institutions.

Whatever be the reasons, as has been observed by the Education Commission, the teacher training institutions stand isolated from the main stream of national life, from the academic life of the universities, from schools, from one another, and what is most serious, from the very community which they are supposed to serve. The isolation from the community at once has acquired the greatest significance in view of the changed political and socio-economic situation in the country.

A sound programme of professional education of teachers is essential for the qualitative improvement of education. Investment in teacher education can yield very rich dividends because the financial resources required are small when measured against the resulting improvements in the education of millions. We all know that no educational reform can be successful unless the quality of the teacher is improved, but in turn the quality of the teacher depends to a large extent on the quality of the teacher education. In reality the teacher education is the sine qua non of all educational improvements. The status and quality of the teacher education of our country especially at the elementary level is far from satisfactory. May be the existing system has failed to provide meaningful experiences to the prospective teachers, especially at the elementary level. Elementary teacher education should train prospective teachers to take decisions regarding the application of basic educational principles to the existing school situations without overlooking the characteristics of the learners. Thus, the professional education of the elementary teachers must relate to pedagogy and the way instructional materials can be put to a judicious use.

The above contentions have many ramifications and implications for the teacher education curriculum. It is gratifying to note that some significant developments have already taken place in this field. The National Policy on Education (1986) suggested an over-hauling of Teacher Education at all levels. A National Curriculum Framework for Elementary/Secondary School stages was developed by the NCERT keeping in view the major thrusts of National Policy on Education. Setting up of District Institutes of Education and Training (DIETs) at the elementary level and upgrading some Colleges of Education as Institutes of Advanced Studies in Education (IASEs) and strengthening of Colleges of Teacher Education (CTEs) are other significant steps taken in this direction. These institutions are expected to contribute their mite in improving the quality of the teacher education. It is now felt that to make the training experiences of the teacher trainees purposeful and effective different components of teacher education curriculum, especially at the elementary level need to be reviewed and revised.

The teacher training institutes of the primary level

now modified as District Institutes of Education and Training (DIETs) play an important role in producing the required teachers for the primary and the upper primary schools. Great is the task and dynamic is their role indeed! Are these institutes producing quality teachers? Is the pre-service training programme provided by the DIETs effective in all respects? What are the deficiencies in the DIETs? A variety of such questions are to be answered with empirical evidence for the further improvement of the quality of teacher education at the primary level.

It is, therefore, pertinent to collect data about the perceptions of student teachers, lecturers and principals about their training so as to get a better picture of the situation and to identify the means to improve the teacher education further which help produce quality teachers. So the present study is an ardent effort in this direction.

6.1.1 STATEMENT OF THE PROBLEM

The present study is "An Evaluative Study of Primary School Teacher Education Programme in Andhra Pradesh". It is designed to evaluate various aspects of teacher education and the influence of probable intervening variables on the perceptions and attitudes of pupil-teachers and teacher educators.

6.1.2 OBJECTIVES OF THE STUDY

The main objectives of the study were :

1. To study the perceptions of the student teachers of the DIETs on different aspects of their training.
2. To study the attitude of the student teachers towards teaching profession.
3. To note the variations in the perceptions and attitudes of student teachers due to different personal and demographic variables.
4. To study the perceptions of the teacher educators on the different aspects of the DIETs.

5. To study the attitudes of the teacher educators towards the existing teacher education programme.
6. To identify the differences in the perceptions and attitudes of the teacher educators depending upon their personal and demographic variables.
7. To study the perceptions of the principals on different aspects of the DIETs.
8. To record the physical and academic facilities available in the DIETs.
9. To observe and notice the specific deficiencies in the DIETs.
10. To suggest remedial measures to nullify the deficiencies in the existing primary level teacher education programme.

6.1.3 HYPOTHESES

To realise the above objectives the following descriptive and statistical hypotheses were formulated for the purpose of testing. The hypotheses formulated were in 'null-form' as it is akin to statistical testing.

1. The student teachers in general do not possess positive perception on different aspects of the DIETs.
2. The student teachers are not favourable to teaching profession.
3. The personal and demographic variables of student teachers do not influence their level of perceptions on different aspects of the DIETs and their attitude towards the teaching profession. (This major hypothesis is split into different minor hypotheses for the purpose of testing each variable separately).
4. The teacher educators, in general, do not possess positive perceptions on different aspects of the DIETs.

5. The attitude of the teacher educators towards the existing pre-service training programme is not favourable.
6. The personal and demographic variables of the teacher educators do not influence their perceptions on different aspects of the DIETs and attitudes towards the existing teacher education programme. (This major hypothesis is split into different minor hypotheses for the purpose of testing each variable separately).
7. The principals in general, do not possess positive perception on different aspects of the DIETs.
8. The physical facilities available in the DIETs are not satisfactory.
9. The specific observations of the investigator are not serious and they do not form as obstacles for producing quality teachers.

6.1.4 VARIABLES STUDIED

As the present study envisages an evaluation of the primary school teacher education programme in Andhra Pradesh on the basis of the perceptions and attitudes of the student teachers, teacher educators and principals, the dependent variables are as follows:

i. Perception of the student teachers on different aspects of the DIET.
ii. Attitude of the student teachers towards teaching profession.
iii. Perception of the teacher educators on different aspects of the DIET.
iv. Attitude of the teacher educators towards the existing teacher education programme.
v. Perception of the principals on different aspects of the DIET, and

vi. Availability of material and infrastructural facilities.

Independent Variables

The student teacher related independent variables are sex, age, educational qualifications, locality, methodology in subject, methodology in language, family literacy index, father's occupation, mother's occupation and family annual income. The teacher educator's related independent variables are sex, age, educational qualifications, designation and experience as primary school teacher.

6.1.5 MEASUREMENT OF VARIABLES (TOOLS USED)

Perception Scales

As explained earlier the perceptions of the student teachers, lecturers and principals are measured with three perception scales developed by the investigator. For the purpose of collecting items for the above three perception scales the investigator consulted the experts, faculty of the DIETs, student teachers and the related literature. The pilot forms of the scales thus finalised were administered on small samples of principals, lecturers and student teachers of the DIETs. Item analysis was carried out to identify the most appropriate items to be included in the final form. The validity and the reliability of the three scales were also established by using appropriate methods.

Attitude Scales

For the purpose of developing the attitude scales meant for the student teachers and teacher educators, the investigator consulted the principals, lecturers, student teachers and the related literature and developed items on a five point Likert's type of summated ratings. The pilot form of the scales thus finalised was administered on small samples of the student teachers and teacher educators. Item analysis was carried out to identify the most appropriate items to be included in the final form. The validity and the reliability of the scales were also established by using appropriate methods.

Check-List

To identify the availability of the material and infrastructural facilities a Check-List was prepared. For the purpose of developing the Check-List meant for principals, the investigator collected the type of items that come under physical facilities, by referring to the DIET guidelines, by visiting the different DIETs and by having discussions with the principals, teaching and non-teaching staff in the DIETs. Thus, an exhaustive list of items was prepared under Yes/No form. The pilot form was administered on a small sample of principals. The suggestions given by the principals were incorporated in the final form. The content validity was established by using the appropriate method.

Personal and demographic Data-Sheets

The personal information regarding the student teachers and the teacher educators of the DIETs was collected through well planned personal data sheets meant for the two types of subjects separately.

6.1.6 SAMPLE SELECTED

The present investigation is essentially a survey type of research aimed at evaluating the existing pre-service training of the primary school teachers conducted by the 23 DIETs situated in 23 districts of Andhra Pradesh. The investigator considered three categories of subjects namely, student teachers, teacher educators and principals of DIETs and the three sub samples were selected as explained below.

At the first stage the sampling unit was a DIET. The 23 DIETs were divided into three strata based on the three regions of the State of Andhra Pradesh, viz., Coastal Andhra, Telengana and Rayalaseema. 10 DIETs were selected in total from the three strata with not less than 3 DIETs in any stratum.

At the second stage 50 student teachers were selected at randon from each one of the DIETs selected in the first stage so as to make the first sub-sample of the student teachers equal to 500. The second sub-sample of the teacher educators was identified by following the cluster sampling technique which means considering all the available teacher educators from each one of the DIETs selected at the first stage. Thus, a total of 101 teacher educators formed the second sub-sample of the survey. The third sub-sample consisted of 10 principals from 10 DIETs. Thus, the sampling technique employed in the investigation may be called as a two stage stratified random sampling technique.

6.1.7 DATA COLLECTION

The investigator in person visited all the 10 DIETs and with the permission of the Head of the Institution the self explanatory instruments developed were administered on 500 student teachers, 101 teacher educators and 10 principals. The student teachers were given the instructions orally and were also asked to read the instructions given along with the instruments and motivated to respond genuinely to all the items in the data gathering tools.

6.1.8 SCORING

As the instruments used in this investigation were perception scales, attitude scales and check-list, they were scored by giving the following weightages to the alternative responses.

Perception scales were scored on a three-point scale by giving weights 3,2 and 1 in the case of the positive items and 1,2 and 3 in the case of the negative items to the three alternatives, viz., maximum extent, moderate extent and least extent respectively. The grand total of the entire scale was obtained by adding the weights of all the items to each individual.

The Likert type attitude scales were scored on a five-point scale by giving weights 5,4,3,2 and 1 in the case of the positive items and 1,2,3,4 and 5 in the case of the negative items respectively. The grand total to each individual on the entire scale was obtained by adding the weights of all the statements.

As the items in the check-list are Yes/No type, the items available in the DIETs were coded as '1' and the items not available in the DIETs were coded as '0'.

The information provided by the respondents in the personal data sheets was also numerically coded to suit the computer analysis.

6.1.9 ANALYSIS

As the data collected through different statements in the tools from different subjects are specific aspects, the item-wise analysis was carried out to identify the specific deficiencies in the different aspects of the DIETs. Statistics such as frequencies, percentages and chi-square were employed to make the description more precise.

The total scores obtained from all the subjects on all the variables were computed. The data were carefully analysed employing the appropriate statistical techniques. Descriptive statistics such as mean, median, mode, quartile deviation, standard deviation, skewness and kurtosis were used to describe the distribution of scores. The inferential statistical techniques such as 't' test (Critical-ratio) and 'F' test were employed to test different hypotheses. The numerical results obtained were interpreted meaningfully.

6.2 CONCLUSIONS

1. On the basis of the student teachers' perceptions it has been found that the following aspects are quite disturbing:

   — Most of the student teachers have expressed that they have not been encouraged to participate in the physical education activities and even the alloted time for them is considerably much less.

— Most of the student teachers are unhappy that their institution is far away from the teaching practice schools.

— Majority of the student teachers have perceived that the present system of examinations has failed in assessing the teaching skills.

— Majority of the student teaches have expressed that the hostel furniture and its surroundings, laboratories, library and water facilities are not satisfactory.

— It has been identified that the curricular work load is so heavy that there is no leisure time for the student teachers to participate in any co-curricular and cultural activities.

— Most of the student teachers are of the opinion that the demonstration lessons given by the lecturers alone do not improve teaching abilities of the student teachers.

— More than 50 per cent of the student teachers have felt that compulsory apprenticeship would bring about qualitative improvement in teacher preparation.

— Majority of the student teachers opine that the present day teacher education curriculum is out-dated and that it should be restructured and reorganised keeping in view the present day needs and aspirations of the young trainees.

2. From the analysis of the responses it has been noticed that most of the student teachers are unhappy with disobedient students, non-academic additional responsibilities entrusted to them and for the lack of recognition to the teaching profession.

3. On the basis of teacher educators' perceptions the following aspects have been found to be most serious:

— The DIETs are ill-equipped and inadequate in the following aspects: laboratories, modern gadgets, buildings and technical staff; lighting facility, reading room, drinking water facility, staff and furniture in the hostels, teaching-learning material, and sports and games material.

— It has been identified that the existing periods of internship and demonstration classes are insufficient.

— Majority of the teacher educators feel that their promotional opportunities are meagre. They feel that there is a need for an effective recruiting agency to appoint the DIET lecturers and to look into the promotional issues and other service matters.

— It has been identified that the curriculum offered in the DIETs has not been able to meet the young trainees aspirations and the local community needs. Hence, the present curriculum needs to be changed.

— The DIET library is not well furnished with books on methodology, education commission reports, etc., and the co-operative book banks and Library Advisory Committees are ineffective and useful neither to the students nor to the staff. The institutional library has not been kept open beyond the working hours of the institution.

Most of the teacher educators feel that their principals never convene the parents' meet to interact with them, they do not enforce discipline in the institute, they are not able to get any help from the local people, they are not able to involve unemployed youth in the institutional activities, they are not able to correct mistakes and give valuable suggestions, they are unable to tap the potentialities of the lecturers, they resort to destructive criticism and they are not able to solve differences among the members of the staff who are not ideal and hardworking.

4. The teacher educators have expressed their concern over the deteriorating standards in teacher education, the less priority given to physical education, the lack of strict adherence to the administrative rules, the low emphasis on practicals, the meagre chances to participate in co-curricular and cultural activities, the lack of dynamism in in-service programmes, the little correlation between theoretical and practical aspects of training, the ineffective supervision of teaching practice and the outdated curriculum.

5. On the basis of the principals perceptions, it has been found that the following aspects are worth noting :

   — Majority of the principals have perceived that the DIETs have insufficient play-grounds and even the available play grounds are not properly utilised.

   — It has been identified that the teaching-learning material is not adequate.

   — Majority of the principals have accepted that they have not conducted workshops to develop the primary school curriculum and that they never convened parents' meetings.

   — Most of the principals have perceived that the following aspects are alarming in the DIETs: inadequate bulbs, insufficient technical staff in laboratories, inadequate equipment in laboratories, insufficient technical staff to prepare teaching aids, insufficient hostel staff, inadequate sports material, inadequate furniture in office, in hostels and in seminar hall.

   — It has been found that the DIET libraries are suffering from lack of text books. Even the available books are not properly utilised because the lecturers do not guide the student-teachers to use library properly. Moreover, the DIET libraries should be kept open beyond the institutions' working hours for the benefit of both the student teachers and the teacher educators.

— Majority of the principals have perceived that there is no need for an effective recruiting agency to look into the appointment, promotions and other service matters.

6. From the response in the Check List, it has been found that out of 179 items of physical facilities, 34 items are not at all available in the DIETs covered under the investigation. Among them, the most important one is Closed-Circuit Television. If a teacher wants to develop a particular skill, he must have immediate feedback in his teaching-learning process which can be provided with the help of a Closed-Circuit Television. But surprisingly no DIET has this facility.

Similarly, 21 items are available in only 3 DIETs. 13 items are available in 4 DIETs, 42 items are available in 7 DIETs and 69 items are available in all the DIETs. Thus, out of 179 items about one-half of the items are available in all the DIETs and the remaining one-half of the items are not available in many DIETs. This pathetic situation has been revealed by the student teachers, lecturers and principals.

7. The investigator has observed personally the following deficiencies in the DIETs :

— Majority of the DIETs are far away from the district headquarters and the teaching practice schools.

— The DIET principals have been mismanaging the financial resources of the institutes.

— Libraries in the DIETs are in very poor status.

- Majority of the DIETs are not well equipped with sports and games material.
- Majority of the DIETs laboratories are in bad condition.
- Inadequate audio-visual equipment.
- Little coordination among DIETs, SCERT, RIEs, NCTE and NCERT.
- Most of the DIETs have insufficient teaching staff.
- The present day curriculum is outdated and that it should be restructured and reorganised.
- Insufficient teaching practice period.
- Lack of commitment to teaching profession.
- Majority of the student teachers have not been able to acquire any teaching skills during the brief span of one month's teaching practice.
- Lack of staff quarters.
- Majority of the lecturers are not confined to teaching alone.

Most of these deficiencies have also been perceived either by lecturers or by student teachers and in certain cases by both. Therefore, it may be safely concluded that the DIETs are far from satisfactory in general in the following aspects: lack of furniture, insufficient teaching-learning material, ill-equipped laboratories, poor library, poor status of physical education, poorly managed hostels, and weak linkages between the DIETs and the local community.

However, the DIET lecturers have felt that there is greater need for increased number of in-service training programmes in improving the curriculum of T.T.C. But the principals have opposed it. This may be due to their negative perception in managing the institution without staff members. Similarly on the issue of a separate recruitment board also the perceptions of principals and lecturers are mutually contradictory.

The common feature that have been identified in the perceptions of the lecturers and the student teachers are more interesting to note. Both the groups have felt that: the curriculum of the pre-service training programme ought to be changed thoroughly; duration of the course should be increased; there should be more number of demonstration lessons, observation lessons and criticism lessons; and there should be more number of days for internship.

8. The variables namely sex, educational qualifications, mother's occupation have significantly influenced the perceptions of the student teachers whereas only the variable of sex has significantly influenced the attitude of the student teachers towards thc teaching profession. No variable of the teacher educator could influence their perceptions and attitudes.

Thus, from the perceptions of student teachers, lecturers, principals and also from the personal observation of the investigator it has been found that the deficiencies identified are similar.

From the analysis of the less and more effective institutions it has been found that the perceptions of student teachers and teacher educators differed significantly on 23 aspects which are already described and they are mostly related to lack of physical facilities, poor organisational climate, and inadequate practical component in the training programme.

The major findings of the study described in the earlier section prompts, that there are many things to be set right so as to make the T.T.C. programme much more effective so as to produce quality teachers.

6.3 EDUCATIONAL IMPLICATIONS AND RECOMMENDATIONS

The deficiencies in the physical and infrastructural facilities can be met over a period of time if the principal prepares institutional plan carefully every year and motivates the faculty to implement the different developmental activities effectively apart from requesting the Government to provide necessary funds to meet the deficiencies. With constant and committed efforts of both the principal and the staff, the institution will certainly become a model and the beneficiaries will also offer their contribution to their alma matter.

It has been identified that the practical aspects of training such as demonstration lessons, observation lessons, criticism lessons, block teaching, etc., have not been given due importance to develop general and specific skills of teaching in the student teachers. It is true that during the one year course the practical aspects are given less priority due to insufficient time. But from the academic year 1999-2000 onwards the duration of the course is increased to two years and the curriculum is prepared on the lines of the National Council for Teacher Education's guidelines. An aggregate forty per cent of the working days are allocated to practical aspects. Hence, the negative perception of student teachers and teacher educators with regard to the insufficiency of the practical aspects may not be felt by the present batch of student teachers. However, the model lessons or demonstration lessons may be provided by the subject lecturers as well as by the senior and resourceful teachers.

Since most of the DIETs are situated far away from the district headquarters or big municipal towns the teacher educators and the student teachers feel inconvenient and unhappy as they have to travel to distant places to find sufficient number of schools for teaching practice. When the Central Government wants to establish DIETs the responsibility of providing physical and infrastructural facilities lies on the State Government. The State Government has identified the areas where the government buildings are available as the centres for the DIETs. To have the teaching practice for hundred students they feel it difficult to find atleast 30 to 40 schools within the radius of five to ten kilometers from the DIETs. Moreover, most of the DIETs do not run a 'model school' to provide demonstration lessons within the campus, the reason being that they are away even from a village. Apart from this the DIET centres have been planned to provide accommodation to the teacher educators and hostels to student teachers to create a corporate campus life. Unfortunately, this has been totally missing in almost all the DIETs. Thus, the DIETs situated away from the urban locality are feasible neither for implementing the practical aspects of training nor for helping to bring a total behavioural change in the student teachers. Both the faculty and the student teachers have mechanical interaction for five hours during all the working days and desert the campus as it has been done in any primary school.

Therefore, it is recommended that the government should take suitable action in creating campus life to both the student teachers and the teacher educators so that many other negative perceptions observed by student teachers, teacher educators and principals may be remedied.

It is reported that the hostels are in very bad shape with lack of clean surroundings, insufficient ventilation, furniture, water, low quality food, etc. To overcome these deficiencies due responsibilities are to be entrusted to the inmates as was the case in the basic training courses. The students used to manage their own hostels, mess, grow vegetables in the campus, maintain vegetation on the campus, etc. Such activities can be undertaken by the students if they are provided a congenial campus life along with their faculty.

They can find lot of time to participate in co-curricular activities such as sports and games and other cultural events (music, dance, drama, art, painting, clay-modelling, etc.). Even the library functioning hours can be extended beyond the institutional working hours. Of course, it is true that the government has not filled all the faculty positions in the DIETs. The technical and the non-teaching staff are also insufficient in the DIETs. All these aspects need immediate attention and suitable remedial action.

In the teacher preparation programme subject specialised activities do play a significant role in the qualitative improvement of teaching a school subject. For example, students of Mathematics methodology may start Maths Student - Teachers Association which may undertake different activities to promote interest in teaching Mathematics. By conducting such subject-wise special programmes in all school subjects the training programme can become more effective. Hence, the State Department of Education should instruct the DIETs to conduct Subject Association Meetings.

The curriculum for teacher training programme is outdated and overhauling it appeared a serious problem to majority of the respondents. The NCTE has developed a curriculum frame for different levels of teacher education. The two year curriculum for T.T.C. which has been introduced since the academic year 2000 is in line with the curriculum frame of the NCTE. However, to execute all its components creation of campus life in the DIETs is essential. Participation of all the personnel involved in the DIETs in the effective transaction of new curriculum is warranted. Necessary special orientation programmes to the principals and teacher educators of the DIETs are to be conducted to realise the above goal.

It has been observed that majority of the DIETs do not have minimum physical and infrastructural facilities, laboratory equipment, furniture and necessary reference books and reports of education commissions but whether the available academic amenities are properly utilised is a fundamental question. Thus, it is a two fold problem—non availability and non use of the available amenities effectively. To satisfy the first aspect the management should provide more funds to procure the needed equipment/books and reports. However, the second aspect is too serious to find easy solutions. It is here 'the commitment' on the part of the teacher educators and principals has to be revitalised to make use of the available facilities to the fullest extent possible and maximise the social returns of the public investment on these items. Of course, the NCTE has been organising a series of workshops and seminars to reorient the teachers and teacher educators to be committed at all levels.

It is often observed that the administrative and academic matters have not been strictly implemented in the DIETs. No doubt our plans are extremely good but their implementation is not satisfactory. The DIET principals and lecturers should be exposed to appropriate training in interpersonal relationships. The State Department of Education should provide special training courses to the principals for making their administrative styles more acceptable, more effective, more dynamic and more humane.

Thus, producing quality teachers has become a prerequisite to achieve qualitative improvement in education at any level. Both the Central and the State Governments should come forward to enhance the budgetary allocations on teacher education and to recruit highly qualified persons as teacher educators. A separate Directorate in the states may be established for the purpose of teacher education as it has been existing in a very few states. Privatising the teacher education or allowing the existing self financing institutions of teacher education is to be stopped at once and the government should establish a good number of teacher education institutions in accordance with the manpower requirements.

6.4 LIMITATIONS OF THE STUDY AND SUGGESTIONS FOR FURTHER RESEARCH

1. This investigation is limited to a small sample of 500 student teachers, 101 teacher educators and 10 principals, selected from only ten DIETs. Future researchers may undertake studies with large sample covering all the DIETs of the state, so as to make generalisations with regard to the perceptions and attitudes of the principals, teacher educators and student teachers respectively.
2. Similar studies may be undertaken on the DIETs in other states. A comparative assessment of the

DIETs in different states may provide real insights into the problems in the field of teacher education.

3. To identify the deficiencies in the training programme for primary teachers, a study of the perceptions and attitudes of principals, teacher educators and student teachers alone may not give us a comprehensive analysis of the teacher education programmes. The future researchers may take up studies on teacher education covering other aspects.

4. The present study is limited to a few personal and demographic variables pertaining to the student teachers and the teacher educators. Further researches may also concentrate on other psycho sociological variables of the subjects involved.

5. The study has not included any institutional variables such as year of establishment, results produced, and titles and awards obtained, etc. Such institutional variables may help us identify the variations between good and poor institutions. Studies in this direction may help us to improve the status of the teacher education further.

BIBLIOGRAPHY

Allport, G.W. (1929). '*The Composition of Political Attitudes*'. American Journal of Sociology, 35, pp.220-238.

Arora, K., Dasgupta, H., Chopra, R. and Puri, P. (1974). "*National Survey of Teacher Education at Elementary Level*", Department of Teacher Education, NCERT, New Delhi. (in) : *Second Survey of Research in Education*, (1972-78). M.B.Buch (ed.), Baroda : *Society for Educational Research and Development.*

Baldwin, J.M. (1901). *Dictionary of Psychology, New York* : McMillan.

Banerjee, J. C. (1967). "*Training of Primary Teachers in India*", Ph. D. thesis Edu., Maharaja Sauajirao University of Boroda. (in) : A Survey of Research in Education, (1974). M. B. Buch (ed.), M. S. University of Boroda : Centre of Advanced Study in Education.

Barber, P.J. and Legge, D. (1976). *Perception and Information, London* : Methuen.

Best, J.W. (1959). *Research in Education, U.S.A.*, Prentice-Hall, Inc., Englewood Cliffs.

Best, J.W. (1963). *Research in Education, New York* : Prentice Hall International Limited.

Betagiri, Suresh (1996). "*Competencies and Training Needs of DIET faculty members in DPEP districts of Karnataka*", Dissertation, Regional Institute of Education, Mysore.

Buch, M.B. (1974). *A Survey of Research in Education.* Baroda : Centre of Advanced Study in Education and Psychology, M.S. University of Baroda.

Buch, M.B. (1979). *Second Survey of Research in Education.* Baroda : Society for Educational Research and Development.

Buch, M.B. (1987). *Third Survey of Research in Education.* New Delhi : National Council of Educational Research and Training.

Buch, M.B. (1991). *Fourth Survey of Research in Education.* New Delhi : National Council of Educational Research and Training.

Buch, M.B. (1997). *Fifth Survey of Research in Education.* New Delhi : National Council of Educational Research and Training.

Buch, M.B. and Singh, S. (1978). "*Third All India Education Survey : Teachers*", NCERT, New Delhi. (in) : T*hird Survey of Research in Education*, (1978-83). M.B. Buch (ed.), New Delhi : NCERT.

Census of India, 1991.

Chakravarthy, S.R. (1977). *Audio-Visual Aids in Education*, New Delhi : Sagar Publications.

Courtesy—"*Discussion Document on Curriculum Framework for Teacher Education*", National Council for Teacher Education, 16, Mahatma Gandhi Marg, I.P. Estate, New Delhi—110 002.

Department of Post-graduate Studies in Education (1974). "*A study of the Role Expectations of Teachers under Training in the city of Bangalore*", Bangalore University. (Bangalore University financed). (in) : *Second Survey of Research in Education*, (1972-78). M.B. Buch (ed.),

Baroda: Society for Educational Research and Development.

Deve Gowda, A.C.(1973). *Teacher Education in India*, Bangalore : Printersall, (Pvt.) Ltd.

Droba (1933). '*The nature of attitudes*'. Journal of Social Psychology, pp. 4,444.

Edward, A.L. (1969). *Statistical Analysis*, New York : Holt, Rinehard and Winston Inc.,

Edward, A.L. (1969). *Techniques of Attitude Scale Construction*, Bombay : Vakils, Feffer and Simons.

Ellis, R.S. (1965). *Educational Psychology : A Problem Approach*, New Delhi: Affiliated East-West Press (Pvt.) Ltd.

Encyclopaedia of Educational Research, (Fifth Edition), Edited by Harold E. Mitzel, London: Collier Macmillan Publishers, pp.1861 - 1868.

Freeman, F.S. (1962). *Theory and Practicals of Psychological Testing*, 3rd Edition, New Delhi: Oxford and I.B.H. Publishing Company.

Garrett, Henry, E.(1979). *Statistics in Psychology and Education*, Bombay : Vakils, Feffer and Simons Ltd.

Gayatri, A. (1996). "*An Investigation into the Perceptions of Student-Teachers on their Teacher Training*", M.Ed. Dissertation, S.V.University, Tirupati.

——(1959). *Dictionary of Education*, IInd edition, McGraw - Hill, New York.

Gopalacharyulu, R.V.V. (1984). "*A Study of Relationship between Certain Psycho-Sociological Factors and Achievement of Student-Teachers in Teacher Training Institutes of Andhra Pradesh*", Ph.D. thesis, Edu., Sri Venkateswara University. (in) : Fourth Survey of Research in Education, (1983-88). M.B.Buch (ed.), New Delhi : NCERT.

Gopalan, Beena (1993). "*A case study of few District Institute of Education and Training in Kerala*", Kerala.

Government of India (1989). *Guidelines of DIET*, New Delhi: Ministry of Human Resource Development.

Gulford, J.P. (1954). *Psychometric methods*, Haryana : Tata McGraw Hill Publishing Company.

Guilford, J.P. (1978). *Psychometric methods*, Tata McGraw-Hill Publishing Ltd., pp.349.

Guilford, J.R. (1964). *Psychometric methods*, New York: McGraw - Hill Publishing Co.,

Gupta, S.P. (1971). "*A Study of Admission Procedures in Elementary and Secondary Teacher Training Institutions*", NCERT, New Delhi. (in) : A Survey of Research in Education, (1974). M.B.Buch (ed.), Baroda: Centre of Advanced Study in Education.

Harper, E., Dass Gupta, B. and Sangal, S.P. (1962). '*Item -analysis Chart and instructions*', Manasayan, New Delhi.

Hass and Packer (1962). *Preparation and Use of Audio-Visual Aids*, New Delhi: Prentice Hall of India (Pvt.) Ltd.

Hornby, A.S., Cowie, A.P. and Lewis, J.W. (1968). *Oxford advanced learner's dictionary of current English*, The English Language Book Society, London: Oxford University Press.

Jangira, N.K. (1982). "*A Study of Social Cohesion in Elementary Teacher Training Institutions and its Relationship with their Efficiency*", Department of Teacher Education, NCERT, New Delhi. (in) : Third Survey of Research in Education, (1973 -78).M.B.Buch (ed.), New Delhi : NCERT.

Joshi, D.C. (1974). "*A Study of Innovations in Teacher Training Institutions*", V.B.Teachers College, Udaipur.

(USEFI financed). (in) : Second Survey of Research in Education, (1972-78). M.B.Buch (ed.), Baroda : Society for Educational Research and Development.

Kohler, W. (1929). *Gestalt Psychology*, New York : Liveright.

Kollur, Sheela Bai (1990). "*A survey of opinion of the teacher educators regarding the new Teacher Certificate Higher syllabus of 1989*", Disst. Abstr. Intr.,

Krupalatha, D. (1979). "*A study of the relative effectiveness of micro teaching technique in developing teacher competence among trainees at Teachers Training Institute level*", Disst. Abstr. Intr.,

Kundu, C.L. (1997). "*Presidential Address*", President of Indian Association of Teacher Educators, Ponda, Goa.

Likert, R. (1932). '*A technique for the measurement of attitudes*'. (in) : '*An Index of Job Satisfaction*', (1951). Brayfield, A.H. and Rothe, H.F. Journal of Applied Psychology, 35 (5), pp.307 - 311.

Likert, R.A. (1932). '*A technique for the measurement of Attitudes*'. Archieves of Psychology, 140.

Madhavi, G. (1996). "*Attitude of Student Teachers of DIETs Towards Teaching Profession*", Disst. Abstr. Intr., I (1.1.), 1.

Mallaya, V. (1968). "*Teacher's Training in Madhya Pradesh*", Ph.D. thesis, Edu., Saugar University, Madhya Pradesh. (in) : A Survey of Research in Education, (1974).M.B.Buch (ed.), M.S.University of Baroda : CASE.

Manoj Praveen, G. (1993). "*Competencies and Training Needs of DIET Faculty members in DPEP districts of Kerala*", Dissertation, RIE, Mysore.

Ministry of Education, *Report of the Teacher Education Commission—1.* New Delhi : Government of India.

Ministry of Human Resource Development (1986). *National Policy on Education : Programme of Action*, New Delhi : Government of India.

Mohammed Pasha (1988). "*A study of the problems faced by the primary teacher training institutes in practice—teaching in practising schools*", Disst. Abstr. Intr.,

Mooney, R.L. and Gorban, L.V. (1950). *The Mooney Problem Check-list Manual*, New York : The Psychological Corporation.

Morgan, J.J.B. (1934). *Keeping a sound mind*, New York: Mc Millan, second edition.

Mukerjee, R.K. (1951). *Ancient Indian Education*, London: Macmillan and Co.,

Prakash, A. and Mehrotra, R.N. (1974). "*An Exploratory Study of the Use of Audio Cassette Recordings in the Supervision of Student-Teacher*", Central Institute of Education, New Delhi. (in) : Second Survey of Research in Education, (1972-78). M.B.Buch (ed.), Baroda : Society for Educational Research and Development.

Rama Mohan Babu,V. (1992). "*Job satisfaction, attitude towards teaching, job involvement, efficiency of teaching and perception of organisational climate of teachers of residential and non-residential schools*", Ph.D. thesis, Edu., Sri Venkateswara University, Tirupati.

Ramamurthy (1994). "*A study of the problems faced by the trainees in schools during the practice teaching programme*", Disst. Abstr. Intr.,

Rai, V.K. (1982). "*A Survey of the Problems of Teachers' Training Colleges with regard to Practising Schools*", Ph.D. thesis, Edu., Gujarat University. (in) : Third Survey of Research in Education, (1978-83). M.B.Buch (ed.), New Delhi : NCERT.

Reddy, C.R.(1991). "*Quality Improvement of Pre-service Education of Primary School Teachers in Andhra Pradesh*", Unpublished Ph.D. thesis, Osmania University, Hyderabad.

Reddy, P.A. (1990). *Adult Education Programmes in India*. Allahabad: Chugh Publications.

Report of the Calcutta University Commission (1920). New Delhi : Government of India Press.

Report of the Hartog Committee (1936). An Examination of Examinations, London : Macmillan & Co.,

Safia Sultana (1976). "*A Study of Academic Difficulties of Student-Teachers*", Department of Education, Aligarh Muslim University. (NCERT financed). (in) : Second Survey of Research in Education, (1972 - 78). M.B.Buch (ed.), Baroda : Society for Educational Research and Development.

Sharma, M. (1982). "*Progress and Problems of Teacher Education in India*", Ph.D. thesis, Edu., Patna University. (in) : Third Survey of Research in Education, (1978-83). M.B. Buch (ed.), New Delhi : NCERT.

Sharma, R.C. (1984). "*Teaching Aptitude, Intellectual Level and Morality of Prospective Teachers*", Ph.D. thesis, Edu., Mohanlal Sukhadia University. (in): Fourth Survey of Research in Education, (1983 - 88). M.B. Buch (ed.), New Delhi : NCERT.

SIERT, Rajasthan (1966). "*Teacher Education at Primary Level in Rajasthan*". (in): Fourth Survey of Research in Education, (1983 - 88). M.B. Buch (ed.), New Delhi : NCERT.

Singh, L.C. (1990). *Teacher Education in India* : A resource book, New Delhi : National Council of Educational Research and Training.

Singh Raghuram, M. (1998). "*Research in teacher education*", The Hindu Daily News, October, 13,1998.

Sinha, P. (1982). "*An Evaluative Study of Teacher Education in Bihar*", Ph.D. thesis, Edu., Patna University. (in) : Third Survey of Research in Education, (1978 - 83). M.B. Buch (ed.), New Delhi : NCERT.

Srivastava, R.C. (1970). "*Evaluation of Practice Teaching* in Teacher Training Institutions", Central Institute of Education, New Delhi. (in) : A Survey of Research in

Education, (1974). M.B. Buch (ed.), Baroda : Centre of Advanced Study in Education.

State Institute of Education (Gujarat). (1965). "*To Study the Problems of the Trainees of the Primary Teacher's Institutions of Gujarat, and to know their views on present Syllabus*", Ahmedabad. (in) : A Survey of Research in Education, (1974). M.B. Buch (ed.), Baroda : CASE.

State Institute of Education (Gujarat). (1966). "*Case Studies of Primary Teacher Training Institutions of Gujarat*", Ahmedabad. (in) : A Survey of Research in Education, (1974). M.B. Buch (ed.), Baroda : CASE.

Sujatha, B.N. (1979). "*An Enquiry into the Under-graduate Teacher Training Programme in the State of Karnataka*", Ph.D. thesis, Edu., Mysore University. (in) : Third Survey of Research in Education, (1978-83). M.B. Buch (ed.), New Delhi : NCERT.

The Government of Indian Resolution on Education (1904). Ministry of Education, Government of India, New Delhi.

The National Policy on Education (1986). Ministry of Human Resource Development, Government of India, New Delhi.

The Report of the Education Commission (1964-66). Ministry of Education, Government of India, New Delhi.

The Report of the University Education Commission (1948 -49). Ministry of Education, Government of India, New Delhi.

The Secondary Education Commission (1953). Ministry of Education, Government of India, New Delhi.

Thurstone, L.L. and Chave (1929). *The Measurement of Attitude*, Chicago : University of Chicago Press.

Tripathi, S.L. (1964). "*The Training of Teachers of Basic Schools*", Ph.D. thesis, Edu., Vikram University. (in) : Third Survey of Research in Education, (1978 - 83). M.B. Buch (ed.), New Delhi : NCERT.

Upasani, N.K. (1966). "*An Evaluation of the Existing Teacher Training Programme for Primary Teachers in the State of Maharashtra with special reference to Rural Areas*", Ph.D. thesis, Edu., Poona University. (in) : A Survey of Research in Education, (1974). M.B. Buch (ed.), Baroda : CASE.

Verma, D.R. (1979). "*A Study of Teacher Training as a Catalyst of Change in Professional Attitudes of Student -Teachers*", Ph.D. thesis, Edu., Banaras Hindu University. (in) : Third Survey of Research in Education, (1978-83). M.B. Buch (ed.), New Delhi : NCERT.

Viswanathappa (1992). "*An Evaluation Programme of DIET in Andhra Pradesh*", Ph.D. thesis, Edu., Mysore University, Mysore.

Wittich, Walter Arno and Schuller, Charles Francis (1953). *Audio-Visual Materials.* New York : Harper and Brothers Publishers.

Young, K.(1957). *Handbook of Social Psychology*, London : Routledge and Kegan Paul Ltd.

APPENDIX—A_1

The Mean Perception Scores of top and bottom groups of Student-Teachers and Discrimination Values of different items in the Pilot Form.

Items	*Total score of the top group on each item*	*Mean (M_t)*	*Total score of the bottom group on each item*	*Mean (M_b)*	*Discrimination Index DI = m_t-m_b*
1	*2*	*3*	*4*	*5*	*6*
1.	180	3.60	170	3.40	0.20 #
2.	173	3.46	99	1.98	1.48
3.	179	3.58	145	2.90	0.68
4.	190	3.80	129	2.58	1.22
5.	222	4.44	205	4.10	0.34
6.	163	3.26	177	3.54	-0.28 #
7.	162	3.24	138	2.76	0.48
8.	220	4.40	180	3.60	0.80
9.	162	3.24	125	2.50	0.74
10.	144	2.88	103	2.06	0.82
11.	153	3.06	103	2.06	1.00
12.	235	4.70	189	3.78	0.92
13.	168	3.36	127	2.54	0.82
14.	129	2.58	107	2.14	0.44
15.	168	3.36	114	2.28	1.08
16.	190	3.80	128	2.56	1.24
17.	127	2.54	97	1.94	0.60

(Contd...)

1	2	3	4	5	6
18.	167	3.34	88	1.76	1.58
19.	224	4.48	147	2.94	1.54
20.	147	2.94	127	2.54	0.40
21.	130	2.60	96	1.92	0.68
22.	99	1.98	119	2.38	-0.40 #
23.	151	3.02	67	1.34	1.68
24.	222	4.44	168	3.36	1.08
25.	193	3.86	85	1.70	2.16
26.	238	4.76	195	3.90	0.86
27.	188	3.76	161	3.22	0.54
28.	237	4.74	168	3.36	1.38
29.	173	3.46	115	2.30	1.16
30.	220	4.40	86	1.72	2.68
31.	150	3.00	107	2.14	0.86
32.	229	4.58	192	3.84	0.74
33.	200	4.00	111	2.22	1.78
34.	241	4.82	193	3.86	0.96
35.	194	3.88	115	2.30	1.58
36.	124	2.48	109	2.18	0.30
37.	218	4.36	187	3.74	0.62
38.	120	2.40	98	1.96	0.44
39.	237	4.74	205	4.10	0.64
40.	127	2.54	121	2.42	0.12 #
41.	116	2.32	95	1.90	0.42
42.	191	3.82	106	2.12	1.70
43.	185	3.70	97	1.94	1.76
44.	200	4.00	158	3.16	0.84
45.	160	3.20	159	3.18	0.02 #
46.	231	4.62	126	2.52	2.10
47.	121	2.42	88	1.76	0.66
48.	201	4.02	149	2.98	1.04
49.	212	4.24	104	2.08	2.16
50.	159	3.18	75	1.50	1.68
51.	115	2.30	106	2.12	0.18 #
52.	228	4.56	130	2.60	1.96
53.	221	4 42	122	2.44	1.98
54.	183	3.66	127	2.54	1.12
55.	161	3.22	131	2.62	0.60

(Contd...)

1	2	3	4	5	6
56.	219	4.38	193	3.86	0.52
57.	212	4.24	114	2.28	1.96
58.	138	2.76	96	1.92	0.84
59.	186	3.72	101	2.02	1.70
60.	152	3.04	94	1.88	1.16
61.	192	3.84	86	1.72	2.12
62.	147	2.94	72	1.44	1.50
63.	211	4.22	181	3.62	0.60
64.	157	3.14	96	1.92	1.22
65.	182	3.64	102	2.04	1.60
66.	162	3.24	66	1.32	1.92
67.	201	4.02	167	3.34	0.68
68.	222	4.44	145	2.90	1.54
69.	216	4.32	130	2.60	1.72
70.	197	3.94	175	3.50	0.44
71.	219	4.38	193	3.86	0.52
72.	194	3.88	81	1.62	2.26
73.	106	2.12	96	1.92	0.20 #
74.	168	3.36	113	2.26	1.10
75.	151	3.02	70	1.40	1.62
76.	143	2.86	204	4.08	-1.22 #
77.	88	1.76	135	2.70	-0.94 #
78.	170	3.46	112	2.24	1.22
79.	208	4.16	163	3.26	0.90
80.	155	3.10	84	1.68	1.42
81.	236	4.72	217	4.34	0.38
82.	216	4.32	217	4.34	-0.02 #
83.	225	4.50	176	3.52	0.98
84.	159	3.18	145	2.90	0.28 #
85.	226	4.52	146	2.92	1.60
86.	244	4.88	224	4.48	0.40

The items marked with '#' are eliminated in the final form of student teacher's perceptional scale as the discrimination value is less than 0.3.

APPENDIX—A_2

STUDENT TEACHERS PERCEPTION SCALE

Final Form—English Version

Dear student teacher,

This is a research questionnaire related to teacher training. Please read each question carefully in terms of its contribution to your perception on the teacher training and put a (✓) mark in one of the three brackets against the item.

There is no question of right or wrong answer. What you feel in your work is the right answer. Each question has three alternatives. They are :

1. To the Maximum Extent.
2. To the Moderate Extent.
3. To the Least Extent.

No question should be left unmarked. This questionnaire is useful to know your perception on teacher training programme. You should record the response that appropriately refers to your perception on the issue in that question.

This is purely for research purpose and all information will be kept confidential. Right answer is the key to good research. I will be grateful to you for your help.

Yours sincerely,

CHANDRA SEKHAR, K.
Research Scholar,
S.V. University.

	Max. ext.	Mod. ext.	Lea. ext.
1. Do you think that the student teachers face unnecessary problems in the institution?	( )	( )	( )
2. Do you feel that the teachers working in their respective schools do not make any constructive criticism after the teaching practice classes ?	( )	( )	( )
3. Do you think that there are insufficient number of classrooms in your institution ?	( )	( )	( )
4. Do you feel that S.S.C. should be the minimum qualification for the T.T.C. entrance test?	( )	( )	( )
5. Do you feel that the present duration of the training course is enough to make you an ideal teacher ?	( )	( )	( )
6. Do you think that the entrance test which you took before joining the training course is up to the standard ?	( )	( )	( )

7.	Do you feel that the lesson plan prepared earlier cannot be followed, as it is, in the classroom?	( )	( )	( )
8.	Do you think that the physical instructor does not encourage the student teachers to participate in the physical education ?	( )	( )	( )
9.	Do you feel that there is sufficient sports material in your institution ?	( )	( )	( )
10.	Do you feel that your institute is a 'model institute' in terms of institutional climate and clean campus ?	( )	( )	( )
11.	Do you think that the present day examinations fail to test the teaching skills ?	( )	( )	( )
12.	Do you think that it is difficult to go to distant villages for block teaching ?	( )	( )	( )
13.	Do you agree that the teaching methods taught in your training course are not useful in practical teaching ?	( )	( )	( )
14.	Do you feel that the student teachers participate sincerely in work-experience activities ?	( )	( )	( )
15.	Do you feel that the inadequate laboratory facilities in the institution are one of the causes for dissatisfaction of the trainees ?	( )	( )	( )
16.	Do you feel that there is adequate furniture in your hostel ?	( )	( )	( )
17.	Do you accept that the lecturers show commitment to their teaching ?	( )	( )	( )

18. Do you think that too much of record work in the training programme makes you unpleasant? ( ) ( ) ( )

19. Do you agree that the demonstration classes alone do not improve learning in teaching ? ( ) ( ) ( )

20. Do you agree that the post of physical instructor has been vacant for years in your institution? ( ) ( ) ( )

21. Do you feel that the principal of your institute is cooperative ? ( ) ( ) ( )

22. Do you feel that the lecturers do not guide the student teachers in the appropriate use of the library ? ( ) ( ) ( )

23. Are you interested in observing your friend's teaching practice classes ? ( ) ( ) ( )

24. Do you think that there is no need to increase teaching practice period ? ( ) ( ) ( )

25. Do you feel that the lecturers are giving adequate advice and guidance for teaching practice ? ( ) ( ) ( )

26. Are you of the opinion that the present day PSTE curriculum does not meet the local needs of the people ? ( ) ( ) ( )

27. Do you feel that the authorities of the institution do not show concern for the requirements of the student teachers ? ( ) ( ) ( )

28. Are you unhappy with the unhygienic surroundings of the hostel ? ( ) ( ) ( )

29. Do you think that the model lessons taken by your lecturers are helpful in your teaching practice ? ( ) ( ) ( )

30. Do you accept that the lecturers do not explain the student teachers the purpose and use of teaching any topic ? ( ) ( ) ( )

31. Do you feel that the teacher training is interesting and challenging ? ( ) ( ) ( )

32. Do you accept that the student teachers have enough facilities for recreation in the institute ? ( ) ( ) ( )

33. Do you think that there should be paid-apprenticeship of two years after the training for certification ? ( ) ( ) ( )

34. Do you feel that the citizenship training camp is one of the most important programmes in your course ? ( ) ( ) ( )

35. Do you feel that the student teachers are not able to participate in co-curricular activities due to lack of enough leisure ? ( ) ( ) ( )

36. Do you like to write lesson plans ? ( ) ( ) ( )

37. Are the general classes overcrowded with the student teachers ? ( ) ( ) ( )

38. Do you think that there is no correlation between theoretical and practical aspects of training ? ( ) ( ) ( )

39. Do you feel that the writing of ( ) ( ) ( )

observation sheets in observation classes is an eye-wash ?

40. Do the teachers of the respective schools observe teaching practice classes of the trainees with interest ? ( ) ( ) ( )

41. Do you feel that there is cordial relationship between the principal and the student teachers ? ( ) ( ) ( )

42. Do you think that physical education is allotted meagre time in the time-table ? ( ) ( ) ( )

43. Is there adequate water facility in your hostel ? ( ) ( ) ( )

44. Do you think that the lecturers do not show sufficient care in work experience activities ? ( ) ( ) ( )

45. Do you think that the student teachers are not provided with sufficient opportunities to exhibit their talent in cultural activities ? ( ) ( ) ( )

46. Do you think that the lecturers show sufficient care in teaching ? ( ) ( ) ( )

47. Are you of the opinion that the moral values are not properly taught in teacher training ? ( ) ( ) ( )

48. Do you lose good opinion on teacher education due to the overcrowded hostel rooms ? ( ) ( ) ( )

49. Do you think that there is a need to make the duration of the training course two years ? ( ) ( ) ( )

50. Do you get satisfaction when your fellow student teachers appreciate your lesson ? ( ) ( ) ( )

51.	Do you feel that the supervision of the lecturers during teaching practice is an eye-wash?	( )	( )	( )
52.	Do you feel that there is no sufficient toilet facility in the hostel ?	( )	( )	( )
53.	Do you feel that the lecturers are impartial in awarding internal assessment marks ?	( )	( )	( )
54.	Do you think that the student teachers have meagre chances to participate in social activities during their training programme ?	( )	( )	( )
55.	Are you of the opinion that there is no stress on topics like nutrition, health and habits in the syllabus of the training course ?	( )	( )	( )
56.	Do you think that the lecturers do not evince sufficient interest in using audio-visual equipment in their teaching ?	( )	( )	( )
57.	Do you feel that the teachers in the respective schools are very happy during the teaching practice period ?	( )	( )	( )
58.	Do you feel that the students are not served proper food in the hostel ?	( )	( )	( )
59.	Do you think that the lecturers do not give sufficient demonstration classes ?	( )	( )	( )
60.	Do you feel that there are inadequate facilities for reading in the library ?	( )	( )	( )
61.	Do you think that there is	( )	( )	( )

adequate play-ground in your institute ?

62. Do you feel that the present day teaching practice improves the teaching effectiveness ? ( ) ( ) ( )

63. Do you think that the teacher training programme does not develop personality in the teacher trainees ? ( ) ( ) ( )

64. Do you think that the writing of records, preparation of teaching aids should not be made compulsory in teacher training programme ? ( ) ( ) ( )

65. Do you teach the lesson by drawing good figures on the black board during the teaching practice period ? ( ) ( ) ( )

66. Do you think that there is need to increase the number of records from the present level in your training course ? ( ) ( ) ( )

67. Do you feel that the present curriculum offered in the teacher training is outdated ? ( ) ( ) ( )

68. Do you feel that the subject association meetings are not conducted in your institution ? ( ) ( ) ( )

69. Do you think that the rank you got in the entrance test does not show your teaching aptitude ? ( ) ( ) ( )

70. Do you think that the theory papers are new and interesting ? ( ) ( ) ( )

71. Do you feel that the DIET curriculum should be restructured and reorganised ? ( ) ( ) ( )

72.	While observing closely do you think how best the teaching of other student teachers will be useful in your teaching ?	( )	( )	( )
73.	Do you think that the writing of records is definitely useful in your training ?	( )	( )	( )
74.	Do you like the way your lecturers teach ?	( )	( )	( )
75.	Do you aspire to teach new topics by using novel aids to the pupils?	( )	( )	( )

Appendix—B_1

The Mean Attitude Scores of top and bottom groups of Student-Teachers and Discrimination Values of different items in the Pilot Form.

Items	Total score of the top group on each item	Mean (M_t)	Total score of the bottom group on each item	Mean (M_b)	Discrimination Index $DI = m_t - m_b$
1	2	3	4	5	6
1.	245	4.90	214	4.28	0.62
2.	210	4.20	177	3.54	0.66
3.	240	4.80	203	4.06	0.74
4.	222	4.44	184	3.68	0.76
5.	235	4.70	219	4.38	0.32
6.	243	4.86	227	4.54	0.32
7.	213	4.26	158	3.16	1.10
8.	233	4.66	195	3.90	0.76
9.	220	4.40	190	3.80	0.60
10.	172	3.44	115	2.30	1.14
11.	219	4.38	139	2.78	1.60
12.	211	4.22	185	3.70	0.52
13.	227	4.54	216	4.32	0.22 #
14.	70	1.40	81	1.62	-0.22 #
15.	217	4.34	202	4.04	0.30
16.	195	3.90	180	3.60	0.30

(Contd...)

1	2	3	4	5	6
17.	238	4.76	188	3.76	1.00
18.	236	4.72	228	4.56	0.16 #
19.	145	2.90	132	2.64	0.26 #
20.	221	4.42	180	3.60	0.82
21.	241	4.82	218	4.36	0.46
22.	217	4.34	158	3.16	1.18
23.	185	3.70	130	2.60	1.10
24.	68	1.36	61	1.22	0.14 #
25.	62	1.24	83	1.66	-0.42 #
26.	80	1.60	104	2.08	-0.48 #
27.	227	4.54	148	2.96	1.58
28.	215	4.30	162	3.24	1.06
29.	239	4.78	225	4.50	0.28 #
30.	218	4.36	113	2.26	2.10
31.	123	2.46	129	2.58	-0.12 #
32.	238	4.76	200	4.00	0.76
33.	241	4.82	201	4.02	0.80
34.	164	3.28	157	3.14	0.14 #
35.	177	3.54	145	2.90	0.64
36.	218	4.36	188	3.76	0.60
37.	244	4.88	199	3.98	0.90
38.	247	4.94	230	4.60	0.34
39.	248	4.96	194	3.88	1.08
40.	197	3.94	137	2.74	1.20
41.	245	4.90	230	4.60	0.30
42.	216	4.32	207	4.14	0.18 #
43.	235	4.70	171	3.42	1.28
44.	249	4.98	199	3.98	1.00
45.	159	3.18	128	2.56	0.62
46.	179	3.58	120	2.40	1.18
47.	241	4.82	161	3.22	1.60
48.	218	4.36	202	4.04	0.32
49.	196	3.92	177	3.54	0.38
50.	245	4.90	162	3.24	1.66
51.	165	3.30	112	2.24	1.06
52.	247	4.94	236	4.72	0.22 #
53.	165	3.30	99	1.98	1.32
54.	190	3.80	118	2.36	1.44
55.	196	3.92	118	2.36	1.56
56.	237	4.74	202	4.04	0.70
57.	249	4.98	230	4.60	0.38

APPENDIX—B_2

STUDENT TEACHERS ATTITUDE SCALE

Final Form—English Version

Dear student teacher,

This is a research questionnaire pertaining to the attitude of teacher trainees towards teaching profession. Some statements related to various aspects of teaching profession are given below. Please read each statement carefully in terms of its contribution to your attitude on the teaching profession and answer it by putting (✓) mark in the given answer sheet.

If you....

(1)	Strongly Agree with the statement	:	Put a (✓) mark in the first bracket.
(2)	Agree with the statement	:	Put a (✓) mark in the second bracket.
(3)	Undecided with the statement	:	Put a (✓) mark in the third bracket.
4)	Disagree with the statement	:	Put a (✓) mark in the fourth bracket.

(5) Strongly Disagree with the statement : Put a (✓) mark in the fifth bracket.

No question should be unmarked. There is no question of right or wrong answer, what you feel in your work is the right answer. This questionnaire is useful to know your attitude to the teaching profession. You should record the response that appropriately refers to your attitude to the issue in that statement.

This is purely for research use and all information will be kept confidential. Right answer is the key to good research. I will be grateful to you for your help.

Yours sincerely,

CHANDRA SEKHAR, K.
Research Scholar,
S.V. University.

	SA	A	UD	D	SD
1. I am interested in teaching.	( )	( )	( )	( )	( )
2. My school is everything to me.	( )	( )	( )	( )	( )
3. Teaching profession is better than any other profession.	( )	( )	( )	( )	( )
4. Freedom should not be given to the pupils to learn according to their interests.	( )	( )	( )	( )	( )
5. Teacher is an artist who sketches the personality of the pupils.	( )	( )	( )	( )	( )
6. Teaching profession is the mother of all professions.	( )	( )	( )	( )	( )

7. I have no liking for teaching profession as it is neglected both by the government and the public. ( ) ( ) ( ) ( ) ( )
8. Teachers mould pupils as nation's architects. ( ) ( ) ( ) ( ) ( )
9. Teaching is a cultured profession. ( ) ( ) ( ) ( ) ( )
10. Teaching profession is quite tiresome. ( ) ( ) ( ) ( ) ( )
11. Teaching profession is interesting only in the initial stages. ( ) ( ) ( ) ( ) ( )
12. I dislike to be an invigilator during the examinations. ( ) ( ) ( ) ( ) ( )
13. Teaching profession is not that much degraded as being done by everyone. ( ) ( ) ( ) ( ) ( )
14. Teaching profession gives a comfortable life. ( ) ( ) ( ) ( ) ( )
15. Pupils learn more through punishment than affinity. ( ) ( ) ( ) ( ) ( )
16. Teaching is a peaceful profession. ( ) ( ) ( ) ( ) ( )
17. Teaching is a noble profession. ( ) ( ) ( ) ( ) ( )
18. I feel happy when mischievous students are punished. ( ) ( ) ( ) ( ) ( )
19. Society is responsible for the miseries of a teacher. ( ) ( ) ( ) ( ) ( )
20. I took up the teaching profession as I was not able to get any other job. ( ) ( ) ( ) ( ) ( )

21. There is too much freedom in the teaching profession. ( ) ( ) ( ) ( ) ( )

22. Teaching profession is not the first one among my priorities. ( ) ( ) ( ) ( ) ( )

23. The teacher need not consider the personal needs and problems of the pupils. ( ) ( ) ( ) ( ) ( )

24. I like to do any work connected to teaching. ( ) ( ) ( ) ( ) ( )

25. If I have a son who is going to the college I would encourage him to become a teacher. ( ) ( ) ( ) ( ) ( )

26. Fault finding is the duty of the teacher. ( ) ( ) ( ) ( ) ( )

27. Teaching profession makes a person lazy. ( ) ( ) ( ) ( ) ( )

28. Teaching generates new ideas and thoughts. ( ) ( ) ( ) ( ) ( )

29. I feel shy to disclose in public that I belong to the teaching profession. ( ) ( ) ( ) ( ) ( )

30. Like any other profession, teaching profession is a means for livelihood. ( ) ( ) ( ) ( ) ( )

31. In teaching profession both the teacher and student gain knowledge. ( ) ( ) ( ) ( ) ( )

32. Teaching is a routine and monotonous job. ( ) ( ) ( ) ( ) ( )

33. To be in teaching profession is a curse. ( ) ( ) ( ) ( ) ( )

34. Teaching profession is not monetarily beneficial. ( ) ( ) ( ) ( ) ( )

35. Many pupils have no interest in education. ( ) ( ) ( ) ( ) ( )

36. Teaching profession kills active spirit. ( ) ( ) ( ) ( ) ( )

37. Teaching profession influences mankind more than any other profession. ( ) ( ) ( ) ( ) ( )

38. I hate correction work which is a part of teaching profession. ( ) ( ) ( ) ( ) ( )

39. An ideal teacher is a social misfit. ( ) ( ) ( ) ( ) ( )

40. Using teachers for activities other than teaching bothers me. ( ) ( ) ( ) ( ) ( )

41. Now-a-days students are not obedient to the teachers. ( ) ( ) ( ) ( ) ( )

42. Teaching profession has no recognition in the society. ( ) ( ) ( ) ( ) ( )

43. Many students do not respect teachers. ( ) ( ) ( ) ( ) ( )

44. Teaching profession provides self-satisfaction. ( ) ( ) ( ) ( ) ( )

45. A good teacher is respected by all. ( ) ( ) ( ) ( ) ( )

Personal Data

1. Name :

2. Male/Female :

3. Age :

4. Educational Qualifications :

5. Native Place :

6. Methodology Subjects (Selected in T.T.C.) : (1)

   (2)

7. Family Particulars :

S.No.	Relationship	Education	Occupation	Income
1.	Father			
2.	Mother			
3.	Elder Brother			
4.	Younger Brother			
5.	Elder Sister			
6.	Younger Sister			
7.				
8.				

APPENDIX—C_1

The Mean Perception Scores of top and bottom groups of teacher educators and Discrimination Values of different items in the Pilot Form.

Items	*Total score of the top group on each item*	*Mean (M_t)*	*Total score of the bottom group on each item*	*Mean (M_b)*	*Discrimination Index $DI = m_t - m_b$*
1	*2*	*3*	*4*	*5*	*6*
1.	26	2.60	20	2.00	0.60
2.	23	2.30	15	1.50	0.80
3.	12	1.20	11	1.10	0.10 #
4.	28	2.80	28	2.80	0 #
5.	26	2.60	23	2.30	0.30
6.	25	2.50	19	1.90	0.60
7.	30	3.00	22	2.20	0.80
8.	26	2.60	23	2.30	0.30
9.	20	2.00	16	1.60	0.40
10.	22	2.20	20	2.00	0.20 #
11.	11	1.10	12	1.20	-0.10 #
12.	23	2.30	20	2.00	0.30
13.	25	2.50	21	2.10	0.40
14.	24	2.40	23	2.30	0.10 #

(Contd...)

1	*2*	*3*	*4*	*5*	*6*
15.	20	2.00	18	1.80	0.20 #
16.	12	1.20	13	1.30	-0.10 #
17.	27	2.70	20	2.00	0.70
18.	21	2.10	13	1.30	0.80
19.	21	2.10	17	1.70	0.40
20.	29	2.90	25	2.50	0.40
21.	28	2.80	25	2.50	0.30
22.	25	2.50	20	2.00	0.50
23.	26	2.60	21	2.10	0.50
24.	30	3.00	27	2.70	0.30
25.	27	2.70	16	1.60	1.10
26.	29	2.90	24	2.40	0.50
27.	27	2.70	28	2.80	-0.10 #
28.	17	1.70	18	1.80	-0.10 #
29.	16	1.60	13	1.30	0.30
30.	19	1.90	16	1.60	0.30
31.	19	1.90	14	1.40	0.50
32.	30	3.00	26	2.60	0.40
33.	24	2.40	13	1.30	1.10
34.	25	2.50	16	1.60	0.90
35.	27	2.70	23	2.30	0.40
36.	22	2.20	17	1.70	0.50
37.	23	2.30	19	1.90	0.40
38.	19	1.90	13	1.30	0.60
39.	22	2.20	15	1.50	0.70
40.	25	2.50	14	1.40	1.10
41.	26	2.60	29	2.90	-0.30 #
42.	29	2.90	26	2.60	0.30
43.	28	2.80	24	2.40	0.40
44.	21	2.10	18	1.80	0.30
45.	14	1.40	11	1.10	0.30
46.	21	2.10	17	1.70	0.40
47.	27	2.70	19	1.90	0.80
48.	24	2.40	14	1.40	1.00
49.	25	2.50	15	1.50	1.00

(Contd...)

1	*2*	*3*	*4*	*5*	*6*
50.	26	2.60	26	2.60	0 #
51.	27	2.70	28	2.80	-0.10 #
52.	17	1.70	11	1.10	0.60
53.	22	2.20	14	1.40	0.80
54.	28	2.80	16	1.60	1.20
55.	28	2.80	16	1.60	1.20
56.	23	2.30	18	1.80	0.50
57.	18	1.80	11	1.10	0.70
58.	28	2.80	21	2.10	0.70
59.	25	2.50	17	1.70	0.80
60.	27	2.70	23	2.30	0.40
61.	22	2.20	14	1.40	0.80
62.	23	2.30	15	1.50	0.80
63.	28	2.80	25	2.50	0.30
64.	30	3.00	19	1.90	1.10
65.	19	1.90	16	1.60	0.30
66.	15	1.50	11	1.10	0.40
67.	24	2.40	21	2.10	0.30
68.	18	1.80	14	1.40	0.40
69.	29	2.90	28	2.80	0.10 #
70.	24	2.40	19	1.90	0.50
71.	23	2.30	19	1.90	0.40
72.	27	2.70	19	1.90	0.80
73.	25	2.50	17	1.70	0.80
74.	21	2.10	18	1.80	0.30
75.	22	2.20	20	2.00	0.20 #
76.	22	2.20	14	1.40	0.80
77.	22	2.20	16	1.60	0.60
78.	22	2.20	18	1.80	0.40
79.	18	1.80	10	1.00	0.80
80.	17	1.70	12	1.20	0.50
81.	22	2.20	17	1.70	0.50
82.	26	2.60	16	1.60	1.00
83.	29	2.90	19	1.90	1.00
84.	27	2.70	20	2.00	0.70

(Contd...)

1	*2*	*3*	*4*	*5*	*6*
85.	28	2.80	17	1.70	1.10
86.	30	3.00	21	2.10	0.90
87.	25	2.50	19	1.90	0.60
88.	17	1.70	12	1.20	0.50
89.	26	2.60	17	1.70	0.90
90.	19	1.90	17	1.70	0.20 #
91.	24	2.40	20	2.00	0.40
92.	25	2.50	16	1.60	0.90
93.	27	2.70	16	1.60	1.10
94.	27	2.70	14	1.40	1.30
95.	27	2.70	22	2.20	0.50
96.	24	2.40	19	1.90	0.50
97.	25	2.50	18	1.80	0.70
98.	24	2.40	16	1.60	0.80
99.	27	2.70	25	2.50	0.20 #
100.	26	2.60	18	1.80	0.80
101.	12	1.20	11	1.10	0.10 #
102.	26	2.60	27	2.70	-0.10 #
103.	26	2.60	23	2.30	0.30
104.	23	2.30	19	1.90	0.40
105.	21	2.10	13	1.30	0.80
106.	20	2.00	12	1.20	0.80
107.	24	2.40	14	1.40	1.00

Appendix—C_2

Lecturer's Perception Scale

Final Form—English Version

Sir/Madam,

This is a research questionnaire concerning lecturer's perceptions on DIETs physical, academic, administrative, financial and interpersonal aspects. Please read each question carefully in terms of its contribution to your perception on the DIET and put a (✓) mark in one of the three brackets against the item.

There is no question of right or wrong answer. What you feel in your work is the right answer. Each question has three alternatives. They are :

1. To the Maximum Extent.
2. To the Moderate Extent.
3. To the Least Extent.

No question should be left unmarked. This questionnaire is useful to know your perception on DIETs various aspects. You should make the response that appropriately refers to your perception on the issue in that question.

This is purely for research purpose and all information will be kept confidential. Right answer is the key for good research. I will be grateful to you for your kind help and cooperation.

Yours sincerely,

CHANDRA SEKHAR, K.
Research Scholar,
S.V. University.

	Max. Ext.	Mod. Ext.	Least. Ext.
1. Do you think that there are sufficient number of classrooms in your institution ?	( )	( )	( )
2. Do you agree that there is comfortable furniture in your classrooms ?	( )	( )	( )
3. Do you accept that there is a beautiful campus for your institution ?	( )	( )	( )
4. Do you agree that your principal is overburdened in your DIET ?	( )	( )	( )
5. Do you want to conduct sports competitions for the students to draw-out their talents ?	( )	( )	( )
6. Does your institution have a play ground to play different field games ?	( )	( )	( )

7. Do you think that there is enough equipment in the educational technology laboratory ? ( ) ( ) ( )

8. Do you have adequate power facility in your DIET? ( ) ( ) ( )

9. Do you think that you have good books in your institution's library ? ( ) ( ) ( )

10. Do you think that there is need for increasing the number of demonstration classes ? ( ) ( ) ( )

11. Do you feel that there is adequate furniture in the reading room ? ( ) ( ) ( )

12. Are you of the opinion that you have enough equipment in your biology laboratory ? ( ) ( ) ( )

13. Do you feel that the present block teaching practice is not sufficient to improve teaching skills among the student teachers ? ( ) ( ) ( )

14. Do you think that the principal does not provide sufficient academic and resource support to the DIET lecturers ? ( ) ( ) ( )

15. Do you think that there are adequate reference books in your library ? ( ) ( ) ( )

16. Do you like to use necessary 'projected-aids' in your demonstration classes ? ( ) ( ) ( )

17. Do you feel that the training should be provided to the

student teachers in all the school subjects ? ( ) ( ) ( )

18. Do you think that there are opportunities to reach higher level ? ( ) ( ) ( )

19. Is your campus clean and green ? ( ) ( ) ( )

20. Do you feel that the non-teaching staff are over-burdened in your DIET ? ( ) ( ) ( )

21. Do you think that the approval of the lesson plan is an eye-wash ? ( ) ( ) ( )

22. Do you have adequate electric lighting facility in your classrooms ? ( ) ( ) ( )

23. Do you feel that wearing uniform at the time of block teaching is useful ? ( ) ( ) ( )

24. Do you feel that there are adequate buildings for the hostel ? ( ) ( ) ( )

25. Do you think that there is adequate furniture in your library ? ( ) ( ) ( )

26. Are you of the opinion that by conducting teaching practice classes in model school you can improve the teaching skills of the student teachers ? ( ) ( ) ( )

27. Do you feel that there is need for revitalising the present day curriculum in your institute ? ( ) ( ) ( )

28. Do you feel that the trainees use sufficient teaching aids in their teaching practice classes ? ( ) ( ) ( )

29. Do you feel that the internal assessment marks should be raised from the present level ?	( )	( )	( )
30. Are you of the opinion that there is enough equipment in the physical science laboratory ?	( )	( )	( )
31. Do you think that there are sufficient buildings for laboratories in your institution ?	( )	( )	( )
32. Do you feel that there is need for an effective recruiting agency for appointing the DIET lecturers ?	( )	( )	( )
33. Do you like to organise activities to keep your campus clean ?	( )	( )	( )
34. Do you think that the computer evaluation is the only solution to avoid biased attitude of the lecturers ?	( )	( )	( )
35. Do you think that there are sufficient technical staff members in your laboratories ?	( )	( )	( )
36. Is your institution financially sound ?	( )	( )	( )
37. Do you have adequate drinking water facility in your DIET ?	( )	( )	( )
38. Do you think that the principal utilises the grants for the academic development of the institution ?	( )	( )	( )
39. Do you feel that the cooperative book bank maintained by your library is useful to both the teachers and trainees ?	( )	( )	( )

40. Are you of the opinion that the local philanthropists have helped your institution in its development ? ( ) ( ) ( )

41. Do you agree that there is adequate furniture in the staff rooms ? ( ) ( ) ( )

42. Do you think that there is adequate space for office use ? ( ) ( ) ( )

43. Do you agree that the institution buildings are used for community festivals every year ? ( ) ( ) ( )

44. Do you feel that there are well defined service rules for your teaching staff ? ( ) ( ) ( )

45. Do you agree that the principal of the institution conducts parents meetings and reminds them of their responsibilities towards their children ? ( ) ( ) ( )

46. Do you encourage work related habits for developing your campus ? ( ) ( ) ( )

47. Do you accept that the principal of your institution maintains strict administrative rules to create good atmosphere in your institution ? ( ) ( ) ( )

48. Do you feel that the usage of multi-media brings more comprehension in the classroom interaction? ( ) ( ) ( )

49. Are there any occasions in which your principal seeks the

help of the local people to develop your institution? ( ) ( ) ( )

50. Do you think that there is sufficient teaching learning material in your DIET ? ( ) ( ) ( )

51. Do you like to help the local people in giving them educational information ? ( ) ( ) ( )

52. Do you think that there is a spacious building for seminar hall ? ( ) ( ) ( )

53. Do you encourage the unemployed youth and seek their help in the institutional activities ? ( ) ( ) ( )

54. Do the local people help you in solving your personal problems ? ( ) ( ) ( )

55. Do you have adequate water supply in the garden of your institution ? ( ) ( ) ( )

56. Do you think that there is strong political pressure in the appointments, transfers and promotions in your institution ? ( ) ( ) ( )

57. Are you of the opinion that your principal shows keen interest in maintaining the garden of your institution ? ( ) ( ) ( )

58. Do you believe that the technical staff are essential in preparing teaching aids ? ( ) ( ) ( )

59. Are you of the opinion that the principal encourages the student teachers in preparing the teaching aids ? ( ) ( ) ( )

60. Do you feel that there is sufficient furniture in your office room ? ( ) ( ) ( )

61. Do you feel that the student teachers avoid the topics that they find difficult to teach in their teaching practice classes ? ( ) ( ) ( )

62. Do you think that there are sufficient number of Education Commission Reports in your institute's library ? ( ) ( ) ( )

63. Are the guest lectures on health and moral education very common in your institution? ( ) ( ) ( )

64. Do you think that the curriculum offered in your institution meets the local needs ? ( ) ( ) ( )

65. Is your institution's library kept open even after the working hours for the facility of the student teachers ? ( ) ( ) ( )

66. Do you think that there are sufficient hostel staff in your DIET ? ( ) ( ) ( )

67. Is your institute's principal a model to other lecturers ? ( ) ( ) ( )

68. Do you think that there are sufficient books on teaching in your institution ? ( ) ( ) ( )

69. Do you think that your principal always observes the behaviour of the lecturers in your institution ? ( ) ( ) ( )

70. Do you feel that there is need for complete overhaul of the present day PSTE curriculum ? ( ) ( ) ( )

71. Do you feel that your institute's principal corrects the mistakes of lecturers with his valuable suggestions ? ( ) ( ) ( )

72. Do you feel that there is sufficient ventilation in your library ? ( ) ( ) ( )

73. Do you feel that your principal always works hard and thereby inspires others ? ( ) ( ) ( )

74. Do you think there is sufficient furniture in the hostel ? ( ) ( ) ( )

75. Do you agree that your principal ensures that the lecturers utilise their full potentialities ? ( ) ( ) ( )

76. Do you feel that your principal's criticism is always constructive ? ( ) ( ) ( )

77. Are you of the opinion that there are sufficient maps in your institution ? ( ) ( ) ( )

78. Do you feel that there are sufficient chairs and tables in your seminar-hall ? ( ) ( ) ( )

79. Does your principal help the staff members in setting their minor differences ? ( ) ( ) ( )

80. Do you feel that the student teachers fail to use the teaching aids in their teaching practice ? ( ) ( ) ( )

81. Do you feel that your colleagues exhibit their cooperative attitude atleast in their teaching ? ( ) ( ) ( )

82. Do you think that there are

sufficient text books in your institution's library ? ( ) ( ) ( )

83. Do you feel that your principal reminds the lecturers of their responsibilities very often ? ( ) ( ) ( )

84. Do you feel that the principal of your institution makes the lecturers more alert and work-minded through effective supervision ? ( ) ( ) ( )

85. Do you have a sufficient play-ground ? ( ) ( ) ( )

86. Do you utilise your institution's play-ground optimally ? ( ) ( ) ( )

87. Do you feel that your institution's Library Advisory Committee functions well ? ( ) ( ) ( )

88. Do you have adequate sports equipment in your institution ? ( ) ( ) ( )

89. Do you feel that there are sufficient almirahs and racks in your institution's library ? ( ) ( ) ( )

APPENDIX—D_1

The Mean Attitude Scores of top and bottom groups of teacher educators and Discrimination Values of different items in the Pilot Form.

Items	*Total score of the top group on each item*	*Mean (M_t)*	*Total score of the bottom group on each item*	*Mean (M_b)*	*Discrimination Index DI = m_t-m_b*
1	*2*	*3*	*4*	*5*	*6*
1.	30	3.00	29	2.90	0.10 #
2.	43	4.30	34	3.40	0.90
3.	39	3.90	16	1.60	2.30
4.	45	4.50	34	3.40	1.10
5.	46	4.60	33	3.30	1.30
6.	40	4.00	26	2.60	1.40
7.	25	2.50	17	1.70	0.80
8.	25	2.50	13	1.30	1.20
9.	39	3.90	20	2.00	1.90
10.	32	3.20	26	2.60	0.60
11.	21	2.10	20	2.00	0.10 #
12.	46	4.60	45	4.50	0.10 #
13.	33	3.30	16	1.60	1.70
14.	29	2.90	15	1.50	1.40

(Contd...)4

1	*2*	*3*	*4*	*5*	*6*
15.	48	4.80	47	4.70	0.10 #
16.	30	3.00	38	3.80	-0.80 #
17.	39	3.90	25	2.50	1.40
18.	34	3.40	24	2.40	1.00
19.	39	3.90	42	4.20	-0.30 #
20.	41	4.10	22	2.20	1.90
21.	40	4.00	22	2.20	1.80
22.	40	4.00	44	4.40	-0.40 #
23.	28	2.80	14	1.40	1.40
24.	33	3.30	19	1.90	1.40
25.	50	5.00	46	4.60	0.40
26.	49	4.90	45	4.50	0.40
27.	45	4.50	41	4.10	0.40
28.	25	2.50	23	2.30	0.20 #
29.	37	3.70	21	2.10	1.60
30.	46	4.60	32	3.20	1.40
31.	36	3.60	25	2.50	1.10
32.	43	4.30	28	2.80	1.50
33.	40	4.00	49	4.90	-0.90 #
34.	31	3.10	19	1.90	1.20
35.	48	4.80	44	4.40	0.40
36.	43	4.30	19	1.90	2.40
37.	31	3.10	20	2.00	0.10
38.	28	2.80	46	4.60	-1.80 #
39.	40	4.00	30	3.00	1.00
40.	32	3.20	33	3.30	-0.10 #
41.	45	4.50	20	2.00	2.50
42.	41	4.10	17	1.70	2.40
43.	43	4.30	28	2.80	1.50
44.	43	4.30	24	2.40	1.90
45.	43	4.30	41	4.10	0.20 #
46.	45	4.50	33	3.30	1.20
47.	26	2.60	39	3.90	-1.30 #
48.	42	4.20	21	2.10	2.10

APPENDIX—D_2

LECTURER'S ATTITUDE SCALE

Final Form—English Version

Sir/Madam,

This is a research questionnaire related to the attitude of lecturers towards teacher training programme. Some statements related to various aspects of teacher training are given below. Please read each statement carefully in terms of its contribution to your attitude to the teacher training and answer it by putting (✓) mark in the given answer sheet.

If you...

(1) Strongly Agree with the statement : Put a (✓) mark in the first bracket.

(2) Agree with the statement : Put a (✓) mark in the second bracket.

(3) Undecided with the statement : Put a (✓) mark in the third bracket.

(4)	Disagree with the statement	:	Put a (✓) mark in the fourth bracket.
(5)	Strongly Disagree with the statement	:	Put a (✓) mark in the fifth bracket.

No question should be left unmarked. There is no question of right or wrong answer. What you feel in your work is the right answer. This questionnaire is useful to know your attitude towards the existing teacher education programme. You should record the response that appropriately refers to your attitude to the issue in the statement.

This is purely for research purpose and all information will be kept confidential. Right answer is the key for good research. I will be ever grateful to you for your help.

Yours sincerely,

CHANDRA SEKHAR, K.
Research Scholar,
S.V. University.

	SA	A	UD	D	SD
1. The teaching methods taught in training programme are not useful in practical teaching.	( )	( )	( )	( )	( )
2. The standards of teacher education are rapidly deteriorating day by day.	( )	( )	( )	( )	( )
3. By insisting on the lecturers to participate in in-service programmes only we can					

improve their skills in teaching. ( ) ( ) ( ) ( ) ( )

4. Workshops/Seminars are the occasions to enjoy parties with government money. ( ) ( ) ( ) ( ) ( )

5. There are no assessment classes after demonstration classes. ( ) ( ) ( ) ( ) ( )

6. Physical education is allotted very little time in the time-table. ( ) ( ) ( ) ( ) ( )

7. The quality of teacher education is not able to maintain its standard due to lack of strict adherence to the administrative rules. ( ) ( ) ( ) ( ) ( )

8. Topics like nutrition, health and habits are not included in the syllabus of the training course. ( ) ( ) ( ) ( ) ( )

9. In general, psychology is a difficult subject to most of the student teachers. ( ) ( ) ( ) ( ) ( )

10. There is no correlation between theoretical and practical aspects of training. ( ) ( ) ( ) ( ) ( )

11. Student teachers during their training period have a few chances to participate in social activities. ( ) ( ) ( ) ( ) ( )

12. Student teachers are not taught new topics with the help of innovative aids. ( ) ( ) ( ) ( ) ( )

13. To improve the teaching skills, in-service training programme lacks the needed dynamism. ( ) ( ) ( ) ( ) ( )

14. Student teachers do not evince proper interest in teaching practice. ( ) ( ) ( ) ( ) ( )

15. Student teachers do not take interest in classroom discussions. ( ) ( ) ( ) ( ) ( )

16. Though the practicals are more important than theory in teacher training they are not given much importance. ( ) ( ) ( ) ( ) ( )

17. As the student teachers in their training programme do not have sufficient leisure, they are not able to participate in co-curricular activities. ( ) ( ) ( ) ( ) ( )

18. The DIET is the guiding factor in improving the quality of primary education. ( ) ( ) ( ) ( ) ( )

19. If there are efficient resource persons, in-service training achieves desirable results. ( ) ( ) ( ) ( ) ( )

20. Writing of records, preparation of teaching aids should not be made compulsory in teacher training programme. ( ) ( ) ( ) ( ) ( )

21. Even though DIET spends a lot of money to impart

primary teacher education, it is unable to achieve the desired goals. ( ) ( ) ( ) ( ) ( )

22. Student teachers have no freedom in their institution. ( ) ( ) ( ) ( ) ( )

23. Audio-visual aids are not used when student teachers are taught. ( ) ( ) ( ) ( ) ( )

24. The present day teacher training institutes fail to impart quality teacher education in our country. ( ) ( ) ( ) ( ) ( )

25. Supervision in teaching practice is nothing but an eye-wash. ( ) ( ) ( ) ( ) ( )

26. I get nervous at the time of conducting model classes. ( ) ( ) ( ) ( ) ( )

27. The present day teacher education does not develop creativity among the pupils. ( ) ( ) ( ) ( ) ( )

28. General Classrooms are overcrowded. ( ) ( ) ( ) ( ) ( )

29. Too much record work makes me feel uneasy. ( ) ( ) ( ) ( ) ( )

30. The present day teacher education neglects the personality development of the student teachers. ( ) ( ) ( ) ( ) ( )

31. Teacher education does not attract the attention of scholars in our society. ( ) ( ) ( ) ( ) ( )

32. The present day in-service programme lacks clear cut policies and priorities. ( ) ( ) ( ) ( ) ( )

33. The present day teacher training curriculum is outdated. ( ) ( ) ( ) ( ) ( )

34. Teacher education does not provide an opportunity to improve the communicative skills. ( ) ( ) ( ) ( ) ( )

35. Lack of accountability makes the teacher educators lethargic. ( ) ( ) ( ) ( ) ( )

Personal Data

1. Name :

2. Male/Female :

3. Age :

4. Educational Qualifications

   a) General :

   b) Professional :

5. Designation :

6. Experience as Primary School Teacher :

APPENDIX—E

PRINCIPAL'S PERCEPTION SCALE

Final Form—English Version

Sir/Madam,

This is a research questionnaire relating to the principal's perceptions on DIETs physical, academic, administrative, financial and interpersonal aspects. Please read each question carefully in terms of its contribution to your perception on the DIET and put a (✓) mark in one of the three brackets against the item.

There is no question of right or wrong answer. What you feel in your work is the right answer. Each question has three alternatives. They are :

1. To the Maximum Extent.
2. To the Moderate Extent.
3. To the Least Extent.

No question should be left unmarked. This questionnaire is useful to know your perception on DIETs various aspects. You should record the response that appropriately refers to your perception on the issue in that question.

This is purely for research purpose and all information will be kept confidential. Right answer is the key for good research. I will be ever grateful to you for your help.

Yours sincerely,

CHANDRA SEKHAR, K.
Research Scholar,
S.V. University.

		Max. Ext.	Mod. Ext.	Least Ext.
1.	Do you utilise your institution's play-ground optimally ?	( )	( )	( )
2.	Do you feel that you have adequate classrooms?	( )	( )	( )
3.	Do you agree that you have comfortable furniture in classrooms ?	( )	( )	( )
4.	Do you want to conduct sports competitions for students to exhibit their talents ?	( )	( )	( )
5.	Do you have sufficient teaching-learning material in your DIET ?	( )	( )	( )
6.	Do you think that you have good books in your library ?	( )	( )	( )
7.	Do you have sufficient play-ground in your campus?	( )	( )	( )
8.	Do you have adequate power facility in your DIET?	( )	( )	( )

9. Do you think that you have sufficient lecturers in your DIET ? ( ) ( ) ( )

10. Do you feel that there is need for conducting sufficient workshops to develop primary school curriculum in your DIET ? ( ) ( ) ( )

11. Do you accept that you have adequate furniture in reading room ? ( ) ( ) ( )

12. Do you think that there is need to increase the number of demonstration classes ? ( ) ( ) ( )

13. Do you feel that the present block teaching is insufficient to improve the teaching skills of the student teachers ? ( ) ( ) ( )

14. Do you have adequate buildings for the hostel ? ( ) ( ) ( )

15. Do you have adequate furniture in your library ? ( ) ( ) ( )

16. Do you accept that the usage of multi-media brings more comprehension in the classroom interaction? ( ) ( ) ( )

17. Do you agree that the lecturers are overburdened in your DIET ? ( ) ( ) ( )

18. Do you suggest that the trainees should be provided training in the methods of teaching in all school subjects ? ( ) ( ) ( )

19. Do you have adequate reference books in your library ? ( ) ( ) ( )

20. Do you have adequate furniture in staff rooms ? ( ) ( ) ( )

21. Do your lecturers use adequate 'non-projected aids' in their classes ? ( ) ( ) ( )

22. Do you feel that the competence of lecturers is not up to the mark in your DIET ? ( ) ( ) ( )

23. Do your trainees use a large number of teaching aids in their teaching practice ? ( ) ( ) ( )

24. Do you feel that the non-teaching staff are over-burdened in your DIET ? ( ) ( ) ( )

25. Do you have sufficient maps in your institution? ( ) ( ) ( )

26. Do you feel that the lecturers do not know how to use teaching aids in your institution ? ( ) ( ) ( )

27. Do you feel that the approval of lesson plan is an eye-wash ? ( ) ( ) ( )

28. Do you have a beautiful garden in your DIET ? ( ) ( ) ( )

29. Do you agree that uniform should be made compulsory in block-teaching ? ( ) ( ) ( )

30. Do you have sufficient electric bulbs in your classrooms ? ( ) ( ) ( )

31. Do you have sufficient buildings for laboratories? ( ) ( ) ( )

32. Do you agree that the lecturers are not provided with sufficient academic and resource support in your DIET ? ( ) ( ) ( )

33. Do you feel that the internal assessment marks should be raised from the present level ? ( ) ( ) ( )

34. Do your lecturers render their services to the student teachers for proper use of the library ? ( ) ( ) ( )

35. Do you agree that there are sufficient technical staff in your laboratories ? ( ) ( ) ( )

36. Do you feel that the DIET lecturers are not trained as per DIET regulations ? ( ) ( ) ( )

37. Does your institute publish sufficient number of Newsletters and Institutional Journals ? ( ) ( ) ( )

38. Do you agree that the internal assessment is impartial in your DIET ? ( ) ( ) ( )

39. Are you interested in organising activities for cleaning your campus ? ( ) ( ) ( )

40. Do you have enough equipment in your educational technology laboratory ? ( ) ( ) ( )

41. Do you feel that the computer evaluation is the only solution to avoid biased attitude of the lecturers ? ( ) ( ) ( )

42. Do you think that the curriculum offered in your DIET meets the local needs ? ( ) ( ) ( )

43. Do you conduct parents' meetings and remind them of their responsibilities towards their children ? ( ) ( ) ( )

44. Do your lecturers are not doing justice to the job of teaching because of their heavy administrative duties in the institution ? ( ) ( ) ( )

45. Do you feel that it will be more useful to the student-teachers if the cooperative book bank is maintained by your institutional library ? ( ) ( ) ( )

46. Do you have sufficient pre-service teacher education lecturers in your DIET to improve the quality of pre-service teacher education ? ( ) ( ) ( )

47. Do your lecturers show keen interest in maintaining the institute's garden ? ( ) ( ) ( )

48. Do you feel that the technical staff are essential in preparing the teaching aids ? ( ) ( ) ( )

49. Do you have adequate space for office use ? ( ) ( ) ( )

50. Are your lecturers always ready to clear the doubts of the student teachers ? ( ) ( ) ( )

51. Do the local people help you in solving your personal problems ? ( ) ( ) ( )

52. Do you feel that the lecturers are under qualified in your DIET ? ( ) ( ) ( )

53. Do you feel that the Education Commission Reports should be in your library for the benefit of the student teachers ? ( ) ( ) ( )

54. Do you agree that the local

philanthropists have helped your institution in its development ? ( ) ( ) ( )

55. Are the guest lecturers on 'health and moral education' very common in your institution ? ( ) ( ) ( )

56. Is your campus clean and green ? ( ) ( ) ( )

57. Do you have spacious building for the seminar hall? ( ) ( ) ( )

58. Do you feel that the lecturers talk irrelevant things in small separate groups in staff meetings ? ( ) ( ) ( )

59. Do you feel that there is a lot of political pressure in the appointments, transfers and promotions in your institution ? ( ) ( ) ( )

60. Do you have sufficient hostel staff in your DIET? ( ) ( ) ( )

61. Do you have adequate drinking water facility in your DIET ? ( ) ( ) ( )

62. Do you have enough equipment in the biological science laboratory ? ( ) ( ) ( )

63. Do the lecturers in your institution have the feeling that the institution is theirs ? ( ) ( ) ( )

64. Do the lecturers in your institution have adequate opportunities to reach higher positions ? ( ) ( ) ( )

65. Do you have adequate sports material ? ( ) ( ) ( )

66. Do you have sufficient furniture in your office ? ( ) ( ) ( )

67. Do your lecturers maintain cordial relationship among themselves ? ( ) ( ) ( )

68. Do the lecturers encourage student teachers in preparing the teaching aids ? ( ) ( ) ( )

69. Do you have adequate water supply for the garden in your institute ? ( ) ( ) ( )

70. Do your staff members exhibit their cooperative attitude atleast in teaching ? ( ) ( ) ( )

71. Do you feel that your lecturers avoid the topics that they find difficult to teach ? ( ) ( ) ( )

72. Do you feel that there is need for complete overhaul of the present day pre-service teacher education curriculum ? ( ) ( ) ( )

73. Is the library in your institution kept open even after working hours for the maximum benefit of the students ? ( ) ( ) ( )

74. Do you feel that there is necessity for an effective recruiting agency for appointing the DIET lecturers? ( ) ( ) ( )

75. Is your institution financially sound ? ( ) ( ) ( )

76. Do you like to use adequate 'projected aids' in your demonstration classes ? ( ) ( ) ( )

77. Do the inefficient lecturers cause any hindrance to the efficient lecturers in your institution ? ( ) ( ) ( )

78. Do the lecturers leave the institution before the working hours ? ( ) ( ) ( )

79. Do you have the required equipment in physical science laboratory ? ( ) ( ) ( )

80. Do you have sufficient ventilation in your institution's library ? ( ) ( ) ( )

81. Do you take interest in the welfare of the lecturers? ( ) ( ) ( )

82. Do you accept the local community's help to improve your institution ? ( ) ( ) ( )

83. Do you have sufficient furniture in your hostel? ( ) ( ) ( )

84. Do you have sufficient text books in your library? ( ) ( ) ( )

85. Do your lecturers solve the personal problems of student teachers even after the working hours of the institution ? ( ) ( ) ( )

86. Do you agree that the buildings of your institution are used for social activities every year? ( ) ( ) ( )

87. Do you have books on teaching methodologies? ( ) ( ) ( )

88. Does your institution have play-grounds for different types of field games ? ( ) ( ) ( )

89. Do you have strict administrative rules to create good atmosphere in your institution ? ( ) ( ) ( )

90. Do you feel that there is always cordial relationship between

the teaching and non-teaching staff in your institution ? ( ) ( ) ( )

91. Do you have well defined service rules ? ( ) ( ) ( )

92. Do you like to serve as a source of educational information to the local people ? ( ) ( ) ( )

93. Do you think that your DIET has conducted sufficient number of workshops for developing teaching-learning material ? ( ) ( ) ( )

94. Do you have adequate furniture in your seminar hall ? ( ) ( ) ( )

95. Do you feel that there should be a Library Advisory Committee in your institution ? ( ) ( ) ( )

96. Suppose there is a comment that the teaching aids are not effectively used in your DIET. Do you accept it ? ( ) ( ) ( )

97. Do you promote work related habits for improving your campus ? ( ) ( ) ( )

APPENDIX—F

PRINCIPALS' CHECK–LIST

Final Form—English Version

Sir/Madam,

This is a research Check-List Questionnaire pertaining to the principal's opinion about DIETs infrastructural facilities like the physical plant, furniture, teaching-aids, sports and games equipment, etc. Please read each item carefully in terms of its availability, usage and its contribution to your DIET and put a (✓) mark in one of the two brackets against the item.

There is no question of right or wrong answer. What you feel in your work is the right answer. No question should be left unmarked.

This is purely for research purpose and all information will be kept confidential. Right answer is the key for good research. I will be ever grateful to you for your help.

Yours sincerely,

CHANDRA SEKHAR, K.
Research Scholar,
S.V. University.

		YES	NO
1.	Own buildings	( )	( )
2.	Rented buildings	( )	( )
3.	Air and ventilation (Describe)	( )	( )
4.	Separate principal's room	( )	( )
5.	No. of classrooms	( )	( )
6.	Reading room	( )	( )
7.	Biological science laboratory	( )	( )
8.	Physical science laboratory	( )	( )
9.	Psychology laboratory	( )	( )
10.	Social Studies laboratory	( )	( )
11.	Educational technology laboratory	( )	( )
12.	Separate staff rooms	( )	( )
13.	Staff quarters	( )	( )
14.	Separate rooms for the non-teaching staff	( )	( )
15.	Separate quarters for the non-teaching staff	( )	( )
16.	Store room	( )	( )
17.	Canteen building	( )	( )
18.	Seminar Hall	( )	( )
19.	Library building	( )	( )
20.	Computer room	( )	( )
21.	Gymnasium	( )	( )
22.	Sports training room	( )	( )
23.	Toilets for girls	( )	( )
24.	Toilets for boys	( )	( )
25.	Lavatories for girls	( )	( )
26.	Lavatories for boys	( )	( )
27.	Fire Extinguishers	( )	( )
28.	Fire buckets	( )	( )
29.	Hostel building	( )	( )
30.	Compound wall	( )	( )
31.	Foot-paths	( )	( )

		YES	NO
32.	Approach roads	( )	( )
33.	Meadow	( )	( )
34.	Drinking water facility	( )	( )
35.	Beautiful garden	( )	( )
36.	Water facility to garden	( )	( )
37.	Garden care	( )	( )
38.	Electricity	( )	( )
39.	Electric Generator	( )	( )
40.	Journals	( )	( )
41.	Co-operative Book Bank	( )	( )
42.	Sufficient number of racks in the Library	( )	( )
43.	Sufficient number of tables in the Library	( )	( )
44.	Sufficient number of chairs in the Library	( )	( )
45.	Publication of Newsletters	( )	( )
46.	Reports of Education Commissions	( )	( )
47.	Books on teaching methodology	( )	( )
48.	Sufficient number of text books	( )	( )
49.	Chairs with hands	( )	( )
50.	Tables with drawers	( )	( )
51.	Iron safes	( )	( )
52.	Benches in the classrooms	( )	( )
53.	Telephone facility	( )	( )
54.	Screw guage	( )	( )
55.	Vernier Calliperse	( )	( )
56.	Metre-scale	( )	( )
57.	Simple pendulum	( )	( )
58.	Micro balance	( )	( )
59.	Beakers	( )	( )
60.	Measuring jars	( )	( )
61.	Liquid measuring jars	( )	( )

		YES	NO
62.	Microscope	( )	( )
63.	Electrodes	( )	( )
64.	Pippets	( )	( )
65.	Burettes	( )	( )
66.	Spirit lamps	( )	( )
67.	Spring balances	( )	( )
68.	Test tubes	( )	( )
69.	Vaccum tubes	( )	( )
70.	Rubber tubes	( )	( )
71.	Mirrors	( )	( )
72.	Lenses	( )	( )
73.	Dissection boxes	( )	( )
74.	Science blocks	( )	( )
75.	Kipps apparatus	( )	( )
76.	Chemicals	( )	( )
77.	Film-strip Projector	( )	( )
78.	16 m.m. Film Projector	( )	( )
79.	Slide Projector	( )	( )
80.	Overhead Projector	( )	( )
81.	Opaque Projector	( )	( )
82.	Epidiascope	( )	( )
83.	Micro-Projector	( )	( )
84.	Television	( )	( )
85.	Closed Circuit Television	( )	( )
86.	Vedio Tape Recorder	( )	( )
87.	Audio Tape Recorder	( )	( )
88.	Projection Screen	( )	( )
89.	Record Player	( )	( )
90.	Still Photograph Camera	( )	( )
91.	Photo darkroom equipment		
92.	Letter press, offset and other printing equipment	( )	( )
93.	Slide and Filmstrip making equipment	( )	( )

		YES	NO
94.	Slide and Filmstrip copying equipment	( )	( )
95.	Radio	( )	( )
96.	Gramophone Records	( )	( )
97.	Public Address System equipment :		
	(i) Microphone	( )	( )
	(ii) Amplifier	( )	( )
98.	16 m.m. Sound Films	( )	( )
99.	16 m.m. Silent Films	( )	( )
100.	Filmstrips	( )	( )
101.	Slides	( )	( )
102.	Still Pictures	( )	( )
103.	Transparencies	( )	( )
104.	Globes	( )	( )
105.	Cartoons	( )	( )
106.	Posters	( )	( )
107.	Comics	( )	( )
108.	Folding Cards	( )	( )
109.	Diagrams	( )	( )
110.	Flash Cards	( )	( )
111.	Pictures of National Leaders and Scientists	( )	( )
112.	Models	( )	( )
113.	Objects	( )	( )
114.	Specimens	( )	( )
115.	Mock-Ups	( )	( )
116.	Diorama	( )	( )
117.	Puppets	( )	( )
118.	Mobiles	( )	( )
119.	Study Kits	( )	( )
120.	Black Boards	( )	( )
121.	Bulletin Boards	( )	( )
122.	Magnetic Boards	( )	( )
123.	Flannel Boards	( )	( )

		YES	NO
124.	Chalk Boards	( )	( )
125.	Peg Boards	( )	( )
126.	Museum	( )	( )
127.	Micro-teaching facility	( )	( )
128.	Flow Charts	( )	( )
129.	Stream Charts	( )	( )
130.	Time Line Charts	( )	( )
131.	Strip Charts	( )	( )
132.	Tree Charts	( )	( )
133.	Line Graphs	( )	( )
134.	Bar Graphs	( )	( )
135.	Circle Graphs	( )	( )
136.	Pictorial Graphs	( )	( )
137.	Flannel Graphs	( )	( )
138.	Contemporary Maps	( )	( )
139.	Historical Maps	( )	( )
140.	Survey Maps	( )	( )
141.	Pictorial Maps	( )	( )
142.	Topographical Maps	( )	( )
143.	Outline Maps	( )	( )
144.	Political Maps	( )	( )
145.	Weather Maps	( )	( )
146.	District Maps	( )	( )
147.	State Maps	( )	( )
148.	Country Maps	( )	( )
149.	World Maps	( )	( )
150.	Uniform	( )	( )
151.	Badminton Court	( )	( )
152.	Hockey Court	( )	( )
153.	Basketball Court	( )	( )
154.	Foot Ball Court	( )	( )
155.	Throw Ball Court	( )	( )

	YES	NO
156. Volley Ball Court	( )	( )
157. Cricket Court	( )	( )
158. Soft Ball Court	( )	( )
159. Baseball Court	( )	( )
160. Circle Game Court	( )	( )
161. Deep Frog Court	( )	( )
162. Kabaddi Court	( )	( )
163. Kho-Kho Court	( )	( )
164. Tennis Court	( )	( )
165. Badminton Equipment	( )	( )
166. Hockey Equipment	( )	( )
167. Basketball Equipment	( )	( )
168. Football Equipment	( )	( )
169. Ringtennis Equipment	( )	( )
170. Throwball Equipment	( )	( )
171. Volleyball Equipment	( )	( )
172. Cricket Equipment	( )	( )
173. Softball Equipment	( )	( )
174. Baseball Equipment	( )	( )
175. Tennis Equipment	( )	( )
176. Gymnasium Equipment	( )	( )
177. Asanas	( )	( )
178. Yoga	( )	( )
179. First Aid Box	( )	( )

APPENDIX—G_1

The response pattern of Perceptions of Student Teachers.

Items & S. No.	*1*	*2*	*3*	X^2		*Item Totals*
1	*2*	*3*	*4*	*5*		*6*
1.	92	227	181	57.14	**	1089
2.	147	185	168	4.56	@	1021
3.	154	101	245	64.47	**	1091
4.	51	30	419	576.25	**	1368
5.	105	152	243	59.87	**	1138
6.	50	128	322	236.80	**	1272
7.	96	151	253	77.04	**	1157
8.	233	120	147	42.50	**	914
9.	259	136	105	80.56	**	846 #
10.	75	122	303	175.20	**	1228
11.	168	180	152	2.53	@	984
12.	188	128	184	13.74	**	996
13.	128	186	186	13.66	**	1058
14.	155	167	178	1.72	@	1023
15.	288	120	92	136.04	**	804 #
16.	289	118	93	137.76	**	804 #
17.	95	201	204	46.61	**	1109
18.	95	153	252	76.50	**	1157

(Contd...)

1	2	3	4	5		6
19.	190	201	109	30.65	**	919
20.	247	69	184	98.53	**	937
21.	82	157	261	97.90	**	1179
22.	240	107	153	55.52	**	913
23.	39	78	383	427.51	**	1344
24.	136	104	260	82.43	**	1124
25.	68	176	256	107.68	**	1188
26.	120	196	184	20.35	**	1064
27.	160	159	181	2.02	@	1021
28.	275	88	137	113.90	**	862 #
29.	40	120	340	291.10	**	1300
30.	106	138	256	75.82	**	1150
31.	55	116	329	249.78	**	1274
32.	191	175	134	10.65	**	943
33.	276	77	147	123.35	**	871 #
34.	78	143	279	127.34	**	1201
35.	183	174	143	5.47	@	960
36.	42	78	380	415.22	**	1338
37.	237	182	81	75.82	**	844 #
38.	118	135	247	59.80	**	1129
39.	140	115	245	57.93	**	1105
40.	125	164	211	22.74	**	1086
41.	84	151	265	101.47	**	1181
42.	224	111	165	38.95	**	941
43.	247	103	150	65.54	**	903
44.	168	155	177	1.59	@	1009
45.	199	155	146	10.02	**	947
46.	79	195	226	72.62	**	1147
47.	141	145	214	20.74	**	1073
48.	99	111	290	138.54	**	1191
49.	141	73	286	143.19	**	1145
50.	32	143	325	263.96	**	1293
51.	123	137	240	49.77	**	1117
52.	205	88	207	56.08	**	1002
53.	205	145	150	13.74	**	945

(Contd...)

1	2	3	4	5		6
54.	201	178	121	20.73	**	920
55.	196	127	177	15.57	**	981
56.	267	110	123	92.13	**	856 #
57.	190	115	195	24.40	**	1005
58.	221	147	132	27.84	**	911
59.	310	79	111	189.32	**	801 #
60.	150	92	258	86.10	**	1108
61.	69	190	241	94.36	**	1172
62.	108	164	228	43.92	**	1120
63.	100	110	290	138.41	**	1190
64.	48	123	329	255.49	**	1281
65.	343	93	64	283.92	**	721 #
66.	190	175	135	9.96	**	945
67.	271	109	120	99.39	**	849 #
68.	175	142	183	5.86	@	1008
69.	103	185	212	39.14	**	1109
70.	220	139	141	26.20	**	921
71.	22	77	401	505.09	**	1379
72.	60	103	337	268.18	**	1277
73.	70	209	221	85.02	**	1151
74.	11	33	456	756.84	**	1445
75.	68	198	234	92.13	**	1166

Note : '#'Items marked with the symbol were the aspects on which the student teachers were unhappy.

APPENDIX—G_2

The response pattern of Attitudes of Student Teachers towards Teaching Profession.

Items & S. No.	1	2	3	4	5	X^2	
1	2	3	4	5	6	7	
1.	4	2	6	82	406	1219.85	**
2.	11	47	31	242	169	406.20	**
3.	13	9	22	101	355	872.96	**
4.	26	66	44	88	276	411.58	**
5.	4	1	15	105	375	1022.38	**
6.	10	6	14	67	403	1176.02	**
7.	47	94	74	119	166	83.54	**
8.	10	12	18	171	289	635.82	**
9.	18	28	42	170	242	405.40	**
10.	80	135	46	127	112	54.74	**
11.	51	87	56	137	169	107.53	**
12.	47	62	29	103	259	348.33	**
13.	38	21	31	154	256	423.26	**
14.	31	71	68	179	151	155.96	**
15.	18	59	36	121	266	407.49	**
16.	18	42	34	194	212	359.77	**
17.	14	11	4	79	392	1106.02	**

(Contd...)

1	2	3	4	5	6	7	
18.	36	91	78	143	152	93.00	**
19.	83	141	103	93	80	25.06	**
20.	32	63	37	118	250	330.21	**
21.	67	74	60	175	124	96.97	**
22.	78	81	58	87	201	136.00	**
23.	35	44	21	102	298	531.01	**
24.	7	13	27	139	314	691.54	**
25.	53	48	81	145	173	127.49	**
26.	49	63	50	129	209	193.72	**
27.	23	29	32	111	305	580.35	**
28.	12	3	8	90	387	1084.44	**
29.	18	34	22	104	322	667.75	**
30.	70	115	52	128	135	54.98	**
31.	11	4	9	65	411	1237.39	**
32.	17	48	51	145	239	335.52	**
33.	13	11	35	77	364	902.88	**
34.	96	120	66	119	99	19.69	**
35.	49	135	78	129	109	52.92	**
36.	29	40	35	135	261	402.54	**
37.	24	29	22	85	340	750.57	**
38.	60	78	56	132	174	106.48	**
39.	43	22	24	78	333	702.08	**
40.	140	136	53	86	85	55.96	**
41.	118	197	61	82	42	151.07	**
42.	68	175	44	98	115	101.45	**
43.	81	154	58	130	77	65.66	**
44.	18	14	24	132	312	661.56	**
45.	7	2	2	28	461	1637.57	**

APPENDIX—G_3

The response pattern of Perceptions of Teacher Educators.

Items & S. No.	1	2	3	X^2		Item Totals
1	2	3	4	5		6
1.	7	48	46	31.74	**	241
2.	24	53	24	16.65	**	202
3.	19	26	56	22.95	**	239
4.	26	35	40	2.99	@	216
5.	20	26	55	20.81	**	237
6.	22	42	37	6.44	*	217
7.	27	55	19	21.23	**	194
8.	11	39	51	25.03	**	242
9.	12	49	40	22.12	**	230
10.	38	45	18	11.66	**	182
11.	36	50	15	18.43	**	181
12.	33	53	15	21.46	**	184
13.	37	41	23	5.31	@	188
14.	15	30	56	25.56	**	243
15.	24	42	35	4.89	@	213
16.	5	33	63	49.98	**	260
17.	5	16	80	97.44	**	277

(Contd...)

1	2	3	4	5		6
18.	38	33	30	0.97	@	194
19.	16	34	51	18.20	**	237
20.	9	35	57	34.29	**	250
21.	12	40	49	22.12	**	239
22.	36	48	17	14.51	**	183
23.	6	25	70	64.17	**	266
24.	20	38	43	8.69	*	225
25.	28	43	30	3.94	@	204
26.	4	28	69	64.17	**	267
27.	35	49	17	15.29	**	184
28.	21	64	16	41.36	**	197
29.	14	34	53	22.59	**	241
30.	40	44	17	12.61	**	179
31.	35	32	34	0.14	@	201
32.	51	25	25	13.38	**	176 #
33.	8	41	52	31.15	**	246
34.	28	38	35	1.56	@	209
35.	77	19	5	86.57	**	130 #
36.	33	52	16	19.27	**	185
37.	34	38	29	1.21	@	197
38.	32	31	38	0.85	@	208
39.	40	37	24	4.30	@	186
40.	76	17	8	81.04	**	134 #
41.	39	52	10	27.46	**	173 #
42.	14	40	47	17.96	**	235
43.	37	35	29	1.03	@	194
44.	30	43	28	3.94	@	200
45.	76	20	5	83.18	**	131 #
46.	6	47	48	34.12	**	244
47.	39	29	33	1.50	@	196
48.	14	39	48	18.43	**	236
49.	53	33	15	21.46	**	164 #
50.	20	62	19	35.78	**	201
51.	8	36	57	35.90	**	251
52.	22	34	45	7.86	*	225
53.	58	31	12	31.74	**	156 #

(Contd...)

1	2	3	4	5		6
54.	75	15	11	76.35	**	138 #
55.	43	28	30	3.94	@	189
56.	20	28	53	17.60	**	235
57.	35	31	35	0.32	@	202
58.	26	53	22	16.89	**	198
59.	30	42	29	3.11	@	201
60.	23	56	22	22.24	**	201
61.	26	49	26	10.47	**	202
62.	65	31	5	53.78	**	142 #
63.	50	46	5	36.85	**	157 #
64.	36	52	13	22.83	**	179
65.	78	20	3	91.85	**	127 #
66.	71	23	7	65.89	**	138 #
67.	34	38	29	1.21	@	197
68.	31	48	22	10.36	**	193
69.	30	32	39	1.33	@	211
70.	46	39	16	14.63	**	172 #
71.	37	34	30	0.73	@	195
72.	11	30	60	36.25	**	251
73.	33	41	27	2.93	@	196
74.	44	38	19	10.12	**	177 #
75.	31	40	30	1.80	@	201
76.	41	35	25	3.88	@	186
77.	32	56	13	27.58	**	183
78.	38	27	36	2.04	@	200
79.	45	33	23	7.21	*	180
80.	13	57	31	29.07	**	220
81.	19	53	29	18.14	**	212
82.	29	46	26	6.91	*	199
83.	23	40	38	5.13	@	217
84.	35	40	26	2.99	@	193
85.	22	39	40	6.08	*	220
86.	46	41	14	17.60	**	170 #
87.	55	34	12	27.46	**	159 #
88.	35	55	11	28.83	**	178
89.	25	50	26	11.90	**	203

APPENDIX—G_4

The response pattern of Attitudes of Teacher Educators towards existing teacher education programme.

Items & S. No.	*1*	*2*	*3*	*4*	*5*	X^2	
1	*2*	*3*	*4*	*5*	*6*	*7*	
1.	5	30	0	35	31	53.01	**
2.	26	33	4	29	9	32.81	**
3.	3	12	6	44	36	68.36	**
4.	6	20	7	42	26	43.80	**
5.	7	37	2	36	19	51.43	**
6.	22	52	4	19	4	76.28	**
7.	33	48	5	12	3	75.78	**
8.	15	25	11	36	14	20.93	**
9.	7	37	5	33	19	42.22	**
10.	11	41	8	33	8	48.46	**
11.	24	50	4	20	3	72.32	**
12.	7	35	5	40	14	52.22	**
13.	9	42	8	36	6	59.45	**
14.	7	36	1	44	13	69.84	**
15.	4	39	5	40	13	63.90	**
16.	22	37	5	27	10	33.01	**
17.	12	51	4	24	10	69.15	**

(Contd...)

1	*2*	*3*	*4*	*5*	*6*	*7*	
18.	4	3	2	31	61	132.22	**
19.	3	2	3	37	56	123.11	**
20.	0	7	4	44	46	102.81	**
21.	14	35	9	32	11	30.04	**
22.	4	10	5	49	33	78.75	**
23.	12	34	5	34	16	34.50	**
24.	4	26	8	46	17	55.49	**
25.	22	39	3	28	9	41.52	**
26.	0	5	4	35	57	122.51	**
27.	4	40	8	34	15	50.53	**
28.	24	48	5	20	4	63.41	**
29.	2	20	8	50	21	67.76	**
30.	4	30	13	32	22	27.37	**
31.	12	46	8	25	10	49.94	**
32.	9	29	11	38	14	31.82	**
33.	8	40	10	35	8	50.14	**
34.	2	30	7	44	18	58.06	**
35.	14	32	7	26	22	19.25	**

APPENDIX—G_5

The response pattern of Perceptions of Principals.

Items & S. No.	*1*	*2*	*3*	*Item Totals*
1	*2*	*3*	*4*	*5*
1.	3	7	—	23
2.	1	3	6	15
3.	3	4	3	20
4.	—	3	7	13
5.	—	9	1	19
6.	—	5	5	15
7.	2	1	7	15
8.	—	5	5	15
9.	1	3	6	15
10.	9	1	—	11
11.	2	6	2	20
12.	4	3	3	19
13.	2	5	3	21
14.	1	4	5	16
15.	1	4	5	16
16.	—	6	4	16
17.	1	7	2	19
18.	1	—	9	12
19.	—	7	3	17
20.	1	5	4	17

(Contd...)

1	2	3	4	5
21.	—	8	2	22
22.	1	5	4	23
23.	—	10	—	20
24.	1	8	1	20
25.	2	7	1	21
26.	—	3	7	27
27.	—	4	6	26
28.	1	7	2	19
29.	—	3	7	13
30.	3	5	2	21
31.	2	3	5	17
32.	1	3	6	25
33.	—	7	3	23
34.	5	4	1	24
35.	4	5	1	23
36.	2	5	3	21
37.	2	6	2	20
38.	1	5	4	17
39.	—	4	6	14
40.	2	7	1	21
41.	3	4	3	20
42.	1	8	1	20
43.	7	2	1	26
44.	—	7	3	23
45.	—	5	5	15
46.	1	2	7	14
47.	2	5	3	19
48.	2	7	1	19
49.	1	5	4	17
50.	—	3	7	13
51.	6	—	4	22
52.	—	3	7	27
53.	—	4	6	14
54.	5	4	1	24
55.	5	4	1	24
56.	1	6	3	18
57.	2	5	3	19
58.	2	3	5	23
59.	2	4	4	22

(Contd...)

1	*2*	*3*	*4*	*5*
60.	5	4	1	24
61.	2	3	5	17
62.	2	4	4	18
63.	1	5	4	17
64.	1	5	4	17
65.	3	6	1	22
66.	2	7	1	21
67.	1	5	4	17
68.	—	3	7	13
69.	1	6	3	18
70.	2	5	3	19
71.	—	3	7	27
72.	1	7	2	21
73.	7	3	—	27
74.	2	7	1	19
75.	3	5	2	21
76.	—	5	5	15
77.	1	2	7	26
78.	1	4	5	24
79.	1	7	2	19
80.	—	6	4	16
81.	—	6	4	16
82.	1	9	—	21
83.	4	6	—	24
84.	2	7	1	21
85.	2	5	3	19
86.	4	5	1	23
87.	2	7	1	21
88.	2	7	1	21
89.	—	7	3	17
90.	—	8	2	18
91.	2	7	1	21
92.	—	5	5	15
93.	1	3	6	15
94.	3	5	2	21
95.	—	5	5	15
96.	1	4	5	24
97.	—	4	6	14

APPENDIX—G_6

The response pattern of Principal's Check-List

S.No.	Items	KN	RC	KL	NL	RR	WL	MN	BP	MP	PP
1.	Own buildings	1	1	1	1	1	1	1	1	1	1
2.	Rented buildings	0	0	0	0	0	0	0	0	0	0
3.	Air and ventilation (Describe)	1	1	1	1	1	1	1	1	1	1
4.	Separate principal's room	1	1	1	1	1	1	1	1	1	1
5.	No. of classrooms	6	4	3	3	4	5	3	4	3	4
6.	Reading room	1	0	1	1	1	1	1	1	1	1
7.	Biological science laboratory	1	0	1	0	1	1	1	1	1	1
8.	Physical science laboratory	1	0	1	0	1	1	1	1	1	1
9.	Psychology laboratory	1	0	1	0	1	1	1	0	0	0
10.	Social Studies laboratory	1	0	0	1	1	1	0	1	0	0
11.	Educational technology laboratory	1	0	0	0	0	0	0	0	0	1
12.	Separate staff rooms	1	1	1	1	1	1	1	1	1	1
13.	Staff quarters	0	0	1	0	0	1	0	0	0	0
14.	Separate non-teaching rooms	1	1	1	1	1	1	1	1	1	1
15.	Separate non-teaching quarters	0	0	1	0	0	1	0	0	0	0
16.	Store room	1	1	1	1	1	1	1	1	1	1

(Contd...)

S.No.	*Items*	*KN*	*RC*	*KL*	*NL*	*RR*	*WL*	*MN*	*BP*	*MP*	*PP*
17.	Canteen building	0	0	1	0	1	1	0	0	0	0
18.	Seminar Hall	1	1	1	1	1	1	1	1	1	1
19.	Library building	1	0	1	1	1	1	1	1	1	1
20.	Computer room	0	0	0	0	1	1	0	1	0	1
21.	Gymnasium	0	0	0	0	0	0	0	0	0	0
22.	Sports training room	1	0	0	0	0	0	0	0	0	0
23.	Toilets for girls	1	0	1	1	1	1	1	1	0	1
24.	Toilets for boys	1	0	1	1	1	1	0	1	0	1
25.	Lavatories for girls	1	0	1	1	1	1	0	1	1	1
26.	Lavatory for boys	1	0	1	1	1	1	0	1	1	1
27.	Fire Extinguishers	1	1	1	1	1	1	1	1	1	1
28.	Fire buckets	1	0	0	1	1	1	1	1	1	1
29.	Hostel building	1	0	1	1	1	1	1	1	0	1
30.	Compound wall	1	1	1	1	1	1	1	0	0	1
31.	Foot-paths	1	1	1	1	1	1	1	1	1	1
32.	Approach roads	1	1	1	1	1	1	1	1	1	1
33.	Meadow	1	0	1	1	1	1	1	1	1	1
34.	Drinking water facility	1	0	1	0	1	1	0	1	0	1
35.	Beautiful garden	1	0	0	0	1	1	0	0	1	0
36.	Water facility to garden	1	0	0	0	1	1	0	0	1	1
37.	Garden care	1	0	0	0	1	1	0	0	1	0
38.	Electricity	1	1	1	1	1	1	1	1	1	1
39.	Electric Generator	0	0	0	0	0	0	0	0	0	0
40.	Journals	1	1	1	1	1	1	1	1	1	1
41.	Co-operative Book Bank	1	0	0	0	0	0	0	0	0	0
42.	Sufficient racks in the Library	1	0	1	0	1	1	0	1	1	0
43.	Sufficient tables in the Library	1	0	1	0	1	1	0	0	0	0
44.	Sufficient chairs in the Library	1	0	1	0	1	1	0	0	0	0
45.	Publish Newsletters	1	1	1	1	1	1	0	1	0	0
46.	Reports of Education Commissions	1	0	0	0	0	0	0	0	0	0
47.	Books on teaching methodology	1	1	1	1	1	1	1	1	1	0
48.	Sufficient text books	1	1	1	1	1	1	1	1	1	0
49.	Chairs with hands	1	1	1	1	1	1	1	1	1	1
50.	Tables with drawers	0	1	1	1	1	1	1	1	1	1

(Contd...)

S.No.	Items	KN	RC	KL	NL	RR	WL	MN	BP	MP	PP
51.	Iron safes	1	1	1	1	1	1	1	1	1	1
52.	Benches in the classrooms	1	0	1	1	1	1	1	1	1	1
53.	Telephone facility	1	1	1	1	1	1	1	1	1	1
54.	Screw guage	1	1	1	1	1	1	1	1	1	1
55.	Vernier Calliperse	1	1	1	1	1	1	1	1	1	1
56.	Metre-scale	1	1	1	1	1	1	1	1	1	1
57.	Simple pendulum	1	1	1	1	1	1	1	1	1	1
58.	Micro balance	1	1	1	1	1	1	1	1	1	1
59.	Beakers	1	1	1	1	1	1	1	1	1	1
60.	Measuring jars	1	1	1	1	1	1	1	1	1	1
61.	Liquid measuring jars	1	1	1	1	1	1	1	1	1	1
62.	Microscope	1	1	1	1	1	1	1	1	1	1
63.	Electrodes	1	1	1	1	1	1	1	1	1	1
64.	Pippets	1	1	1	1	1	1	1	1	1	1
65.	Burettes	1	1	1	1	1	1	1	1	1	1
66.	Spirit lamps	1	1	1	1	1	1	1	1	1	1
67.	Spring balances	1	1	1	1	1	1	1	1	1	1
68.	Test tubes	1	1	1	1	1	1	1	1	1	1
69.	Vaccum tubes	1	1	1	1	1	1	1	1	1	1
70.	Rubber tubes	1	1	1	1	1	1	1	1	1	1
71.	Mirrors	1	1	1	1	1	1	1	1	1	1
72.	Lenses	1	1	1	1	1	1	1	1	1	1
73.	Dissection boxes	1	1	1	1	1	1	1	1	1	1
74.	Science blocks	1	1	1	1	1	1	1	1	1	1
75.	Kipps apparatus	1	1	1	1	0	1	0	1	1	1
76.	Chemicals	1	1	1	1	1	1	1	1	1	1
77.	Film-strip Projector	0	1	1	0	1	1	0	0	0	0
78.	16 m.m. Film Projector	0	0	0	0	1	0	0	0	0	0
79.	Slide Projector	1	1	1	1	1	1	1	1	1	1
80.	Overhead Projector	1	0	1	1	1	1	1	1	1	0
81.	Opaque Projector	0	0	0	0	1	0	0	0	0	0
82.	Epidiascope	0	0	0	0	0	0	0	0	0	0
83.	Micro-Projector	0	0	0	0	1	1	0	0	0	0
84.	Television	1	0	1	0	1	1	0	1	1	1
85.	Closed Circuit Television	0	0	0	0	0	0	0	0	0	0
86.	Video Tape Recorder	0	0	0	0	0	0	0	0	0	0
87.	Audio Tape Recorder	1	0	1	1	1	1	1	1	1	1

(Contd...)

S.No.	Items	KN	RC	KL	NL	RR	WL	MN	BP	MP	PP
88.	Projection Screen	1	0	0	0	1	1	0	1	0	0
89.	Record Player	1	0	0	0	1	0	0	0	0	0
90.	Still Photograph Camera	1	0	0	0	0	0	0	0	0	0
91.	Photo darkroom equipment	0	0	0	0	1	0	0	0	0	0
92.	Letter press, offset and other printing equipment	0	0	0	0	0	0	0	0	0	0
93.	Slide and Filmstrip making equipment	0	0	0	0	0	0	0	0	0	0
94.	Slide and Filmstrip copying equipment	0	0	0	0	0	0	0	0	0	0
95.	Radio	1	1	1	1	1	1	1	1	1	1
96.	Gramophone Records	0	0	0	0	0	0	0	0	0	0
97.	Public Address System equipment:										
	(i) Microphone	1	1	1	1	1	1	1	1	1	1
	(ii) Amplifier	1	1	1	1	1	1	1	1	1	1
98.	16 m.m. Sound Films	0	0	0	0	0	0	0	0	0	0
99.	16 m.m. Silent Films	0	0	0	0	0	0	0	0	0	0
100.	Filmstrips	0	1	1	1	1	1	1	1	1	0
101.	Slides	1	1	1	1	1	1	1	1	1	1
102.	Still Pictures	1	1	0	0	1	1	1	1	1	1
103.	Transparencies	1	1	1	1	1	1	1	1	1	1
104.	Globes	1	1	1	1	1	1	1	1	1	1
105.	Cartoons	1	1	1	1	1	1	1	1	1	1
106.	Posters	1	1	1	1	1	1	1	1	0	1
107.	Comics	1	1	1	0	1	1	0	1	1	1
108.	Folding Cards	1	1	1	1	1	1	1	1	1	1
109.	Diagrams	1	0	0	0	1	1	0	1	0	1
110.	Flash Cards	1	1	1	1	1	1	1	1	1	1
111.	Pictures of National Leaders and Scientists	1	1	1	1	1	1	1	1	1	1
112.	Models	1	1	1	1	1	1	1	1	1	1
113.	Objects	1	1	1	1	1	1	1	1	1	1
114.	Specimens	1	1	1	1	1	1	0	1	1	1
115.	Mock-Ups	0	0	0	0	0	0	0	0	0	0
116.	Diorama	0	0	0	0	0	0	0	0	0	0
117.	Puppets	0	0	0	0	1	0	0	0	0	1

(Contd...)

S.No.	Items	KN	RC	KL	NL	RR	WL	MN	BP	MP	PP
118.	Mobiles	0	0	0	0	1	0	0	0	0	1
119.	Study Kits	1	1	1	1	1	1	1	1	1	1
120.	Black Boards	1	1	1	1	1	1	1	1	1	1
121.	Bulletin Boards	1	0	1	1	1	1	0	1	1	1
122.	Magnetic Boards	0	0	0	0	1	1	0	0	0	0
123.	Flannel Boards	1	1	1	0	1	0	1	1	0	1
124.	Chalk Boards	1	1	1	1	1	1	1	1	1	1
125.	Peg Boards	0	0	1	0	0	1	0	0	0	1
126.	Museum	0	0	0	0	0	0	0	0	0	0
127.	Micro-teaching facility	1	0	0	0	1	0	0	0	0	0
128.	Flow Charts	1	1	1	1	1	1	1	1	1	1
129.	Stream Charts	1	1	1	1	1	1	1	1	1	1
130.	Time Line Charts	1	1	1	1	1	1	1	1	1	1
131.	Strip Charts	1	1	1	1	1	1	1	1	1	1
132.	Tree Charts	1	1	1	1	1	1	1	1	1	1
133.	Line Graphs	1	1	1	1	1	1	1	1	1	1
134.	Bar Graphs	1	1	1	1	1	1	1	1	1	1
135.	Circle Graphs	1	1	1	1	1	1	1	1	1	1
136.	Pictorial Graphs	1	1	1	1	1	1	1	0	0	1
137.	Flannel Graphs	0	0	0	0	0	0	0	0	0	1
138.	Contemporary Maps	1	0	1	0	1	1	1	1	0	1
139.	Historical Maps	1	0	1	1	1	1	1	1	0	1
140.	Survey Maps	1	1	1	0	1	1	0	0	1	1
141.	Pictorial Maps	1	1	1	0	1	0	0	0	0	1
142.	Topographical Maps	1	0	0	0	1	0	0	1	0	1
143.	Outline Maps	1	0	0	0	1	0	0	0	0	1
144.	Political Maps	1	1	1	1	1	1	0	1	1	1
145.	Weather Maps	1	0	0	1	1	1	0	1	1	1
146.	District Maps	1	1	1	1	1	1	1	1	1	1
147.	State Maps	1	1	1	1	1	1	1	1	1	1
148.	Country Maps	1	1	1	1	1	1	1	1	1	1
149.	World Maps	1	1	1	1	1	1	1	1	1	1
150.	Uniform	1	1	1	1	1	1	1	1	1	1
151.	Badminton Court	1	0	1	1	1	1	1	1	1	1
152.	Hockey Court	0	0	0	0	0	0	0	0	0	0
153.	Basketball Court	0	0	0	0	0	0	0	0	0	0
154.	Foot Ball Court	0	0	0	0	0	0	0	0	0	0
155.	Throw Ball Court	1	1	1	1	1	1	1	1	1	0
156.	Volley Ball Court	1	1	1	1	1	1	1	1	1	1

(Contd...)

S.No.	Items	KN	RC	KL	NL	RR	WL	MN	BP	MP	PP
157.	Cricket Court	0	0	0	0	0	0	0	0	0	0
158.	Soft Ball Court	0	0	0	0	0	0	0	0	0	0
159.	Baseball Court	0	0	0	0	0	0	0	0	0	0
160.	Circle Game Court	0	0	0	0	0	0	0	0	0	0
161.	Deep Frog Court	0	0	0	0	0	0	0	0	0	0
162.	Kabaddi Court	1	1	1	1	1	1	1	1	1	1
163.	Kho-Kho Court	1	1	1	1	1	1	1	1	1	0
164.	Tennis Court	0	0	0	0	0	0	0	0	0	0
165.	Badminton Equipment	1	0	1	1	1	1	1	1	1	1
166.	Hockey Equipment	0	0	0	0	0	0	0	0	0	0
167.	Basketball Equipment	1	0	0	0	0	0	0	0	0	1
168.	Football Equipment	0	0	0	0	0	0	0	0	0	1
169.	Ring Tennis Equipment	1	1	0	1	1	1	0	1	1	0
170.	Throwball Equipment	1	1	1	1	1	1	1	1	1	1
171.	Volleyball Equipment	1	1	1	1	1	1	1	1	1	1
172.	Cricket Equipment	1	0	0	0	1	1	0	0	0	0
173.	Softball Equipment	0	0	0	0	0	0	0	0	0	0
174.	Baseball Equipment	0	0	0	0	0	0	0	0	0	0
175.	Tennis Equipment	0	0	0	0	0	0	0	0	0	0
176.	Gymnasium Equipment	1	1	1	1	1	1	1	1	1	0
177.	Asanas	1	0	1	0	1	0	0	0	0	0
178.	Yoga	1	0	1	0	1	1	0	0	0	0
179.	First Aid Box	1	1	1	1	1	1	1	1	1	0

KN	=	Karvetinagar	WL	=	Warangal
RC	=	Rayachoty	MN	=	Mahaboob Nagar
KL	=	Kurnool	BP	=	Boyapalem
NL	=	Nalgonda	MP	=	Mynampadu
RR	=	Ranga Reddy	PP	=	Pallepadu

INDEX